Spirituality Seeking Theology

Spirituality
Seeking Theology

ROGER HAIGHT, S.J.

ORBIS BOOKS
Maryknoll, New York 10545

ORBIS BOOKS
Maryknoll, New York 10545

Fathers and Brothers
MARYKNOLL

Founded in 1970, Orbis Books endeavors to publish works that enlighten the mind, nourish the spirit, and challenge the conscience. The publishing arm of the Maryknoll Fathers and Brothers, Orbis seeks to explore the global dimensions of the Christian faith and mission, to invite dialogue with diverse cultures and religious traditions, and to serve the cause of reconciliation and peace. The books published reflect the views of their authors and do not represent the official position of the Maryknoll Society. To learn more about Maryknoll and Orbis Books, please visit our website at www.maryknollsociety.org.

Manufactured in the United States of America

Library of Congress Cataloging-in-Publication Data

Haight, Roger.
   Spirituality seeking theology / by Roger Haight, S.J.
       pages cm
   ISBN 978-1-62698-077-8 (pbk.)
   1. Spirituality—Catholic Church. 2. Jesus Christ. 3. Catholic Church—
Doctrines. I. Title.
   BX2350.65.H35   2014
   248—dc23
                                                          2013034521

To my Jesuit Community at
America House

Contents

Preface

This book is written as a companion volume to *Christian Spirituality for Seekers* (CSS).[1] In that book I used the Spiritual Exercises of Ignatius Loyola as a framework for representing a spirituality of following Jesus that could be entertained by anyone. Because Jesus is a public figure captured in the four Gospels, anyone seeking spiritual wisdom can turn to these collected stories of Jesus to be inspired by his teachings and recorded actions. This could work for people of any age, whether they be religious or not, no matter the religious tradition to which they belong, or the amount of experience they bring to the quest. This book does not depend on the earlier one, in the sense that *Christian Spirituality for Seekers* would have to be read first for this one to make sense, but it does go back to the same spirituality, based on the ministry of Jesus of Nazareth.

This book is designed to address a specific problem in the Western church in our day, namely, the decline of Christianity and the steady flow of people out of the churches. Americans who visit Europe quickly become aware of what secularization has wrought across nations and denominations. The same forces are at work in North America even though the rates of alienation are less severe. No single factor accounts for this slow withdrawal from the church; complex shifts in culture do not yield to simple analysis. But it can be said, because it is almost synonymous with the decline itself, that Christian doctrine has lost traction with the faithful. Few young people understand Christian doctrine, and when they have some idea of it, they fail to see its bearing on their immediate lives.[2] This book addresses this problem. But it is crucial to understand how it goes about the project.

One can compare and contrast two methods of addressing the decline of Christianity. One way would take account of contemporary

---

1. Roger Haight, *Christian Spirituality for Seekers: Reflections on the Spiritual Exercises of Ignatius Loyola* (Maryknoll, NY: Orbis Books, 2012).

2. These generalizations are borne out by sociological studies that speak in percentages. There will always be a recognizable minority of churched young people who are enthusiastic about their Christian lives. One statistic, however, is particularly striking: "the proportion of Americans expressing no religious affiliation has almost tripled since the late 1990s." William V. D'Antonio, Michele Dillon, and Mary L. Gautier, *American Catholics in Transition* (Lanham, MD: Rowman & Littlefield, 2013), 67.

culture and deliberately analyze and reappropriate the traditional symbols and doctrines of the Christian faith in a way that translates them into a relevant language that can be appropriated today. This is the theological project; it goes directly to the beliefs of the church and critically reformulates them in order to preserve their truth in a culture and language that are different from those in which they were originally formulated. This path is not being followed in this book. A second and different route passes through spirituality. The meaning of the term "spirituality" will be explained in greater detail in the introduction. But a first description of the meaning of spirituality and of some of its characteristics will help clarify the logic and rationale of the argument here.

This book remains on the level of spirituality. "Spirituality" refers to the way persons and groups live their lives with reference to something that they acknowledge as transcendent. In Christianity, spirituality consists of following Jesus as the revealer of God and God's rule. All Christians will agree that being a Christian somehow entails being a follower of Jesus Christ. This simple, straightforward conception of spirituality, however, contains a structure that allows it to open up a distinctive approach to Christian faith. This book uses the following elements of spirituality to make its case for the relevance of Christianity to present-day Western culture and practical life in our complex societies:

First and foremost, spirituality is a form of behavior. It consists in the sum total of a person's actions as he or she moves along in life. Our actions gradually define us, so that our identities are tied up in the history of our actions. Spirituality thus appears as something that profoundly entails who we are.

Second, spirituality so defined has to be understood as a narrative. Jesus' life of ministry serves as a paradigm. Instead of cataloguing the virtues that constitute a virtuous Christian life, one looks to the story of a person and the consistent pattern of a person's commitment. One's relationship to transcendence is constructed by the daily activities that shape a person's life.

Third, spirituality is intrinsically developmental. Spirituality is a living thing that grows through time and through the life cycle of human experiences. The idea of a static spirituality in no way corresponds to reality.

Fourth, spirituality is prior to the church. This will be demonstrated further in chapter 8, but the proposition can be gleaned off the surface of history. The followers of Jesus gathered after the death and resurrection of Jesus as a group of Jews who, through a loyal following of Jesus, gradually developed into a church. This historical narrative shows how the spirituality of following Jesus forms the basis out of which the church initially developed, and a social analysis of the organizational church will show that the lived faith life of the followers of Jesus is the ground of the church itself.

Fifth, this means that spirituality is also prior to and the basis of the theology and the doctrines of the church. The elementary source out of which the doctrines developed was the lived tradition of the existential life of the church, that is, its corporate spirituality. Theology and what arises out of such reflection, doctrines, emerge out of spirituality and reflect the spirituality to which they give expression.

Finally, because of the status of spirituality as prior to and the basis of doctrine, it provides a bridge for ecumenical communication and mutual understanding. All Christians share the same spirituality of being followers of Jesus, so that spirituality conceived in these broad terms provides a common language of communication and understanding. This is most important in the current situation of creeping alienation that affects all the churches.

These six characteristics of Christian spirituality show that fixing attention on this specific aspect of Christianity or of the church as a whole provides a new vantage point for addressing the problem of the decline of the church. This needs to be underlined at the outset of this book because its method places it within the sphere of spirituality and not of theology. To be forceful about this point, this book is a work not of theology but of spirituality.[3] This recognition allows several things to fall into place and shows why this approach has distinct advantages.

The appeal to spirituality gives this work a direct relevance to human life. It both describes and addresses Christian life. This work does not appeal to doctrines to explain human life. It probes Christian praxis and the life of faith itself to show where the doctrines have their source. Many Christians today live in a situation that is analogous to first-century followers of Jesus who did not yet possess the theological or doctrinal framework that developed in the centuries that followed. Analogously, this book relates directly to a following of Jesus. It appeals to the same Christian life as a following of Jesus of Nazareth "prior" to the development of doctrine.[4]

---

3. In the introduction that follows I will distinguish spiritual reflection from the discipline of theology. In ordinary language many different kinds of discourse are blended together in the general term "theology." But it is important to distinguish between different kinds of closely related forms of reflection.

4. The imaginative framework of this book is set with regard to someone who is not a believer but a seeker. He or she has been introduced to Jesus of Nazareth through the Spiritual Exercises of Ignatius Loyola as these are presented in *Christian Spirituality for Seekers*. This book follows and lays out in the form of a grand narrative a spirituality of following Jesus prior to internalizing Christian faith in the objective terms represented

This book is ecumenical, because Christian spirituality is shared in common across the churches. All Christians are followers of Jesus of Nazareth. This definition of what all Christians share gives this book an ecumenical coinage that allows cross-denominational appreciation and exchange at a level prior to the differences of doctrine and theological biases. The description of Christian spirituality offered here should not be measured by *The Small Catechism* of Martin Luther, or *The Institutes* of John Calvin, or *The Catechism of the Council of Trent*, or *The Catechism of the Catholic Church*. What is being described in this book is not doctrine but spirituality, the following of Jesus of Nazareth, which unfolds in good measure prior to and innocent of theology and doctrines. These lived experiences are given a reflective existence by the concepts and analyses offered on these pages, but these are proposed in a way that is descriptive and not normative. The point is to ferret out relevant meaning, not to define doctrines. Everything in this book can be reviewed by formal, critical, and dialectical theology and found wanting or affirmed with new vigor by the standards of different churches. But the substance of what is described here is spirituality that exists prior to theology, as existence is to reflection upon it, and certainly does not compete with it.

The following chapters are searching for a place where Protestant, Catholics, Orthodox, those committed to other faith traditions, and unbelievers can speak about Jesus of Nazareth and what he inserted into history. The premise for this revolves around spirituality, a concern for transcendent values worthy of attracting a commitment. Many people who generally are not being addressed today live in this place. Given that audience, those who read this book as a book about beliefs and doctrines, or as a work of Protestant or Catholic theology, misinterpret it by asking it to respond to questions it is not addressing, somewhat like asking church music to explain the hypostatic union.[5] This book accompanies the two disciples who are still on their way from Jerusalem to Emmaus. They have to keep walking, but on their

---

in the confessional and doctrinal forms of particular churches. In other words, this book has to be read as a first address to people who are searching for a synthesis, and not as a reductionist version of the synthesis possessed by the churches.

5. One of the reasons why spirituality can provide a forum for ecumenical and interreligious conversation springs from the primal existential level of experience that spontaneous spirituality represents. Entering into this frame of reference allows people to recount their experiences and listen to the experience of others in a way that resonates more directly with actual lives. This is a sphere of interchange that is freer because it is prior to and often completely unaware of various ideological interpretations of how this experience would develop or should be construed. That important conversation comes later, after the interchange about the things that people in the spiritual conversation share.

way they also have to keep talking about their experiences and what they hope for.

This book, then, is open to further development, to theological debate and critical appropriation. It is also open to dialogue and to being used as a lens for trying to understand what is truly important in Christian faith and where it illumines human life and encourages human flourishing.

The structure of this book mirrors the Christian story. This refers to the large story of the rise of the Christian community through explicit encounters with God as creator, as saving power in Jesus of Nazareth, and as constant presence as Spirit. The book loosely follows the grand sacred narrative by which Christianity understands reality as it comes from the hands of the creator and is visited by God in the ministry of Jesus, which gives rise to the church and a hope in an absolute destiny for humankind. Beneath that narrative superstructure are the personal and collective lives of Christians across the centuries that I call spirituality. But this will be explained in the introduction.

The book is roughly divided into three parts. The first part includes chapters 1-3 and describes the story of the emergence of the universe and of the human species within it. Being a part of that story, for it is the story of our own creation, gives rise to the question of the "whence?" of the universe in transcendent terms. From questions like this come the ideas of creation and a creator God. In the Christian framework, God and creator have become almost synonymous.

The second part turns to Jesus of Nazareth, and in four chapters I speak about various aspects of Jesus of Nazareth as the centering inspiration of Christian spirituality. These chapters discuss how Jesus became the particular focus of Christian faith by his preaching the rule of God and attracting followers. I draw out contours or aspects that Jesus revealed of God and of human existence in the light of God. Then, from the perspective of spirituality as distinct from theology, I meditate on the death and resurrection of Jesus.

The third part, chapters 8 and 9, turns to the Christian story after Jesus. Chapter 8 discusses the foundations of the church as a movement of the corporate spirituality of the followers of Jesus, first within Judaism, but then gradually developing into a religious organization distinct from Judaism. This took much more time than we tend to think.[6] The concluding chapter describes how the doctrine of trinity developed and how it has its roots in the corporate spirituality that

---

6. One should think of Christianity and Judaism becoming separate religions sometime around the fourth century. Daniel Boyarin, *Border Lines: The Partition of Judaeo-Christianity,* Divinations (Philadelphia: University of Pennsylvania Press, 2004), 6.

is the church.[7] I end with that other all-encompassing prospect that provides a counterpart to creation, that is, eschatology. Conceptions of beginning and the end are the bookends of the story that leads through Jesus of Nazareth and the church.

This panoramic overview shows that this book does not offer formal theological answers to the questions raised by Christian spirituality. Rather it strives honestly to demonstrate how Christian spirituality is a question to itself, a question that reaches out toward the discipline of theology.

I am grateful to a number of people who have helped me in the course of this project. Elizabeth Johnson, who is expert in the dialogue between theology and science, read the chapters on creation and method and suggested basic distinctions that clarified the argument in crucial ways. John Keating and Donald Moore, fellow Jesuits, read the manuscript, and in comment and conversation helped me smooth out the text at several points. Patrick Amer, a clear-thinking and careful-reading lawyer and theologian, reviewed the text and suggested several moves to sharpen the logic. I am also grateful to the editor of this work, James Keane, for ably shepherding it through the process of publication.

---

7. The word "trinity" is usually not capitalized because it is not a name of God but designates a doctrine.

Introduction: Spirituality Searching for Theology

This book occupies the space between two distinct aspects of the Christian life. On the one side is spontaneous Christian living, perhaps learned in the course of growing up or propelled by the story of Jesus but nurtured with little instruction. Persons in this group use ordinary language to express to themselves and others the various dimensions of their spirituality. On the other side lies the world of theologians. Theologians know what the key words of the Creed and various Christian doctrines mean, and they use a technical language that is critical and analytical to express the height and depth of reality as it is behind the appearances. The vast majority of Christians belong to the first group of people, who live their faith unselfconsciously. They know that a discipline of theology exists, but they are not sure whether it would make any difference in their lives if they knew anything about it.

This book is written from the perspective of Christian spirituality. It is neither a mere report on Christian life nor a work of theology. Between a Christian life spontaneously lived and the work of theologians lies the vast sphere of conscious witness and reflection on Christian practice. That practice essentially consists of following Jesus, a third place between everyday behavior and focused intellectual reflection that is both distinct from and related to both. The goal of the book is to show how following Jesus gives rise to a self-consciousness and language that are prior to what is taken up by Christian theologians in the formal, critical discipline of theology.

This will become clear in the four considerations that follow. First, like all reality, human life is constantly in motion, and this movement never ceases to give rise to new questions. Second, for many people the one constant in their lives consists of a basic faith that, although it too develops, has a consistent formal structure. Third, "faith in action" is a good way of describing spirituality. Spirituality is a way of life that constantly faces questions that are genuinely new. And, fourth, when these three factors are taken together, they account for the notion of a "Spirituality Seeking Theology."

Searching

"Searching" has become a common descriptor of human life in the Western world. Whether our culture is described as late modern or postmodern, it has lost many of the certainties upon which its stability rested. Those who have internalized an evolutionary worldview recognize the role of randomness in life processes, and how that randomness threatens a sense of purpose. Historical consciousness means that no idea or value can be understood apart from its particular human context. All ideas and values are linked to some particular culture. Many are not transportable. Being has yielded to becoming; process rather than permanence characterizes the world as we know it. Plato's vision of an eternal superstructure of reality clashes not only with everything people see, hear, and opine, but also now with everything that is critically examined. Each person's life is a narrative, a particular story within the larger story of a particular group. Narratives are constructed by constant decisions, either/or, and each path leads in a new and different direction. Yet, precisely because constant motion is as unsettling as seasickness, because it occludes permanent moorings, it highlights by contrast a desire for coherent meaning that drives the phenomenon of searching. Searching is no longer merely implicit in life; it becomes an overt striving for something solid that will help define the self by the self's relating to it, identifying with it, and appropriating its permanent value. Searching shows that human existence needs to be embraced by something stable that offers coherence and permanence.

Faith as Existential Stability within Change

The religious word for clinging to something permanent in a finite and changing world is "faith." With a few but profound distinctions, Paul Tillich has shown how the commitment of faith is a reasonable option.

Tillich defines faith as "the state of being ultimately concerned."[1] The definition has two equally important senses. The ultimacy refers both to the subjective act of a person's being concerned and to the object about which the person is concerned. The two correlate with each other. Reversing the order, that which can legitimately elicit an ultimately responsive commitment must itself be worthy of it: it must be of supreme and final importance.[2] Conversely, the value response

---

1. Paul Tillich, *Dynamics of Faith* (New York: Harper & Row, 1957), 1, 4.

2. Tillich attends to this in a more pointed definition of faith in which the passive voice indicates the influence of the object on the subject: "In a short formula, one can say

to the object must be that which organizes a person's life; all other concerns revolve around the centering dedication. This short description of faith as "ultimate concern" begins to reveal its formative importance. Faith comes very close to defining the particular identity of an individual person.

Three qualities of faith that Tillich's analysis helps to draw out have particular relevance for the development of this book: faith is a common subjective phenomenon; its problematic character lies in its object; and it most clearly manifests itself in action.

Because of its centering character within the human person, Tillich insists that all human beings have faith. Far from being rare, some faith provides all responsible people with the coherence and integrity of their lives. Faith as a subjective attitude and a formal disposition "is basic and universal."[3] "In this formal sense of faith as ultimate concern, every human being has faith. Nobody can escape the essential relation of the conditional spirit [human existence] to something unconditioned [transcendent and ultimate]."[4]

Second, the problem underlying faith today relates more to its object than to its existential embodiment. The only thing worthy of ultimate concern must itself be ultimate. But what in our expanded consciousness of so many different religions and movements is truly transcendent and ultimate, relative to all others? On the objective or material side, "there have been faiths with unworthy contents. They invest something preliminary, finite, and conditional with the dignity of the ultimate, infinite, and unconditional."[5] The classic name for this is idolatry; it hides behind many accepted forms of behavior today. The difficulty of determining what is truly ultimate means that faith is always searching to know better its proper object.

Third, in the case of many persons, the condition of being grasped by ultimate concern may not appear on the surface of their confessional statements. Some people are explicitly committed unbelievers, and others do not follow their stated beliefs. A better indication of where a person's or a group's faith really lies may be found in their consistent behaviors. Faith actualizes itself most authentically and surely in people's consistent practice. This means that action more than any other expression measures the existence and authenticity of faith.

---

that faith is the state of being grasped by an ultimate concern." Paul Tillich, *Systematic Theology*, vol. 3, *Life and the Spirit; History and the Kingdom of God* (Chicago: University of Chicago Press, 1963), 130.

3. Tillich, *Systematic Theology*, 3:130.
4. Tillich, *Systematic Theology*, 3:130.
5. Tillich, *Systematic Theology*, 3:130.

Spirituality as Faith in Action

Faith and spirituality are closely aligned. Reflecting on the correlation between spirituality and faith will bring out the searching character of spirituality.

In this book spirituality is understood as the way persons and groups live their lives in the face of what they consider to be ultimate reality. This dynamic, activist understanding of spirituality takes into account that the logic or fundamental direction of people's lives reveals in the surest practical way where their deepest commitments lie. In many ways people gradually define themselves by their consistent activities: we are what we do. This phrase does not subvert the ability of humans to stand back and take a reflective look at themselves: we are also more than our actual performance. But this does not lessen the ability of behavior patterns to reveal the accuracy or the deception in our self-descriptions that may be apparent to others from our actions. The location of spirituality in action assumes some measure of responsible freedom being operative in the patterns of people's decision making. Action is where decisions become real.

Spirituality should not be reduced to an observable lifestyle or to a synthesis of the sum total of a person's activities. Spirituality refers to the way these activities reflect what a person takes to be supremely important and transcendent. It is another word that attempts to find the categories for measuring the set of factors that together define the inner being of a person or group. Spirituality refers to the way persons and whole groups organize their lives around what is transcendently important. Reciprocally, self-disposition relative to transcendent value defines both the importance of the object and the inner driving force or character of personhood.

That spirituality is cognate with faith appears in all their essential characteristics. Both revolve around the fundamental commitment that defines a person's identity. Both require a transcendent quality in the object of commitment. And both manifest themselves practically in the character of the behavior that their transcendent or ultimate object calls forth. Faith as a subjective disposition could be defined by the self-transcending center of gravity driving the sum total of a person's decisions and actions. And spirituality could be defined as the ultimate concern that is displayed in one's actions. Spirituality is the playing out of one's faith in action.

Spirituality Seeking Theology

From the consideration of the searching character of life that has appeared dramatically in developed Western societies, and from the correlations of basic faith and the conception of spirituality used here, one can begin to understand the phrase "spirituality seeking theology." It attempts to define the terrain of this book and the space from which its questions and answers arise. This can be illustrated with a description of how the relatively spontaneous language of the New Testament was generated out of the movement of the spiritual followers of Jesus.

Research on the origins and development of Christianity shows that it began as a movement of the followers of Jesus of Nazareth after his death and resurrection, a corporate spirituality of following Jesus wholly contained within Judaism. Only gradually did distinctive characteristics of the spirituality of following Jesus emerge that began to differentiate this movement from the Jewish temple and synagogues, as "Christians" searched, gradually became aware of, and began to formulate the qualities that distinguished them from Jewish communities.[6] In this whole process, but especially during the first and into the second century, one can see how spirituality provided the substratum for the process of reflection that gradually clarified Christian positions vis-à-vis Jewish beliefs. Definitions of modern Christian theology often characterize it as appealing to religious experience. On the basis of this initial historical process, a more accurate description might be an appeal to the full range of the spirituality of following Jesus. Liberation theologians are right in describing theology as reflection on Christian praxis or spirituality.

Christian spirituality consists of following Jesus. Christians are those who have shaped their lives after the pattern of Jesus in their belief in God and God's rule. Christian spirituality includes a set of beliefs, an ethical code, and a number of practical spiritual behaviors, such as worshiping God in Christian assembly, prayer, other devotions, and good works. But the basis or ground for the whole of Christian spirituality across the many churches consists in following Jesus. Christianity began with following Jesus, and this is what it has continued to be and always will be.

Christian spirituality always reflects the historical context in which it exists. This can be demonstrated by a consideration of the history of Christian spirituality, where we see very different ways of living Christian life. In other words, the common core of following Jesus,

---

6. The word "Christians" has to be carefully parsed to avoid the anachronism of a reference to a clearly defined religion distinct from the "Judaism" that gave birth to the Jesus movement. It took centuries for a clear social and cultural differentiation to become solidified. This development is studied by Daniel Boyarin, *Border Lines: The Partition of Judaeo-Christianity,* Divinations (Philadelphia: University of Pennsylvania Press, 2004).

that is, living out Christian faith in God in a way that is determined by Jesus' teaching and example and the hope he inspires, assumes different forms and styles in different historical cultures and environments.

Christian spirituality absorbs different cultural systems into itself and remains the same spirituality in its base of following Jesus. One Christian faith or spirituality picks up different shapes, expressions, and beliefs along the way. In the present period of searching, Christian spirituality will gradually reformulate its beliefs in God, define its ethical norms, and express its worship of God in a manner that is derived from the source of Christian life but is fitted into this new culture in the same way Christian spirituality has always done.

The basal character of Christian spirituality raises the question of the nature of the theology from which it differs. What is the theology that is distinct from spirituality and for which spirituality is searching?[7] This question would yield an easier answer if theology were a single discipline with a unified method. In reality, the analogous term "theology" refers to many disciplines: the study of the Bible, which employs a variety of methods; the study of the history of doctrines and how they were generated in different ways in different ages and contexts; and a host of present-day disciplines. Some of these disciplines are academic and others are not; some use methods that appeal to specific audiences; some are hybrids forged in a dialogue with non-theological disciplines; some have a specific goal for a specific audience. For example, both constructing and teaching a catechism today in different Christian traditions require careful attention to representing particular church traditions and to addressing specific audiences. Sometimes this activity would be called theological in a generic sense, but as a discipline with its own method, catechetics is quite different from theology, as theology is understood here.

In this book theology refers to the academic discipline of understanding reality critically through the symbols of Christian faith. The word "symbol" speaks in a wide sense of the persons, events, writings, words, concepts, institutions, doctrines, and actions that make up the living tradition through which a corporate spirituality or a religion preserves itself as it passes through time. The theologian uses these symbols of the faith tradition to interpret the meaning of all reality. The subject matter of theology is thus not limited to its transcendent object, God, because theology also interprets the world in terms of conceptions of God that are stimulated by revelation and handed down in a tradition.

---

7. I answer this question in an extended discussion in *Dynamics of Theology* (Maryknoll, NY: Orbis Books, 2001).

Criticism plays an essential role in this intellectual discipline. Theology interprets the world critically, and, in the light of a tradition of revelation, it frequently interrupts the standard reigning opinions about reality. But criticism also moves in the other direction as well. All Christians agree that scripture is the norm of the church and not vice versa. But when theology enters into dialogue with the world, the world reflects back upon theological symbols critically and questions whether they are generating a language that accurately characterizes the world or truly interprets Christian faith as it exists in today's cultural context. Theology, then, transcends expressions of faith and spirituality and asks the question of truth. Does spiritual experience correspond to reality, as best it can be determined, by using both the norms of secular knowledge and the norms of faith's tradition in relevant correlation?

This question shows how closely theology as construed here relates to spirituality: theology is inseparable from spirituality, and spirituality always reaches out for critical reflection upon itself. One can pinpoint what theology "adds" to spirituality on the levels of method and appropriation. On the one hand, spirituality is a discipline whose language gives expression to the existential practice of a way of life, sometimes in a reflective and organized way as in a school of spirituality or in a systematically organized treatise. On the other hand, theology attends to the questions of the truth of such expressions by critically measuring a way of life and its language against the symbols of Christian revelation, and measuring interpretations of those symbols against the reality of the world known through other sources and disciplines. Christian spirituality is a reflective discipline aimed at expressing in a clear, functional way an understanding of an existential Christian way of life. As such, Christian spirituality gives rise to theology. Christian theology, which has its source in Christian spirituality, asks the question of truth: what understandings of the faith and the world represented in spirituality most adequately correspond to reality?

The point of this digression on theology is to be clear where this book does not go. It consistently stops short of critical theological analysis of how to justify a functional spiritual language. It does not examine the intelligibility of Jesus' divinity in relation to his historical human existence, nor analyze the concept of resurrection as distinct from an Easter experience, nor examine the coherence of the doctrine of the immanent trinity as distinct from the experience of an economic trinity, nor investigate the various doctrines connected with the end-time. Theological language, when borrowed, is placed in service of the expression of a spirituality of following Jesus.

This should throw some light on the dynamics of Christian spirituality seeking theology. The foundational base of Christian faith has
always consisted of a continuous and consistent spirituality of following Jesus. Out of this corporate spirituality have emerged organization, reflection on spiritual experience in the light of new cultures, and
the gradual formulation of beliefs through theological reflection on
the living experience of the community, as this has been codified in
the scriptures and in every historical period and place. Again, this
process illustrates the meaning of spirituality searching for theology.
This book deals with Christian spirituality as individual and ecclesial
following of Jesus as that opens up questions for reflection and formulation. The point here is not to interpret teachings or doctrines, or to
defend them as true, but to link Christian vocabulary to the sources of
its meaning in a living spirituality that is always facing fresh problems
and asking questions from new perspectives.

CHAPTER ONE

The Human as Spirit of the World

It seems right that the quest for meaning begin with a description of human existence within the story of the universe. During the course of the twentieth century, combined sciences such as astronomy, physics, biology, and paleontology have fashioned a new picture of our universe and the planet earth. This astonishing new story of our cosmos, our earth, the rise of life in it, and the appearance of the human species is our story because we are part of it, and it describes us. This story of the universe sets a new context for our understanding ourselves, God, and the bonds that tie God, the world, and human existence together.

Compared with premodern and modern understandings, the new scientific story involves a significant shift in our understanding of the world and the human. Scholars generally note a transition from a static view of the world to a recognition of its historicity and development at the end of the eighteenth and through the nineteenth century. In the course of the twentieth century, this historical consciousness has subsequently been drawn up analogously into a much wider picture of the universe, the planet earth, and the evolution of life. This has resulted in a dramatically new framework for human self-understanding and for situating the self–world–God relationships. The doctrines that give formal expression to Christian faith have to be reappropriated within this new imaginative framework of understanding.

The following discussion loosely follows a narrative line that moves from the Big Bang to anthropology. The story is not told in scientific detail; most are familiar with it in nonscientific lay terms. The story provides a framework for commentary on some of the ways in which the resulting new picture of things affects the presuppositions of spiritual reflection. This chapter thus respects the distinction between science and religious thinking, and at the same time it provides background for the more explicitly spiritual reflection on the idea of creation that lies ahead. Here the analysis aims at raising up aspects of the story of the universe that should condition the imagination when the discussion moves to formal reflection on transcendence and ultimacy. The chapter draws from philosophers of science and theologians who

attend to the interaction between science and theology methodologi-
cally and in terms of content.

These reflections loosely correlate with three stages of the development of higher and more complex forms of being resulting in human
existence. The passage moves through time from inorganic matter, to
life, to the human species, and the question of the human.

The Story of the Universe

The standard story of creation in Christianity is found in two versions in the first book of the Hebrew scriptures, Genesis: it is the story
of the creation of Adam and Eve, the first archetypal human beings.
Most Christians recognize the mythic and symbolic character of this
story, that it stimulates meaning in response to deep human questions
about the ultimate ground of being and does not describe empirical or
historical beginnings. It is a little story that carries large significance.
By contrast, the awesome narrative of the beginning and development
of our cosmos unfolds in a different register and may seem to some
to challenge religious belief. Educated people worldwide know this
story well; it has become the presupposition of science education and
a framework for human self-understanding. The story is not retold
here but is presupposed. The chapter aims rather at raising up various
salient characteristics of the new story of the universe that will have
a bearing on the distinct but not completely unrelated spiritual questions of creation and anthropology.

Age of the universe. A consensus among scientists establishes the age of
the universe at between thirteen and fourteen billion years as we measure time. Various strands of evidence and mathematical calculation
enable this retrojection to the point at which our universe began in an
explosion of energy. We have no data on anything before that time,
so the birth of the cosmos was also the birth of time. This moment is
somewhat irreverently and ironically called the Big Bang. Out of that
event or happening there developed all that is contained in our universe: the ingredients or elements of the whole of it exploded out of
this burst of being.

Some significant implications about our world can be drawn from
the fact that it had a beginning in time and is a product of development. A bit of reflection leads to an elusive sense of how long a time
thirteen plus billion years is. The chronology also indicates that the
human species appeared only at the very end of the history of our
universe to date. Various comparisons impress this on the imagination. For example, if the duration of the universe was compared to a

single year, *Homo sapiens* made its appearance only on the last day of December late in the evening. From our perspective we tend to consider ourselves the apex or climax of evolution, but from a more neutral point of view we are only the latest in a very long and busy history that generated and is still generating countless other forms of being.

Another lesson that may be drawn from this narrative lies implicit in the story itself. Time and especially development over time represent constitutive dimensions of the universe: its being does not just subsist *in* time but also *is* temporal. The significance of this stands out more clearly when opposed to a static conception of the universe. A universe with a fixed structure does not negate time, but it depicts development through time as passage through structures that remain the same. By contrast, recognition of the intrinsically temporal and developmental character of being makes it essentially unstable and changing.[1] This will become clearer in the consideration of the engine of development further on.

The size of the universe. Given global economics today, the image or idea of a billion has been tamed: we can reach out toward the thirteen-billion-year-old universe. But the size of the universe accompanies its age, and despite its finitude the human mind cannot begin catch up with it.

Various authors try to represent the size of the ever-expanding universe. "What are we to make of a universe that we now know consists of some 125 billion galaxies? . . . That has a diameter of 30 billion light years? The distance light travels in a year is about six trillion miles, so to reach a diameter of 30 billion light years, one multiplies 30 billion by six trillion to get some 180 sextillion miles."[2]

Cognizance of the size of the universe bends back to influence our conception of the human. One consideration, anthropocentric in character, tries to soften the shock of what seems like infinite finitude. This idea folds the age and size of the universe into human self-understanding as what was needed to generate our planet, life on it, and finally the human species; it is simply our prehistory. We are the result of this magnificent, breathtaking story.[3] This reflection will return later in the discussion of various suggestions of teleology in the universe.

---

1. Nature is not a structure but a story. It is constituted as a narrative. "For the 'being' of the world is always also a 'becoming' and there is always a story to be told, especially as matter becomes living and then conscious and, eventually, social too." Arthur Peacocke, *Theology for a Scientific Age: Being and Becoming—Natural and Divine,* Signposts in Theology (Oxford: Basil Blackwell, 1990), 62.

2. David Toolan, *At Home in the Cosmos* (Maryknoll, NY: Orbis Books, 2001), 139.

3. John Polkinghorne, *Beyond Science: The Wider Human Context* (Cambridge: Cambridge University Press, 1996), 84, as cited by Toolan, *At Home in the Cosmos,* 139.

But another reflection holds any easy anthropocentrism in check. The sheer magnitude of the universe simply forbids a human claim to being the center of reality; it enforces cosmic humility. One cannot insist that life analogous to our own does not exist in other contexts within our universe when the probabilities favor it, not to mention forms of life and worlds that may be more "advanced" than our own. This is one of several precise points where the new coordinates of our self-understanding will have a definite impact on the forms of religious expression that were generated in a smaller and stabler world.[4]

The energy of the universe. The imaginative symbol pointing to the beginning of the universe represents it as a burst of energy. This energy, this power that makes the universe work, explodes and expands. The force of this energy continues to sustain the universe; energy is of the very substance of what is. The universe itself is this unimaginable expanding flow of cosmic energy that keeps on creating new space. Yet expansive energy is conditioned by a gravity that pulls the elements of the universe together by attraction. Disparate pieces of matter communicate with each other by this other force that draws them to each other. On a cosmic level one can imagine a dynamic interplay between expansive energy and a constricting gravitational force between bodies that together establish a massive regulating system governing the flow of energy.

On a more "local" organizational level, where energy is structured by a closer orderly pattern or system, another rule affecting the flow of energy becomes manifest. The second law of thermodynamics states that "with the elapse of time, the organized, kinetic energy available for mechanical work—whether electrical, chemical, or thermal—inevitably has to be paid for in waste, irretrievable structural dissipation, decay, and aging."[5] It is as if all forms of being consist of bundles of energy that are harnessed or organized in active patterns of interchange. On the one hand, the organization promotes integrated,

---

4. Science's account of the Big Bang cannot fail to have an impact on the imagination. Kant's turn to the subject resulted in an anthropocentrism that left the universe and the world in the sense of planet a mere background for a concern for the human drama of history. Science has so altered the imagination relative to our habitat that the story of the cosmos has reduced somewhat the position of the human. "In fact, the universe is itself the principal creative adventure, and there is no reason to assume that our species is the sole reason for its existence," writes John Haught. In fact, he continues, human existence is "a small part of the universe, but we are not the whole story" (*Christianity and Science: Toward a Theology of Nature* [Maryknoll, NY: Orbis Books, 2007], 127). The story of the universe contains its own awesome resonances that almost engulf the human; the human has been drawn into a larger narrative.

5. Toolan, *At Home in the Cosmos*, 161.

focused, and organic application of forces that enable in turn an incre-
ment in the level of capacity and operation. Energy becomes organized to perform specific tasks that constitute distinct forms of being.
On the other hand, the whole system steadily expends energy so that
gradually in the long run the system itself is condemned to wear down
and die.

We will return to the tension between system and energy in a later
discussion of law and randomness. But at this point the significance of
the substantive role of energy in the constitution of reality for anthropology deserves mention. The new world projected by current science
transcends the deterministic, mechanistic universe of the Newtonian synthesis. Energy can never be fully controlled; reality is never
fixed or completely predictable. By contrast, in the period formative
of Christian doctrines and thereafter, conceptual definition and stasis
reflected permanence, and immobility suggested eternal complete-
ness. By definition change meant deficiency in being, and temporal
being was associated with a path to death. The retrieval of the value
of indeterminacy and change associated with energy does not reverse
the values and turn structure and stability into disvalues. But recognizing the constitutive value of energy relativizes structure by always
pairing it with energy. Both its temporal character and its nature as
dynamic energy mean we live in a fluid world that is constantly in
motion.

Process and complexity. Two dimensions or characteristics of the dynamism of the world are process and complexity. The old story of the
universe did not really allow for deep change. Western thought pos-
tulated a higher world above, or a metaphysical world of laws, but
the ideal world did not include constant generation of new forms of
being.[6] Of course, human beings have always had some sense of historicity, in different depths and degrees. No one could ignore the way
human beings constantly adjust their social arrangements and the
diversity among groups. But change always occurred within permanent structures, forms of being that organized the world universally
or by nature. The world itself was not moving, only individual items
within it changed as they came and went. By contrast, the current picture of the world depicts change at the level of the structures of nature.
New possibilities affect seemingly permanent patterns, so that change
constitutes the very character of nature. This is a world of process,

---

6. The term "metaphysical" refers to a sphere of reality that is not empirical but
seems to be required as the condition of the possibility of what appears on the surface
of the world and its history, as a deeper or a higher realm that one interprets to be
entailed in what happens empirically.

a world that is always becoming, where substance and permanent structures only appear so at a given time but not over vast periods of time or in radically changed conditions. Creation becomes an ongoing process that constantly introduces novelty to the given. If creation is ongoing, then the world at any given time is always imperfect, and deficiency is concomitant with being itself.[7]

Reality is dynamic, and the dynamism entails complexity. Toolan describes this complexity in terms of constant interchange between system and new data. Reality for the most part is made up of "systems that exchange energy and matter with their environment; they are open to turbulence, fluctuation, and a degree of random chance."[8] Systems are never self-enclosed so that they admit no variables. The influx of energy and the ways of processing new data allow a given system to withstand and even move against the tide of entropy. "The typical dynamical system—physical, chemical, biological, or neurological—is almost never truly isolated or self-contained; it is, first, an 'open' system exchanging matter and energy with its environment."[9]

The complexity of being is exemplified in the amazing variety of organizational patterns that reality assumes. This is especially true on the biological level. Kinds of being in the flow of reality keep adjusting to their environment by an internalization of new variables. The world can be perceived as layered through various strata in a scale of being according to different criteria of measurement and complexity. Some self-organizing systems are more differentiated than others and are capable of new and different kinds of activity. There seems to be a clear trajectory in evolution toward more differentiation and "higher" forms of being. The history of evolution "shows an overall trend toward greater complexity, responsiveness, and awareness. The capacity of organisms to gather, store, and process information has steadily increased. Who can doubt that a human being represents an astonishing advance over an amoeba or a worm."[10]

This last reflection has jumped ahead in the story. Up to now we've described the age, size, and motion of the cosmos that generated and constitutes us. The commentary now attends to the transition from inorganic being to life.

---

7. John F. Haught, *God after Darwin: A Theology of Evolution* (Boulder, CO: Westview Press, 2000), 38.

8. Toolan, *At Home in the Cosmos*, 167.

9. Toolan, *At Home in the Cosmos*, 167.

10. Ian G. Barbour, *When Science Meets Religion* (San Francisco: HarperSanFrancisco, 2000), 111.

The Emergence of the Earth, Life, the Human

The next part of the long story of the cosmos as we know it tells how our galaxy was formed and in it the little planetary system revolving around our sun. Our planet emerged through various random events that left us with a moon, oceans of water, and a gradual process of shifting landmasses to form the continents as we know them. The conditions for life on the planet also fell into place, and at this stage of the story evolutionary biologists and paleontologists take over the narrative. This phase of the story contains fundamental principles for understanding our world and ourselves: the motor of evolution in the dynamic interchange between law and random occurrence, the generation of novelty, and from that the emergence of life and the human.

Law and randomness. Process or becoming describes the essential quality of reality from the beginning. This dynamism becomes more specifically defined in the process of evolution. Among others, three important principles can be observed interacting in the evolutionary process. First, contingency and randomness elicit development. The universe cannot be fully rationalized; because of its complexity the interactivity of events cannot be predicted. Meteorological events offer a good example of this randomness. But, second, unexpected random events operate within a set of relatively stable chemical and physical laws and systems. Systems always exist in larger environments that interact with them. Thus, system and isolated events do not negate each other; they coexist and interact with each other. Third, this interactive process extends over the long period of time that was indicated earlier.[11] It is difficult to adopt a neutral or object framework of time outside a human point of reference. But to imagine the age of the universe is to notice that cosmic development and evolution have had an enormous framework of time and space to work their way.

One of the main resistances to evolutionary thinking occurs among Christian believers, and the sticking point seems to be the idea of randomness in the process of coming to be, especially of human life. This injects a strong dose of instability and with it a threat of ultimate unintelligibility into the formation of human existence that religion addresses. Is the human species the result of an accident? This will have to be addressed when the spiritual notion of God as creator arises. But at this point one can note that, even in a dynamic world of evolution, relatively stable systems of being, organized according to laws, coexist with random happenings and operate in a relatively consistent manner. "Chance and law are complementary rather than

---

11. Haught, *God after Darwin*, 36.

conflicting features of nature. Random events on one level may lead to statistical regularities on a higher level of aggregation. Redundancy and thresholds may limit the effects of random events on integrated systems. On this reading, chance would be part of the design, and not incompatible with it."[12] "Chance, consequently, is not an alternative to law, but the very means whereby law is creative. The two are strongly interrelated and the universe evolves through their interplay."[13]

The picture of the universe and, more pointedly, of human life on our planet is certainly affected by this understanding of the dynamic engine of evolution. In other words, it is not so large a concept that it becomes irrelevant for self-understanding and actual life. These structures do have bearing on how we conceive of ourselves. On one level, Elizabeth A. Johnson finds an analogy between the dynamics of system and chance in the operation of human freedom. Because the human is part of the world, one can see in the freedom of human existence an echo of the indeterminacy of the universe.[14] On another level, that of life in relation to the future, the interaction of routinized pattern and random interventions opens up reality to constant new being. This dynamism floods human existence with potential meaning.

Forward direction and novelty. The idea of unpredictability that appeared in the consideration of process and complexity, especially in the interaction between law and random happening, describes the open character of the universe. This is associated in science with the principle of uncertainty. The universe is moving not only by expansion but also, within human ken, by complexification and the generation of novelty. This invites reflection.

Turning first to the open character of being, what is called the principle of uncertainty is associated with the discovery that one cannot subject the basic elements of the physical world to exact measurement. It was then concluded "that indeterminacy is *an objective feature*

---

12. Barbour, *When Science Meets Religion*, 113. "Today we can think of God as the designer of a self-organizing system." God respects the integrity of the system as it moves toward higher complexity, emergent life, through the dialectic of randomness and law. "A patient God could have endowed matter with diverse potentialities and let it create more complex forms on its own. In this interpretation God respects the integrity of the world and lets it be itself" (ibid.). This integrates pain, suffering, and death into the system. "Competition and death are intrinsic to an evolutionary process" (ibid.). This issue will come up again in the next chapter.

13. Elizabeth A. Johnson, "Does God Play Dice? Divine Providence and Chance," *Theological Studies* 57 (1996): 8.

14. Johnson, "Does God Play Dice?" 8.

of nature and not a limitation of human knowledge."[15] This makes the cosmos and the planet an open system that includes a range of possibilities that are really new and undecided.

> The future is not simply unknown; it is "not decided." More than one alternative is open, and there is some opportunity for unpredictable novelty. Time involves a unique historicity and unrepeatability; the world would not repeat its course if it were restored to a former state, for at each point a different event from among the potentialities might be actualized.[16]

This represents a considerably different understanding of reality from what was presupposed in the period when Christian doctrines were formulated. The processes of the world and of ideas were then seen within the framework of a design that was already in place, in the eternal ideas of God according to Plato, or in the stable teleological patterns recognizable in nature according to Aristotle. In these systems indeterminacy and chance are the antithesis of design. When one shifts the suppositions of the discussion to include real openness to the new, the concept of evolution "suggests another understanding of design—an understanding that postulates a general direction but no detailed plan. . . . In this view there is increasing order and information but no predictable final state."[17]

Ian Barbour describes how the emergence of novelty may be understood in an evolutionary framework. First of all, within the framework of an interaction between law and chance, "novel forms of order emerged that not only could not have been predicted from laws and theories governing previously existing forms, but also gave rise to genuinely new kinds of behavior of and activity in nature." This represents from a certain perspective a jump in the level of being. The theories that explain this simply describe it as happening in situations "where disorder at one level leads to *order at a higher level*, with new laws governing the behavior of structures showing new types of complexity." In some cases it seems that "order emerges spontaneously in complex systems, especially on the border between order and chaos. Too much order makes change impossible; too much chaos makes continuity impossible. Complexity at one level leads to simplicity at another level. Disorder is often the precondition for the appearance of a new form of order." The whole process involves both continuity and discontinuity. "The formation of such self-organizing, self-perpet-

---

15. Barbour, *When Science Meets Religion*, 69.
16. Barbour, *When Science Meets Religion*, 69.
17. Barbour, *When Science Meets Religion*, 112–13.

uating systems at the molecular level was perhaps the first step in the emergence of life."[18]

This idea of an unfinished universe could have a major impact on any given person's consciousness. It gives one a rather different conception of one's place in the world compared with its opposite, a world with unchanging forms of being. It "suggests that the universe is habitually open to further increase in being and value."[19] This could generate a spirituality in which people realize that they are part of, and take part in, "the great work of increasing the *universe's* own being," making it more than what it was.[20] Pierre Teilhard de Chardin's thought, which is not anthropocentric but cosmocentric, adopted this point of view: we live within a cosmic drama and we are part of it. Without this, life takes on a character of "killing time." Our action in the world would ultimately be futile. If the universe were complete and unchanging, leaving no room for new being, human action could not contribute to an absolute future, and human creativity would ultimately be an illusion. But within a dynamic universe spirituality can trust that we actually contribute to the end-time, "that our efforts can have a *lasting* impact on the whole of things."[21]

Life and the human. The considerations of the interaction between patterns of being structured statistically by law and random events abstractly describe how new forms and levels of being arise. Such was the passage from inorganic being to organic life. The path "upwards" through vegetative and animal life in their myriad forms to the threshold of *Homo sapiens* and then over it provides a story as complex and dramatic as can be told. How did evolution come to arrive at the human? As was just noted, there is some agreement that randomness means that time cannot repeat itself. Elizabeth Johnson says that science is virtually unanimous on the proposition that if the process of the emergence of life were "replayed," it would turn out differently because of the huge role of random factors in the process. Order and pattern are chastened by randomness and novelty; laws are statistical and descriptive, not prescriptive and determinative. Randomness, on the micro and macro levels and in its all pervasiveness in science, "undermine[s] the idea that there is a detailed blueprint or unfolding plan according to which the world was designed and now operates."[22]

---

18. Barbour, *When Science Meets Religion,* 109, 104, 105, respectively.
19. Haught, *Christianity and Science,* 78.
20. Haught, *Christianity and Science,* 78.
21. Haught, *Christianity and Science,* 81.
22. Johnson, "Does God Play Dice?" 6–7.

Yet this has not prevented cosmologists from pushing the question of overall purpose in the universe. Indeed, the universe from the very beginning seems to have been fine-tuned for the possibility of life to emerge. Development successfully passed through many narrow gates, the improbable stages that govern the possibility of life as we know it. In other words, looking backwards from the present, we are able to recreate the improbable journey that in fact arrived at life and, over and above that, the human. In a stronger version of this "anthropic principle" some retrieve a kind of back-door teleology that reads a concrete plan from the beginning into the whole development. But even with the softer version, purposefulness is not ruled out.[23] In the end, a purposeful view of the universe is a matter of faith. Science does not establish that the evolution of life on our planet is teleological. Some scientists outrightly deny that the de facto drift toward complexity and consciousness entails design. But neither does science exclude the possibility of purpose. Thus, one can say more definitely that this ambiguity raises the question of purpose and that the person who denies the possibility of purpose also does so on the basis of faith.

Barbour defends the human in the face of science. Science has been seen as waging an assault on the place and dignity of the human in the world and cosmos. First Copernicus and Galileo decentered the earth within the cosmos; then Darwin demoted the human by stressing its emergence out of matter and lower forms of life. The human seems smaller within the immensity of the cosmos, "insignificant in the midst of vast stretches of time and space."[24] Yet, by contrast, Teilhard applies a different measure of dignity than quantitative size, namely, complexity of being: by this criterion nothing we know compares with the human. If through science our universe has been enlarged, the human is enlarged with it. The human evolved into something distinctive amid all the beings of which we are aware. "Above all, human beings possess consciousness, which is the necessary condition for speech. Thus they are characterized by a capacity to think and speak purposefully. The possession of a complex syntactical language is unique."[25] Only human beings "have the capacity for reflection. Consciousness and language are the presuppositions for abstract thought

---

23. If it is too strongly formulated, the anthropic principle appears anthropocentric in its conception of the relation of God to the universe. "Wouldn't it be enough to understand the principle in the soft sense: that in retrospect one recognizes how the cosmos is in fact as it is so that life and life with mind became possible?" This is not a scientific principle or proof, but neither is it an illegitimate reflection. There is nothing that forbids the construal of purposefulness. Hans Küng, *The Beginning of All Things: Science and Religion* (Grand Rapids: Eerdmans, 2007), 148.

24. Barbour, *When Science Meets Religion*, 61.

25. Küng, *Beginning of All Things*, 162.

and directed, intentional states of mind such as love and hate, hopes and fears, convictions and wishes. All this is the basis for cultural development, for religion, philosophy, and science."[26]

In the light of the science of the cosmos and evolution of the human species, one can describe human existence as the cosmos conscious of itself. On the one hand, the human is completely connected with all of reality and interdependently constituted. The developed universe and the evolution of life provided the parts that constitute human existence. On the other hand, the human enjoys a self-consciousness that can objectify the world and distinguish objects outside the self as other than the self, even though we are in fact immersed in the cosmos. "We are part of an ongoing community of being; we are kin to all creatures, past and present."[27] The continuity and interconnectedness of everything refer both to the basic elements that constitute our world and the principles and laws that describe their actions. The extended story of emergent reality reinforces the interdependence of things. Human beings are created of the same stuff as the cosmos.[28]

The Place of the Human in the Cosmos

We have seen how the new narrative of the genesis of the universe induces "cosmic humility." This story makes it difficult to place human existence at the center of all reality. Leaving that premise in place, people would at the same time surely err if they did not recognize the distinctive character of the human in its spiritual and reflec-

---

26. Küng, *Beginning of All Things*, 163. Science has been encroaching on the uniqueness of the capacities that Küng refers to. It is statistically likely that other planets in our universe have other forms of intelligent life, perhaps more advanced than our own. And on our own planet, research finds analogues to human intelligence in various animal species.

27. Barbour, *When Science Meets Religion*, 62. Frequently enough those who come to this awareness of the continuity of the human with the world, of the essential bodily character of the human, especially out of an appreciation of evolution, argue this position by contrast with "dualism," a way of characterizing classical positions especially of a Platonic or Cartesian vintage. But the term "dualism" is too blunt an instrument to communicate anything very precise; and every precise account of the human should include a distinction between spirit and matter, but not a separation. We know no spirit apart from matter. Thus, for example, mind-brain research has had a major influence on theories of knowledge. See Wesley Wildman, *Religious and Spiritual Experiences* (Cambridge and New York: Cambridge University Press, 2011).

28. See Peacocke, *Theology for a Scientific Age*, 42–43; Elizabeth A. Johnson, *Quest for the Living God: Mapping Frontiers in the Theology of God* (New York: Continuum, 2007), 184. See also Barbra Fiand, *Awe-Filled Wonder: The Interface of Science and Spirituality* (Mahwah, NJ: Paulist Press, 2008) for an extended commentary on how the interconnection of the elements of realty bind the human to all the layers of our physical world.

tive connectedness to all that is. They would be wrong if they did not appreciate the singular sense of responsibility to and for the world that emerges from a *prise de conscience* of humanity's relation to the world. The concluding section of this commentary on the story of the universe raises the larger meta-scientific problem of the place of the human in the world. Two issues loom large. The first has to do with the moral relation of the human to the world. The second concerns basic human attitudes toward entropy and death.

History: the human spirit of the world. One way of trying to grasp the massive, complex story of the genesis of the universe and the human consists in noting thresholds and stages in its formation. From the perspective of the human species, major markers would be the formation of the planet in such a way that it could sustain life. The development of life itself, leading to the human, also passed through various stages that were necessary conditions for the end product. Obviously the transition to *Homo sapiens* that launches the human as it is today was a crucial step or jump. From the broad perspective of the whole story, however, one cannot isolate a single phase because all together make up one story, and the lack of any key element would have negated all the others.

There is a stage of human development that has been mediated so recently in the human story that in relation to the whole it has to be dated "now." This is the emergence in Western culture of historical consciousness in the late eighteenth and throughout the nineteenth century. Teilhard de Chardin depicts this protracted event in an allegory, a modern equivalent to Plato's allegory of the cave, except that it moves in an opposite direction. Human beings suddenly become aware that they exist in a contingent history in which they have responsibility for themselves, this planet, and human life itself. Human consciousness suddenly assumes responsibility for setting its own values and goals. What could be more important for conceptions about the place and role of the human in the universe? Teilhard writes as follows:

> Up to now human beings have lived apart from each other, scattered around the world and closed in upon themselves. They have been like passengers who accidentally met in the hold of a ship, not ever suspecting the ship's motion. Clustered together on the earth, they found nothing better to do than to fight or amuse themselves. Now, by chance, or better, as a natural result of organization, our eyes are beginning to open. The most daring among us have climbed to the bridge. They have seen the ship that carries us all. They have glimpsed

the ship's prow cutting the waves. They have noticed that the boiler keeps the ship going and a rudder keeps it on course. And, most important of all, they have seen clouds floating above and caught the scent of distant islands on the horizon. It [history] is no longer agitation down in the hold, just drifting along; the time has come to pilot the ship. It is inevitable that a different humanity must emerge from this vision.[29]

This dramatic image describes the gradual rise during the nineteenth century of historical consciousness, an awareness of our condition of existing in a time that is linear and moving forward. Moreover, it appears that we as humans—together, not as individuals—have become the pilots of this movement. This is a staggering new awareness, and many never become aware of it at all. But if one does, it has to make a difference. Two implications involved in this experience are relevant for understanding the place of the human in the cosmos.

First, this allegory transforms the human into a project; humanity is not just a kind of being but also a task to be accomplished. This insight dispels any idea of the place of the human as being outside or above the world. The insight involves recognition that humanity, as the self-conscious part of the world, is the world at a new and distinctive level of being. The dynamic developmental and evolutionary structure of the cosmos becomes internalized in the human so that the human now becomes the cosmos in a self-conscious way. Karl Rahner described the human as "spirit in the world." The phrase emphasizes spirit as non-matter, deeply embedded in matter but transcending it in self-knowledge and freedom.[30] The phrase "spirit of the world" assumes Rahner's meaning and expands it. Because the human is spirit of the world, the world itself in a self-conscious condition, the evolutionary dynamism of the world is rendered conscious in the human. In other words, cosmos or world acts out its evolutionary path in and through the human in the new way of freedom. The human is a project, and the project is the evolutionary trajectory of the world.

Second, the self-conscious and thus self-transcending character of the human entails moral responsibility. The human species has assumed a moral responsibility to and for the world. It is responsible *for* the world because of its freedom in relation to the world; it is responsible *to* the world because the human is part of the world. Because humanity is spirit of the world, the criteria for this moral responsibil-

29. Pierre Teilhard de Chardin, *Activation of Energy* (New York: Harcourt, Brace, 1971), 73-74, cited in Juan Luis Segundo, *The Community Called Church* (Maryknoll, NY: Orbis Books, 1973), 121.

30. Karl Rahner, *Spirit in the World* (New York: Herder & Herder, 1968).

ity are dictated by the integrity of the world. For example, at those points where the health or existence of the planet is threatened, or human beings are socially victimized, the ideals of the integrity of the ecosystem and the world of social life or common good provide criteria to criticize old and encourage new human behavior. The developmental well-being of the world forms the moral conscience of human existence.

The end: death and life. The term "end" at this point refers to the end of the story. It does not yet refer in the first place to a sense of ultimate goal or purpose. This would be a question to which science does not provide an answer. Today, however, science can predict the end of human existence in the sense of the end of our world, that is, when the solar system wears down. In some respects this is an irrelevant piece of information because the event is so far distant that it bears no immediate relevance for human behavior. Yet this extrapolation provides reasons that encourage metaphysical responses to the question of the ultimate purpose of the world and human existence in it. Thus, the deeper sense of "end" may be entailed in this topic.

David Toolan wrote that "we are placed in a radically unfinished universe, where it is our task to bring things to completion."[31] But that raises the question of what or where the term "completion" points to. Some reflections on that issue may be a fitting conclusion to this chapter.

Two principles that have arisen in the course of this chapter may be used to frame the issue. The first is that science has approached the question of the universe through a narrative of its genesis and development. Time thus provides one of the intrinsic building blocks of reality; what exists, exists in time. Our convictions about the nature of reality have to factor time into the equation. The second principle, consonant with the developmental character of reality, recognizes that later stages of reality tend to draw earlier stages up into themselves. The earlier supplies the platform on which the later builds. This provides a basis for cosmological and evolutionary continuity. Each of these principles helps to throw some light on the metaphysical questions of death and life.

Regarding time, there is a tendency in science to read reality today in terms of the past. To explain what exists in the present one examines the antecedent causes that account for what exists. This was certainly the case in the framework of a more mechanistic and predictable model of the universe. In that context one had to be impressed by the

---

31. Toolan, *At Home in the Cosmos*, 218.

seemingly absolute law of entropy: energy is finally used up and systems gradually wear down. But a drift in the story of the universe toward complexification and the emergence of new forms of being has accompanied entropy. Time, then, includes the future because the present consistently reaches into the future. From this perspective the future becomes an integral part of the ongoing story of the universe. In John Haught's view, the future supplies an essential element of what already exists out of the past. "In our futurist metaphysics, the world is in a sense not yet real, and therefore it is not yet intelligible, at least in a complete way."[32] Given the linear character of time, one cannot but think of reality as something intrinsically open to the future, which will be new and potentially, but not necessarily, fuller being. Contingency, law, and time all come together in the movement toward new being. With time the future enters into the calculus of the cosmos and, without disturbing the scientific data, throws light on its intelligibility. "Contingent events are an essential part of any world open to evolutionary novelty. And they are exactly what we should expect in a world whose ultimate ground and source favors the world's emerging independence as it opens itself to the future."[33]

Regarding later stages of development that include the earlier, there has been a tendency in the West to think of human existence as transcendent to and over against the world. We have already addressed this question of discontinuity and continuity: the way the human is completely a part of the world even though it transcends materiality as spirit. But the continuity of the human with the world allows and in fact demands that the human itself function as a window allowing us to peer into the universe. And this allows reflection to pass through human subjectivity en route to making projective statements about the nature of the universe. In short, human hope sheds light on the universe.

Are there any markers along the path of cosmic development and biological evolution that point in the direction of metaphysical hope? One is that the narrative structure of the universe extends into the future, making what has developed to this point incomplete. In its very incompleteness it calls for more intelligibility. Another is "that what has come into being already includes such an intensity of beauty that nature may be read as a great promise of more being and value up ahead."[34] This second point bears some weight. The story of the universe and the evolution of life thus far contain an enormous amount

---

32. Haught, *God after Darwin*, 100.

33. Haught, *God after Darwin*, 102. Haught develops these insights further in *Christianity and Science*, especially pp. 51-64, 153-76.

34. Haught, *Christianity and Science*, 60-61.

of partial meaning and beauty. It has also consistently led in the direction of more beauty and more intense forms of complexity in being. Cosmic purpose, Haught concludes, involves "an overall aim—not always successful, but nonetheless persistent—toward the heightening of beauty."[35]

These data, then, are the grounds for human hope, a hope that, as a disposition of the human, is generated in and by the cosmos itself. "If the cosmos is an unfinished story, it is also a story that at least up until now has been open to interesting and surprising outcomes."[36] To have come thus far is indeed something, and it provides grounds for hope in an ultimately coherent end to the story. This coherence, because of the violent and seemingly vicious logic of evolution, a logic in which all life ultimately ceases to exist, would require that the hoped for meaning have a saving character. In this way, the scientific account of reality leaves us with a spiritual question.

---

35. Haught, *Christianity and Science*, 62.
36. Haught, *Christianity and Science*, 64.

CHAPTER TWO

The Question of the Human

A seeking spirituality operates on the premise not of skepticism but of hope. Its narrative character mirrors the historical nature of human existence; all conscious experience arises out of the particular paths of people's lives. It may seem overdramatic to call human life a quest or a search, but examination of the dynamism driving someone's personal history and, more broadly, human history usually justifies such a description. The premise of a seeking and searching spirituality suggests that a good place to continue the reflection on human existence is with a question. And no more primal question exists than the one human existence poses to itself. Laying out the dimensions of this question will include an appropriation of ourselves, a first sketch of an anthropology. What follows then is a broad descriptive account of the question of the human as a starting point for the narrative and searching spirituality that follows.[1]

The development of this initial anthropology, bounded by the limits of a short chapter, can consist of little more than a suggestive outline. It has five parts, describing human existence as spirit, personally free, socially constituted, damaged by what Christians call sin, and challenged by the radical question of meaning. This question, implicit in the human phenomenon as such, thus raises the religious question.

Human Existence as Spirit

It makes sense for a searching spirituality to begin with the question that human existence itself is. This question does not yield an answer that can adequately encompass the unfathomable mystery of the human species. But it unleashes various kinds of analysis that uncover qualities and characteristics of the human that in return pro-

---

1. This starting point is drawn from Karl Rahner, *Foundations of Christian Faith: An Introduction to the Idea of Christianity* (New York: Crossroad, 1994), 26-32. A starting point should not be confused with foundationalism, the idea that philosophy or theology has an absolute starting point that might in turn yield an inclusive system. Reflection does begin somewhere, and the question that human existence poses to the self provides a number of positive functions that will become clear in the development that follows.

vide a measure of self-possession. What are we? Why are we here? Where are we going? These questions do not go away. While people in fact often ignore them, block them, and live in perpetual distraction from them, they linger, they poke, and they sometimes disrupt human life. This first probe into some understanding of human existence will show how the ability to ask these questions suggests that a first symbol for understanding the human is "spirit."

The term "spirit" does not yield to a ready description. A first definition of spirit locates it by negation as "not material," the non-matter that is real but not corporeal or physical, lacking in itself the measurements applied to things in space and time. Spirit transcends the realm of the imagination and is intrinsically unimaginable. A positive appreciation of spirit can be negotiated only by metaphor and negation. For example, spirit is like electronic waves or streaming particles: invisible but effective. And yet, as spirit, it lacks physicality in itself. The very conception of spirit, therefore, is dialectical: it involves a tension that cannot be resolved. The spirit is pure energy, latent, operative in but transcending the physical. From the outset it should be insisted that distinction from matter, the physical, and things corporeal does not necessarily imply separation. If the spiritual were not deeply embedded in the physical world, we would have no access to it at all. The negative edge of "dualisms" lies less in the distinction of aspects that are held together in a given whole, and more in a separation, prioritizing, and neglect of important dimensions of reality. And so it is in the case of the human. The spiritual character of the human reveals itself only within the physical self that it transcends.

The spiritual dimension of the human best shows itself within the various activities of human consciousness. Recall that spirit, which is intrinsically immaterial, cannot be perceived by the ordinary route of sense perception. But we can begin to appreciate what "spirit" refers to in a description of the process of knowing. A formula describing human existence and highlighting how the spiritual reveals itself in human knowing speaks of knowledge as being-present-to-itself.[2] For example, in the case of a person (or subject) knowing or attending to something (an object), the person becomes aware of the object, the self, and the self-knowing-the-object. This bending of the subject back on itself is itself a manner of being: we are each of us being that is conscious of itself. Knowing is not something that just is; as activity, it is being that *is* knowing and self-conscious. This reflecting back to be present to oneself, so that one does not just know but knows that one knows, transcends the physical and gives a glimpse of spirit or

---

2. See Rahner, *Foundations of Christian Faith*, 17-19.

freedom in the act of reaching out from what deceptively appears to be the passive and inert character of inorganic physicality. Freedom and transcendence do not imply independence of matter: we know of no human knowledge without a brain that is the knowing organism. But neither does spirit-as-self appear to be reducible to the brain. Rather, human consciousness leaps out from the physical, chemical, and organic in self-conscious reflection. Spirit manifests itself as the self-presence of being to itself.

Another indication of how the spirit within the human transcends the material lies in the seemingly infinite scope of its reach. Once again, this dimension does not lie on the surface, because all conscious activity consists in particular acts that intend a specific limited object. The transcendent and unlimited character of spiritual consciousness subsists in the drive of human activity and its scope. It becomes more visible in a consideration of cumulative corporate human achievements such as the explosion of knowledge during the last half of the twentieth century. Human curiosity, questioning, and knowing stretch out toward an infinite horizon; the will desires the good in itself so that no single good exhausts the attraction; human action seems to be driven by an infinite quest to have or be more, even to be absolutely in the face of death and the dissolution of the physical. These standard reflections in a classical teleological philosophy of religion have not lost their suggestive power. They point to a dynamism within the human spirit that breaches the barrier of the totality of material objects by a recognition of their finitude.

Spirit, then, refers to something experienced uniquely and paradigmatically in the human itself. We encounter spirit not as something separated from the physical makeup of human beings but as a dimension of the human itself. Spirit, however, is non-matter, the immaterial, and thus unimaginable; it is definable sheerly by negation of the limitation and containment and routine pattern that is associated with the physical.[3] In contrast to the restrictions of law or repetition, spirit manifests itself as an elementary dimension of active self-transcendence that constitutes human freedom. The human "spirit" so manifests itself as "freedom" transcending determinacy that descriptively

---

3. One should be attentive to the world of science in making these statements. This description is offered within a quite limited framework of phenomenological analysis of subjective conscious life. It is not possible for me to comment on spirit and freedom being analogous concepts that have different but structurally similar parallels in other forms of being than the human, whether organic and inorganic. I do not enter into a discussion of the instability of being at all levels, of the dynamism of random events in the process of evolution that may easily accommodate attenuated notions of freedom and even dynamism and spirit, or *élan vitale*. These questions are not unimportant, but they extend beyond the limits and purpose of this exposition. See chapter 1, n. 27.

they are synonymous. Spirit is the inner freedom of being, which in human existence manifests itself as a "self" that is self-conscious: it knows itself knowing. The next section will analyze in an elementary way some of the diverse levels of this freedom.

Human Existence as Freedom

The point of departure for this description of the human is the question itself as something that sheds light on the ones who ask it. To ask a question, to call the given into question, entails reflection, a bending back on the self by mind and spirit that reveals a certain primal self-transcendence. Calling this self-presence or self-manifestation "freedom" or "spirit" helps to define both of these terms. The brief phenomenologies of various levels of human freedom that follow add some density to this constitutive dimension of human existence. They assume the point of view of the individual person where one can distinguish relatively clearly four distinct levels or spheres of human engagement with the world.

A basic level of the response of human freedom or spirit to the world in which it exists may be characterized as sheer openness to it and dependence upon it. A reflective human consciousness always understands the self in the here and now, as in this world and differentiated from it. There is no need to build a subject–object dualism to recognize that we are always selves in the world, open to the world and influenced by the world. To be a person here and now implicitly entails an open subjectivity that stands in relation to the world. A person gains a sense of self-possession both by being defined by the space-time world in which one is, and by standing over against the world as something other than the self. Here lie the grounds by which one is able to "enter into oneself," reflect on oneself, take stock of one's self, and speak of "self-possession." Such self-possession is actually enabled by one's being in relation to the world, the other, the non-self. At this elemental level of human freedom one can think of self in metaphors like a "clear space," or an "expanding self," or a "transparency." Self-consciousness, self-knowledge, and self-control all presume and rest on being in an open relation to non-self and world.

Another level of freedom consists in what is ordinarily called choice, or free choice. In much of the debates about the nature of freedom the focus rests on choice. This was especially so in the historical debates about the role of human freedom in the process of salvation from God mediated by Jesus Christ.[4] Here freedom refers to the abil-

---

4. The theology of the Christian life has been and frequently remains infected by a simplistic response to the question: Who is responsible for an individual's salvation,

ity to choose among options. Everyday life teems with choices; the human person who lives an active life constantly makes choices; to be free is to be able to choose. At this juncture one measures the degree of freedom precisely by a lack of either internal or external constraint. On the one hand, behaviorist psychology might debate the question of just how free we really are. When one begins to reflect on the remarkable predictability of human behavior, one begins to suspect that hidden drives and invisible compulsions at various levels, both personal and social, are hedging one's options fairly closely. On the other hand, what does an individual in liberal Western culture prize more deeply than his or her own individual freedom? On the level of intuitive self-awareness there opens up within each of us a sphere of individual choices, however narrow their field, which one cherishes with a kind of possessiveness that rivals self-love. Our ability to choose defines our individual identity; it is the presupposition of responsibility.

At its romantic optimum, freedom of choice is often depicted as being absolutely allowed and able to do anything one wants at the moment. This kind of freedom seems to be most itself when one can act on sheer whim to follow any desire. One measures freedom at this level by purely self-initiated action in response to stimuli that attract us but do not drive or control us. Freedom increases inversely to restraint, command or imperative; the thinner the commanding reasons, the greater the freedom; the fullest actualization of this freedom lies in carefree response to what pleases. From the standpoint of free choice, freedom also increases with the range of possible choices and the pleasure derived. Søren Kierkegaard's aesthetes, who follow what attracts, flit from flower to flower and revel in free choice.[5]

A further sphere of freedom, in contrast to the infinite openness of freedom as choice, appears more like a fixation on a deep or encompassing value that is found in the objects chosen. At this level, freedom consists in commitment. If the range of objects suggests the breadth of free will's ability to keep choosing, commitment correlates with the depth and height of freedom's possibilities. To dedicate one's life to one thing, if it is done with constant deliberate intention, involves a self-appropriation and self-actualization that maximize responsibility. Freedom as a responsibility exercised in self-disposition represents

---

God or the individual in his or her freedom? Considering these alternatives on the same plane, as though they were competing freedoms in a zero-sum game, completely muddies these waters. This question will be entertained in a later chapter. Here the point is simply to differentiate free choice from other dimensions of freedom.

5. The descriptions of these spheres or levels of freedom are inspired by, while not reproducing exactly, categories used by Søren Kierkegaard. See, for example, his *Either/Or: A Fragment of Life* (Princeton, NJ: Princeton University Press, 1944).

a fuller and more comprehensive taking hold of oneself that distinguishes itself from free choice as a series of individual acts. Moreover, the value of that to which one gives the self becomes internalized, so that the committed subject shares the qualities of that to which it dedicates the self. The directional dynamics of these free activities may be contrary to each other: the constant exercise of new options suggests an effort to draw value into the self and, never being satisfied, continually to seek more; freedom as commitment to one thing appears to be more satisfied by the constant give and take with the value of the single chosen object. The object becomes part of the self so that commitment, as an act of self-giving, is also an act of self-creating. The passivity of attraction yields to active assumption of responsibility for self. The idea of being more deeply free in a commitment to a single object or way of life probably only becomes meaningful in the doing. From the outside it appears to be a limitation; from the inside it means consistent self-possession and expansive growth, if the object is worthy.

Still another distinct dimension of freedom arose with modernity's deepening experience of historicity and may be associated with the industrial revolution. Karl Marx observed the social behavior of human beings and defined human existence as *Homo faber*. Human beings "begin to distinguish themselves from animals as soon as they begin to *produce* their means of subsistence, a step which is conditioned by their physical organization. By producing their means of subsistence men are indirectly producing their actual material life."[6] Marx deeply intuited the close connection of the human with the world it constructed. He thus discovered the dimension of freedom's creativity and the comprehensive character of its potentiality. Human beings are constantly creating themselves in the act of creating their worlds. One needs a social perspective to appreciate this aspect of freedom; it far transcends the single artist's ability to create the single artifact. Marx recognized that human beings, by making history, are creating new being; not just new things in perennial forms, but refashioning the structures of human existence itself. On this level, human freedom appears to be an exalted and sacred power to cooperate consciously with the power of evolution in the creation of new forms of human existence, for good or evil or some mixture of both.

All of these dimensions of freedom subsist together and flow into each other. One or another dimension may assume ascendancy in a particular life, but together they describe the integral potentiality of

---

6. Karl Marx, *The German Ideology*, in *The Marx-Engels Reader* (New York: W. W. Norton, 1972), 114.

each person's freedom. But that freedom reveals an even greater complexity when viewed from a social perspective.

Human Existence as Social

In a Western culture such as ours, a description of the human spontaneously begins with the individual subject: individualism seems to block perception of the social bonds that constitute the individual as such. Other cultures may presuppose human existence as a social phenomenon, so that being a member of a community charges each one with social responsibility. But no balanced picture of the human can prescind from its sociality, which also appears in a series of different levels.

The social dependence of the human in being is quite striking in the early stages of life. It takes a long time to nurture a human being through the early stages of development. In the culture of small, undeveloped, and intentional communities one may never lose this sense of material solidarity in being. In developed societies, adolescence seems to be a training period for entering a new impersonal world that requires individual autonomy. But the fact that a sense of dependence on a community diminishes in a large, impersonal, and mobile society does not really negate a real dependence on networks of others for our functioning and our existence.[7]

The most serious challenge to any idea of personal autonomy comes from a recognition of the psychic and intellectual solidarity of human existence. From the very beginning of conscious life, the human person is given language and, with it, a social code of meaning and value. Each individual is thus socially constituted as an individual being in his or her actual consciousness. An individual becomes his or her autonomous self by socialization in a community's set of meanings. The worldview and the set of values of any particular individual and at any given time are always constituted by the common meanings and the ideals that are carried by and channeled through the community. But particularity does not necessarily entail idiosyncrasy. Particularity and individuality do not have to be a trap; this or that language creates a social platform and provides leverage for the creativity described earlier. Thus, the social creates, supports, and complements individual initiative. And the longer-term effectiveness of individual creativity depends on its social effects, on bringing others

---

7. A common way to express the social constitution of an individual person uses the language of "relationships." Every human being exists in a complicated web of multiple relationships: different kinds of relationships with different kinds of influence and different levels of consciousness and power.

into a common strategy of meaning and value. Edison was a brilliant individual inventor, but he worked within a community of science and industry.

Each person receives language from the society to which he or she belongs, and this establishes a certain priority of language to any single person's use of it to think. This in turn results in the social construction of reality and the sociology of knowledge itself. Once again Marx came to recognize this early in his career. "Consciousness," he wrote, "is, therefore, from the very beginning a social product, and remains so as long as men exist at all."[8] Today the insights of the sociology of knowledge are presupposed in the academy and more generally in public discourse: people are well aware that anyone who seeks to persuade always has a background and an agenda that largely account for their views. Surely the relatedness of thought to temporal particularities raises the question of relativism, but most people appreciate that the partiality of particular points of view can be reconciled with some elementary contact with reality that can be known and shared. In fact, this represents the general condition of human knowledge, and it is not relativistic.[9] But once again, the feigned autonomy of individualism surrenders all hope of getting at the truth, because important truths can be approached only gradually through conversation.

The phrase "spiritual solidarity" might be used to describe the way individuals can choose their communities and create bonds of community across the lines of material, psychic, or intellectual boundaries. For example, some ethical systems might function within the borders of a certain community based on nation, or race, or class, or social affiliation such as a business. Such limits to one's loyalty may be unconscious; they may also be an explicit part of a cultural code. The idea of a spiritual solidarity means the ability of freedom to transcend such limits and to imagine and construct a universally applicable ethics. Such a socially and culturally self-transcending ethic would become real when people create communities that honor values and promote actual behaviors that transcend the more limited frameworks. A truly universal self-understanding of the human, and an accompanying

---

8. Marx, *German Ideology*, 118-22, at 122.

9. Karl Mannheim (*Ideology and Utopia: An Introduction to the Sociology of Knowledge* [New York: Harcourt Brace, 1985]) and Peter L. Berger and Thomas Luckmann (*The Social Construction of Reality: A Treatise in the Sociology of Knowledge* [Garden City, NY: Doubleday, 1967]) uphold the possibility of truth against the specter of a relativism that abandons the human ability to discover truth simply because it is always appropriated from a certain perspective.

universal ethics, would of course reach out to the whole of humanity and operate out of convictions about a universal common good.[10]

The expansive character of human consciousness and freedom manifests a metaphysical dimension in the experience of solidarity with all the living and the dead. Johann Baptist Metz develops this dimension of human consciousness that accompanies a solidarity with all who have suffered innocently and died in a way unworthy of their dignity as human beings. Such a claim upon us reaches out dramatically in such events as the Holocaust; recognition of such attacks on the human itself always contains an appeal to our responsibility that we be aware and take care that this does not happen again. This level of solidarity has a metaphysical dimension because it reaches out from the past and makes a claim on us. It seems paradoxical to have some responsibility to those who have died. But remembering them and the terrifying negativity they represent can shake people's confidence in the value of their own humanity. That contrast impels a metaphysical hope that victims of such events ultimately find some justice.[11]

The Damaged Human Condition

The description of human existence up to this point has been abstract. It has highlighted in somewhat neutral terms various dimensions of the human that are readily available to everyone's experience. But no writer in the Western Christian tradition fails to notice that the human condition as it actually exists is deeply flawed. What are the manifestations of the damaged human condition and why should they be labeled "damaged"? It may be useful to begin this description on the level of the social and move to the personal and biological.

It would be difficult not to notice that human history has consistently been acted out in bloody conflict. One could chart human history in terms of war and the technological development of weapons. And war with other groups often functions as a distraction from

---

10. This should not suggest a kind of totalitarian ethics. The point is to illustrate the expansive character of human freedom's ability to encompass all human beings in the appeal of something like Kant's categorical imperative. This expansive character of human freedom does not negate the particularity of all human beings but precisely respects it. This will appear in a "metaphysical" dimension of social solidarity.

11. Remembering the victims of especially programmatic injustice provides an interruption of any present consciousness that would justify such acts and ethical leverage to act against it. Metz writes: "A practical fundamental theology tries to hold on to solidarity in its indissoluble mystical-universal and political-particular dual structure, with the goal of protecting universalism from apathy and partial solidarity from forgetfulness and hatred." Johann Baptist Metz, *Faith in History and Society: Toward a Practical Fundamental Theology,* trans. J. Matthew Ashley (New York: Crossroad, 2007), 210-11.

social injustice and oppression within each society. A large evolutionary historical perspective helps to explain this situation. In principle, evolution demonstrates the continuities within reality. The evolution of a species involves drawing simpler forms of life into more complex syntheses, not by entirely replacing them but by integrating simpler patterns into larger organic wholes better adapted to the environment. This process postulates and then displays the connectedness of all things. Conflict and life-and-death struggles, species preying on species for survival, supply the dynamics of existence across the span of biological development. That this cycle continues within the human species at first sight appears to be normal.

When one shifts the perspective to the world and its societies at any given time, the pattern seems to be analogous. The world and societies within it seem to be held together in a constant tension of shifting forces that always have the possibility of breaking out in violence. Reinhold Niebuhr understood the dynamics of social justice as predicated on a balance of power without which some form of oppression inevitably ensues.[12] Human groups do not have a directing center of consciousness in the same way as individual persons do; they are not "personally" responsible for corporate actions. Societies are thus much more subject to the few that use superior power for their own interests. It is not difficult to trace a certain correlation between such social behavior in human society and the dynamics governing other life forms. Social tension, competing interests, and the exercise of power in favor of self-interest frequently against the interests of others seem like natural human behavior consistent with evolutionary history. This does not mean that individuals can simply abdicate responsibility for society, and later in this book the ideas of personal and social sin will be discussed.

Personal self-consciousness possesses a closer and stronger witness to a damaged human condition. It is the subject of simple eloquent description and personal testimony across Christian tradition. Paul wrote: "I do not understand my own actions. For I do not do what I want, but I do the very thing I hate" (Rom 7:15). Augustine was mystified at how the human spirit, which could command the bodily self, could not dispose of its own self (*Confessions* 8.8-9). Luther testified at length to the power of concupiscence and self-seeking that infects human nature itself. An experience of resistance to self-transcendence

---

12. Social injustice is caused by excessive power of one segment of society over others; social justice can be maintained only through a balance of the powers of competing interests; and all social justice has to be held in place by some form of coercion. Reinhold Niebuhr most forcefully introduced these conclusions in his *Moral Man and Immoral Society* (New York: Charles Scribner's Sons, 1932).

and to an altruistic response to value outside the self is without doubt
culturally conditioned; all do not experience it in the same way. But it
would be hard to characterize the human without some acknowledgment of what Christians call sin. Paul Ricoeur sees the myth of an
original sin as an extrapolation of the life experience of not being what
one could and should be, as measured by one's own potentialities.[13]
Still more deeply, when this defect shows up in one's own behavior,
the tendency is to deny guilt or make excuses for it, rather than probing further to discover that a dark potentiality hides within each of us.

Finally, on a biological level a human being, like all living things,
undergoes sickness and death. This terse statement hides the amount
of pain and suffering this involves and the myriad causes for it. One
might think that the universal character of suffering and death under-
cuts any metaphysical appraisal of it as negative: why call the natural
condition of the human damaged? Why is it not simply what it is? Or
what came to be through evolution? Where do the leverage and vantage point lie that enable one to call the human condition damaged?

One could respond to this question by an appeal to revelation, but
revelation itself must pass through and effect some resonance within
human experience and understanding. One way of describing the
experience of the damaged character of the human is through a "negative experience of contrast."[14] This refers to a structure of experience
with three elements: a seriously negative situation or event, an at least
implicit recognition of the contrasting way things should be, and an
impulse to right the wrong or correct the situation. In this framework
a scene of human degradation can evoke such a negative experience
of contrast, whether it be the Jewish Holocaust or other examples of
genocide in the twentieth century, or any one of innumerable insidi-
ous attacks on the human, lesser in size but still with malicious intent.
Against such backgrounds the human spirit can grasp other possibilities of the human, also testified to by certain examples, but urged with
new force against the threats of wholesale cynicism. Edward Schillebeeckx often used the Latin word *humanum* to symbolize the latent
and yet transcendent potentialities of the human. This is an eschatological view of the human, and of what it can be in an ideal future,
that continually breaks in to judge the negative condition as wrong,
as damaged in relation to a higher possibility, and as something to be
changed. Positive experiences of the undamaged *humanum* are only

---

13. Paul Ricoeur, "'Original Sin': A Study in Meaning," in *The Conflict of
Interpretations: Essays in Hermeneutics*, ed. Don Ihde (Evanston, IL: Northwestern
University Press, 1974), 285.

14. See Edward Schillebeeckx, *Church: The Human Story of God* (New York:
Crossroad, 1990), 5-6.

fragmentary and fleeting. But when these values appear by contrast in the negative, they offer a possibility that can interrupt the negativity of the present as something to be resisted.[15]

The Religious Question

Only human beings, as far as we know, can describe themselves and question the meaningfulness of their own existence. Human beings can encounter the inherent mystery of human existence: human existence seems to be transparent to itself, but the deeper that people penetrate their own experience, both personal and common, the deeper the mystery becomes.

The description of the human offered here in bare outline depicts it as, first of all, self-reflecting and self-transcending spirit: the ability to question and call oneself into question reveals this elementary character. As such, human existence can be described as constituted in freedom, where freedom has multiple dimensions on the personal individual level at the same time that persons are socially constituted by intrinsic relations to others and the surrounding world. Individuals as autonomous individuals simply do not exist; the human is intrinsically social. Humans exist as bodies, as parts of the world, ultimately in solidarity with the living and the dead. But it is the damaged condition of humanity that most forcefully thematizes the content of the question that human beings are to themselves.

Human existence lives from crisis to crisis, each calling out for a solution. Can we prevent the wars that cause so much death and human pain to survivors? Will we be able to distribute the food necessary to feed all of earth's inhabitants? Will human beings ultimately close down the ecological system that sustains us? Each crisis becomes the most important for those in its path. But to understand the human *qua* human, one has to go more deeply to those universal issues that embrace everyone at once and help define existence itself, questions like guilt and its implications, death and what it says about existence itself, and meaning, the very intelligibility of existing.

The phenomenon of guilt as an actual experience seems unevenly distributed. It is not clear where the judge who measures guilt sits: is it the superego, or society, or a mixture of these that forms conscience, or a creator who expects more from creatures, or a God who will punish? Many people and cultures are not tortured by guilt, but can a culture completely lack a sense of morality or encourage freedom from any

---

15. Lieven Boeve, *God Interrupts History: Theology in a Time of Upheaval* (New York: Continuum, 2007).

sense of responsibility and obligation? These standards raise the question of that to which human existence is accountable.

Death in its turn is not so natural that people readily accept it or do not resist it. One can still make the case Augustine made about existing: if a person is, he or she will love being and desire to be, and the "more fully you love being, the more you will desire eternal life" (*On Free Will* 3.7.21). Death manifests itself as the apparent annihilation of personal existence, and as such it becomes a mystery intrinsic to life itself.

The question of meaning draws the other problems up into itself: is there a way of making coherent sense of human existence as it presents itself? On a personal level, one has to ask whether one's freedom is meaningful. What is it "for," in the sense of what one is supposed to be doing? And in the sense of its destiny, where is it going? This existential question of "whither" can also be written large when addressed to history itself: is it going anywhere? These questions cannot really be ignored, because all people respond to them implicitly by the style of lives they live. But their universal character and their comprehensiveness on this formal level help to underline the place and character of life's mystery. This mystery truly reflects and also explains a searching, seeking spirituality.

How do we go about answering the question of human existence? Does the individual postulate an answer and then act on it as if it were true? Does one consider some options and choose the one that seems genial? Or challenging? Or plausible? Does one accept the tradition in which one finds oneself, the world that each one enters by birth, and, then, through some form of *bricolage*, adjust its tenets to one's personal usage? Once again, Augustine the seeker offers some guidance for a way of proceeding. Toward the end of his search Augustine realized that he could not resolve these questions on his own: he had to yield to some authority, some community and tradition within which he could operate. Even the most important question of one's own life as a particular individual can only be resolved socially.

Religions are the usual carriers of this common public authority, or some philosophy that plays a religious function. This situating of religion entails two conclusions that determine the character of all the reflection that follows. The first has to do with the question that spirituality raises, and the second concerns the quality of the answer.

As to the question, this chapter has tried to show that the secular question of the meaning of human existence and the religious question coincide.[16] In effect they are the same question. In Christianity

---

16. The defining quality of the term "religious" as it is used here is its explicitly

the religious question is frequently framed in the language of "salvation." But Edward Schillebeeckx recognized that this salvation was precisely a response to the question of human existence itself. "Not to lose faith in man in all his activities, despite all evil experiences, reveals itself, on closer analysis, as a latent, unconditional trust in God, as faith that human existence is a promise of salvation."[17] Other religions will use a different language representing different experiences and conceptions that are functionally equivalent. The religious question of salvation has its primary grounding in the active secular life of human beings in this world. Reciprocally, the salvation that, for example, Christianity holds out is only meaningful insofar as it responds to the secular question of the coherent meaning of human existence itself, including its guilt, sickness, suffering, and death.

Second, and equally important, the plausibility of the meaningfulness of human existence that any religion holds out depends on the way of life that this answer reflects and encourages. There are two aspects to this contention. On the one hand, the concept of God itself elicits an existential relationship to the reality that God stands for. The appealing and imperative character of the very idea of God means that one cannot coherently remain neutral or blasé before God. Positively or negatively, God engages human subjectivity. On the other hand, and following from the first point, language about God that does not reflect an active way of life in response to God is not plausible. Language about God without practical consequences is unconvincing. This supplies the basis for what Metz calls the practical grounding of theology: it must address the spiritual issues that make up the question of the meaning of human existence itself.[18] In short, the Christian response to the question of human existence must spring from, and in turn generate, a spirituality that actually supplies that meaning. The discussion of such a spirituality is the subject matter of this book.

---

transcendent character. All spirituality is lived out in the face of something that functions as an overall organizer of personal energy. When this is explicitly something transcendent, one can refer to it as a religious object.

17. Edward Schillebeeckx, *God the Future of Man* (New York: Sheed & Ward, 1968), 77. He adds: "Acceptance of God is the ultimate, precise name which must be given to the deepest meaning of commitment to this world" (p. 76). It will become clear in the following chapters that "salvation" cannot be limited to eternal life; it has to bestow coherent meaning to life in this world now.

18. Metz, *Faith in History and Society*, 62-65.

CHAPTER THREE

Spirituality in the Face
of God Creator

The history of religions shows that the question of the nature of ultimacy raised in the last chapter has more than one answer. The Christian answer, like its parent Jewish answer, lies in God as creator. The discussion that follows aims at presenting the idea of creation as it correlates with a spirituality in search of ultimacy. The chapter rests on the assumption that this notion holds a good deal of the most fundamental meaning of who and what God is for Christians. This reflection on the idea of creation unfolds in tandem with commentary on the scientific account of the origin of the universe to illustrate both the difference and the interconnections between scientific and spiritual language. The two languages are distinct but not unrelated at certain crucial points where they run together in the human imagination.[1] This chapter will also bring out the way the idea of creation responds to the religious question. It has direct bearing on individual persons and their stories. The idea of creation has its origin in a seeking spirituality asking questions of the transcendent source of being, and it reflects back on the direction a spiritual narrative takes.

This chapter takes shortcuts in what could be a much longer discussion. One of them concerns the complex and contentious area of religious epistemology. This direct plunge into the notion of creation leaves many questions about the character of faith and spiritual knowledge undeveloped.[2] These issues are implicit in the discussion of creation faith, but attention is not drawn to them. Also, the schematic

---

1. The relation between (Christian) beliefs and science is debated from both sides. At one extreme, writers seem to be able to move easily between these two spheres of discourse; the assertions of scientific and religious disciplines communicate directly. At the other extreme, many hold that these are distinct ways of experiencing and reasoning that do not communicate with each other at all. In the middle, one can find various positions that insist on distinctions but find a number of mutual influences. This broad third option is reflected here.

2. For an account of the many presuppositions that underlie this discussion one could consult Roger Haight, *Dynamics of Theology* (Maryknoll, NY: Orbis Books, 2001).

character of this chapter results from the lack of space to develop this topic in the depth it deserves. As a result, the goal of the discussion is focused and limited. It presupposes the background and the horizon of the scientific story of the origin of the universe and the question that human existence poses to itself. In this context, the idea is to show, first, how spiritual faith language about God as creator arises out of spirituality; then, second, to describe how creation language can reflect back and shed meaning on everyday secular life, even as it begs for more answers from formal theological reflection.

The idea of creation conjures up many themes for discussion. The first locates the origin of the religious idea of creation in the depths of human experience itself.[3] The second meditates on the deep implications of the idea that God creates out of nothing and considers the complex and disputed area of how God may be construed as acting in the world. The third section shows how our seemingly objective conceptions of God find meaning in their correlation with narrative experiences of life. This move is crucial for understanding the way reflection on ideas about transcendent reality always correlates with forms of human life. Conceptions of God both emerge out of everyday spirituality and represent God as reaching out and soliciting a personal response. Fourth, the Christian idea that God and all that God creates are good has to be reconciled with experiences of sin. What is the source of the evil that is within us? Sin reveals itself in an encounter with God: the very idea of God may irritate and disrupt the one who thinks it, because one cannot stand neutrally before it.[4] Fifth, because response to God involves some form of action, creation spirituality entails an activist anthropology. The chapter ends with the searching question of the nature of God in the light of the scientific picture of the universe, the human person in it, and the idea of creation.

Archeology of Creation Faith

The metaphor of archeology suggests the underground resources buried in human subjectivity that help generate, or allow the possibility

---

3. Standard Christian theology attributes the ultimate source of religious experience and faith to God's grace and revelation. Although I do not discuss the priority of grace and revelation in this chapter, for I have treated it in *Dynamics of Theology*, it is always presupposed in this phenomenological description of experience.

4. Symbols such as "God," "Jesus Christ," "eternal life," are not merely objective. They affect those who entertain them by calling into question the relation of the person to the object they refer to. Johann Baptist Metz calls this the "appellative and imperative" character of basic religious symbols. *Faith in History and Society: Toward a Practical Fundamental Theology*, trans. J. Matthew Ashley (New York: Crossroad, 2007), 62.

of, experience associated with the phrase "being created." This experience is not a conscious grasp of a particular object but is found within an analysis of human consciousness. This analysis highlights dimensions of human consciousness that all human beings potentially could access. If people do recognize themselves as "created beings," this will naturally become an important part of their narratives. The thought of three religious thinkers who have attempted to describe the structures that give rise to particular experiences of creation help to situate the basic idea.

Friedrich Schleiermacher relates the idea of creation very closely to the experience of absolute dependence that can be unearthed in human subjectivity. By analysis of human consciousness he shows how at a deep level of freedom human beings can experience that they do not have within themselves the power of their own being: we are ultimately dependent in our being. While persons experience some bit of control in relation to themselves and the external world, in relation to their very being and its source they exercise no positive agency: they have no leverage.[5] This is essentially the source of an experience of being created. It entails a consciousness of being absolutely dependent on a creative power of being that we call God. This dimension of spiritual freedom can also be called an implicit and mediated, as distinct from an explicit or direct, consciousness of God. Moreover, Schleiermacher indicates that we then spontaneously go on to "postulate the feeling of absolute dependence as valid for everything without exception, because we apply it to our own existence in so far as we are a part of the world."[6]

Karl Rahner, like Schleiermacher a post-Kantian theologian, describes the structure of the experience underlying the doctrine of creation in terms analogous to those of Schleiermacher. He too finds within the human quest for knowledge an intimation of an infinite, absolute, incomprehensible mystery on the other side of the whole sum total of possible finite objects that we could possibly engage. This absolute or infinite being appears as a background or an open horizon against which one recognizes the finitude of all we can possibly know in this world. Our knowing connects with reality. On the side of knowing, absolute incomprehensible reality always resides in "the ontologically silent" presence within our quest for knowing the world. On the side

---

5. Friedrich Schleiermacher, *The Christian Faith*, ed. H. R. Mackintosh and J. S. Stewart (New York: Harper Torchbooks, 1963), par. 3-5, pp. 5-18. The aspect of experience that Schleiermacher is describing here can be called "transcendental," which means that it is not someone's particular experience but a typical structure of all human consciousness.

6. Schleiermacher, *Christian Faith*, par. 46, p. 170.

of the objects that human subjectivity engages, God appears obliquely as that which absolutely transcends the whole of finite being. God, world, and human consciousness are linked together here: consciousness of creation senses that "the world must be radically dependent on God, without making [God] dependent on it. . . ."[7] As in Schleiermacher, the roots of the religious idea of creation lie in a profound experience of being that is appropriated interiorly. The notion of creation does not correspond to an imaginable event or an empirical object of knowledge but to the unspeakable whence of all finitude.

Edward Schillebeeckx proposes another slant on a human experience that leads to a doctrine of creation and that he calls not a "transcendental" experience but an "anthropological constant."[8] This faith or trust arises out of negative experiences of radical threats to the human that constantly arise in history: sickness, oppression, and ultimately death. But just as constant as these threats are the universal impulse to resist them and the positive conception of humanity and existence that grounds this impulse. "I regard these negative dialectics coming within a positive sphere of meaning which is, however, in its universality only implicit (it is a call to the *humanum*) as the universal pre-understanding not only of the pluralist answers that man gives to this call, but also of Christian talk about God, in other words, of the gospel."[9] The resistance to negativity, especially acting it out, reveals an implicit subjective hope that also gives a glimpse of a possible object of hope. "All our negative experiences cannot brush aside the 'nonetheless' of the trust which is revealed in man's critical resistance and which prevents us from simply surrendering man, human society and the world entirely to total meaninglessness. This trust in the ultimate meaning of human life seems to me to be the basic presupposition of man's action in history."[10] Thus, the groundwork for the doctrine of creation in Schillebeeckx also lies in human subjectivity. It manifests itself in the human bent toward a historical ethical response to negativity on the basis of a basic trust in reality. The creator God assumes the character of the guarantor of the human.

---

7. Karl Rahner, *Foundations of Christian Faith: An Introduction to the Idea of Christianity* (New York: Crossroad, 1994), 78.

8. Schillebeeckx writes that "'faith,' the ground for hope, is an anthropological constant throughout human history, a constant without which human life and action worthy of men and capable of realization becomes impossible." Edward Schillebeeckx, *Christ: The Experience of Jesus as Lord* (New York: Seabury Press, 1980), 741. The two categories, "transcendental" and "anthropological constant," are in some respects analogous.

9. Edward Schillebeeckx, *The Understanding of Faith: Interpretation and Criticism* (New York: Seabury Press, 1974), 92.

10. Schillebeeckx, *Understanding of Faith,* 96-97.

These examples of deep historical-existential analyses of human response to reality that support the religious idea of creation show how distinct it is from the sciences that allow a description of the beginnings of our universe. These are different kinds of affirmations appealing to different kinds of evidence.[11] This archeology shows that the religious idea of creation does not lie on the surface of things. This deserves some more discussion.

Creation out of Nothing

The Christian teaching on creation says that God creates out of nothing. According to Ian Barbour, the strict idea of nothing "was forged in the fourth century in response to several hostile doctrines. Against a Gnostic view that matter was evil, the one God created all; against pre-existent matter, God is the source of all; against pantheism, the world is not God but quite distinct from God; against emanation theory, it asserts that God transcends all finitude."[12] The doctrine states that nothing lies outside of God's creating power; nothing has an existence independently of God's creating power. If there were a primal chaos or formless matter into which God introduced order and intelligibility, this could not have been uncreated by God; it too had to be absolutely dependent upon God. There is no appeal here to physical evidence or reference to a "before" the Big Bang: the mode of understanding is utterly different, and to make appeals across these epistemological bases engenders confusion. "Creation is not so much about chronological origins as about the world's ontological dependence on a beneficent principle of being that exists independently of the cosmos."[13]

Schillebeeckx explains that creation means that God is immediately

---

11. Ian Barbour sums up well the source of the doctrine of creation: "The idea of creation can also be seen as an expression of enduring *human experiences*, such as: (1) a sense of dependence, finitude, and contingency; (2) a response of wonder, trust, gratitude for life, and affirmation of the world; and (3) a recognition of interdependence, order, and beauty in the world. The religious idea of creation starts from wonder and gratitude for life as a gift. Theological doctrines are an attempt to interpret such experiences within the context of a particular historical tradition. The theological meaning of creation can be combined with a variety of physical cosmologies, ancient and modern, and does not require any one cosmology." Ian G. Barbour, *When Science Meets Religion* (San Francisco: HarperSanFrancisco, 2000), 51.

12. Barbour, *When Science Meets Religion,* 49. At the end of the second century both Clement of Alexandria and Tertullian (of Carthage) were insisting that God created out of nothing; that is, everything depends on God's creating. See Jaroslav Pelikan, *The Emergence of the Catholic Tradition (100-600)* (Chicago and London: University of Chicago Press, 1971), 36-37.

13. John F. Haught, *Christianity and Science: Toward a Theology of Nature* (Maryknoll, NY: Orbis Books, 2007), 124.

present to the cosmos and everything in it. Because God creates out of nothing, there is nothing between God and creatures. This premise carries us deep into the subject matter. For example, it leads to two basic points about creation that counter some equally fundamental errors. One is that finitude is not evil. Finitude is precisely what God created, and God created it good. The positive character of God's absolute being and creative act shows that finitude and contingency should not be regarded negatively. The other says that, as transcendent creator and absolute being, God is not distant and absent from God's creation. Creation out of nothing means that there is no medium between God and creation; nothing stands between them. God is directly present to God's creation as its cause and ground. God is immanent within and personally present to God's creation. All things exist within God's creative power so that God in turn is the "within" of all creation. Since one cannot think of a motive other than love for God's creating, God is conceived of as creating out of love.

Very few ideas are as basic and all-encompassing as creation. It entails an absolute closeness of a personal and creating God of love to all creatures. The idea of creation thus functions as the symbol for God's immediate presence to the universe, our world, and human existence.[14] All things exist in God; God permeates all that exists; and yet created reality is not God. Creation holds a radical distinction in being between creator and creature but affirms the mutual interactive presence of creator and creatures to each other. "God is eternal, but it is an eternity that is inclusive of, rather than separate from, temporality. God takes in all the events of the world's temporality, including suffering, weaving them into the fabric of [God's] own everlasting life and thereby preserving their value forever."[15]

The one notion of creation has two dimensions: the one includes the other. On the one hand, creation is often thought of in terms of or in relation to the beginning of finite reality. But, in what has already been said, one can see that the doctrine of creation has no explanatory value relative to actual beginnings. In whatever manner finite reality first came into being, the absolute power of God was the source or ground of its being. On the other hand, the power sustaining all finite reality in being is ongoing, and this elicits the doctrine of preservation of being across time. The logic of the affirmation of creation and that of preservation are the same and differ only with respect to an implied reference to original coming-to-be and ongoing existence.

---

14. Schillebeeckx, *Christ*, 804-21, esp. 809. Dorothy Jacko, "Salvation in the Context of Contemporary Secularized Historical Consciousness: The Later Theology of Edward Schillebeeckx" (Th.D. dissertation, Regis College, University of Toronto, 1987), 83-136.

15. David Toolan, *At Home in the Cosmos* (Maryknoll, NY: Orbis Books, 2001), 149.

Like creation, then, God's action of preserving does not refer to specific operations in history, nor does it operate in particular overt ways, that is, as an empirical, this-worldly cause.

The question of ongoing preservation raises the standard question, particularly acute and contested in the area of the relation of theology and science, of how God acts in the world. Generally speaking, with respect to the hard sciences, theologians do not envision God as an actor in the world in the same way that finite causes operate. If God is God, God cannot be conceived of as an empirical this-worldly causality. Yet some theologians want to insert God into the cracks of scientific unknowing, as, for example, opening up "space" for God's activity in what appears to us as indeterminacy and randomness. The point of this effort is to preserve some "special" or "particular" agency of God, in a place that may be called a "causal joint" between God and some special events of God intervening in history. But this effort seems to depict God as a "finite" or secondary cause that acts within the system of nature. The analysis of the archeology of the idea of creation shows precisely that God as creating cause, out of nothing, operates in a qualitatively different way than finite and interacting agents.[16]

The distinction between primary (divine) causality and secondary (finite) causality, developed by Thomas Aquinas, affirms the autonomy of being and acting within the sphere of finite causes, even though they are dependent on God's primary creating causality for their very being. The following statement sums this up nicely:

> God is radically immanent (interior) to all that is—but in a highly differentiated way, according to the character of each process, relationship or object. God, then, is not an entity, like other entities—God is more like a verb, a continuing action in which everything else participates, but participates according to its own individuality. God's primary causality does not substitute for nor interfere with nor countermand the integrity and adequacy of the (secondary) causal structures of nature or of history—despite being their ultimate foundation and source.[17]

---

16. Elizabeth A. Johnson outlines six distinct ways in which theologians conceive of how God acts in the world in *Quest for the Living God: Mapping Frontiers in the Theology of God* (New York: Continuum, 2007), 191-93.

17. William R. Stoeger, "Conceiving Divine Action in a Dynamic Universe," in *Scientific Perspectives on Divine Action: Twenty Years of Challenge and Progress*, ed. Robert John Russell, Nancey Murphy, and William R. Stoeger (Berkeley: Center for Theology and the Natural Sciences; Vatican City: Vatican Observatory Publications, 2008), 229.

The radical difference in kinds of causality means that the two agencies are not in competition with each other; to assert the causality of finite causes does not subtract from the causality of God; there is no zero-sum game or competition between these two agencies; they actually enhance each other. "In this system of thought it is incoherent to think of God as working in the world apart from secondary causes, or beside them, or in addition to them, or even in competition with them."[18] At the same time, there is a concurrent causality, but it is unique and not a synergy between the same kinds of agency. This last point needs to be emphasized. The causality of God and that of finite agents refer to two radically different spheres of being, that of creator and that of creature. To confuse these begins a series of misunderstandings.

Not everyone accepts the radical character of the distinction. Barbour describes the critique of this position as follows: "The active powers of human agents inescapably limit God's freedom. If some of the causal work is done by natural agents, it cannot *all* be done by God. There cannot be two sufficient causes for one event."[19] But there *can* be two sufficient causes for the same act if they are precisely the creative and sustaining action of God and the finite agency of a creature. Instead of thinking of God working in the world by a special act, God's action may be thought of as God's universal creativity at work simultaneously within secondary causes. This issue was discussed extensively in the Middle Ages in terms of grace and free will, and Bernard of Clairvaux proposed a formula resolving debates that alternatively awarded predominance to God's action or to human action: "Grace does the whole work, and so does free choice—with this one qualification: That whereas the whole is done *in* free choice, so is the whole done *of* grace."[20] The simultaneity is possible because the two agencies do not compete. God is fully the primary cause of the full action of the secondary cause. The formula used by scholastic theology in christology to explain how God acted in Jesus, *mutatis mutandis*, actually describes God acting generally in the created world: this-worldly activity is created actuation by uncreated or divine action. God's creating activity sustains everything that is.

Barbour goes on to note that the idea of the self-limitation of God responds to this objection. But the idea of the "self-limitation" of God has to be recognized as paradoxical relative to God, and little more

---

18. Elizabeth A. Johnson, "Does God Play Dice? Divine Providence and Chance," *Theological Studies* 57 (1996): 11-12, at 12.

19. Barbour, *When Science Meets Religion*, 161.

20. Bernard of Clairvaux, "On Grace and Free Will," in *Treatises*, vol. 3 (Kalamazoo, MI: Cistercian Publications, 1977), par. 14.47, p. 106.

than a concealment of our ignorance. Why God's ongoing creating and empowering of being that is truly other than God's self and the gift of endowing finite reality with creative autonomy within the finite sphere should be conceived negatively as limiting is far from clear. The term can be reduced to two convictions: that finite reality is real, and that it is not God. After that we have to admit that our conceptions do not catch up with the workings of God's creative power. But we can recognize that God does not act in history as a "secondary" or finite agent but as God creating.

Before moving forward, a brief summary of this appropriation of the Christian idea of creation is in order. Creation as a religious doctrine does not refer to a single event that occurred in the past. The doctrine of creation does not offer an explanation of the particular order of things that we see in the world today. Creation is rather a conviction based on a spiritual experience that reality exists and continues to exist sustained by a power of being that transcends the whole finite universe. It is an error to confuse God's creating power with this or that worldly agency; these so-called secondary causes are autonomous determinants within and of a world that is other than God; they are studied by science. At the same time the universe and all the causality in it are always being created and sustained by a power of being called God. This makes God intimately close to creation, and one has to think that God creates out of love because any other motive would make little sense. This vision of all reality being enfolded within the presence and power of a loving, creating God will influence how one might think about the existence of many religions.

Creation Anthropology in Narrative Form

The previous sections explored the roots of creation faith within the depths of human subjectivity in contrast to the scientific story of origins. The very idea of creation out of nothing makes God the inner and vital ground of all that exists. Whereas this idea of creation seems to be abstract and analytical, it can correlate with an affective experience that generates an active responsive life. This section will describe an example of this correlation between the idea of God as creator and a dynamic existential spirituality. The logic of this spirituality moves through the themes of presence, communication, response, dialogue, and narrative.

The discussion showed how God is immediately present to creation as the very ground and power of being. The archeology of creation showed that human beings have the capacity to be so reflectively conscious of their own being that they can discover within their dependence in being the presence of God as the power that sustains them. A reflective account of human subjectivity can reveal a tacit or implicit presence of God to the human subject. This amounts to communication. This communication, however, does not resemble the give-and-take between persons, or a deep communication mediated by a work of art. In this case God transcends the mediation. One knows that God to be God must also be other than the medium making God present. Because God is God, the infinite transcendent mystery, human beings have no ability whatsoever to know God directly or to comprehend God in concepts and language. Human beings more accurately may be said to have a sense of God, experience intimations of God, feel God's presence, project language about God that tries to bring God's reality to expression, intuit God, encounter God beneath or above all words, within the marvels of creation, and so on. God may be also be encountered in various forms of negative experience as the one who guarantees that the repulsion to which the negativity gives rise is grounded in an adjudicator of genuine value. Thus, one has the paradoxical situation in which God can be known in a mediated way in the created world around us and within us. But one cannot positively read off the surface of events an understanding of God's absolute transcendent mystery.[21]

These somewhat abstract reflections on the spiritual experience entailed in the idea of creation describe the transcendent dimension of a lively creation spirituality. But because each person is the object of God's creating, a creation spirituality has the positive, immanent dimension that can be called a communication. Ignatius of Loyola provides a good example of such a creation spirituality, and his representation of his own encounter with the creator God shows its spiritual power.

Ignatius explicitly personalizes the idea of creation in his "Contemplation to Attain Love" in *The Spiritual Exercises*.[22] Ignatius transposes the objective idea of creation into personalized statements of what God has done for each individual person, out of love, in such a way that creation in its objective forms becomes God's personal gift, and the gift requires a personal response of gratitude. Creation relative to

---

21. This describes the dialectical character of a religious symbol: the things of this world, and the words and concepts that we use to describe them, are all we have to make the infinitely transcendent God reflectively present to consciousness. We know that these symbols refer to a God who presses in on us. But we also know that God so transcends all finite mediations that such symbols cannot be construed literally. Rather, they draw human consciousness into absolute mystery.

22. Ignatius Loyola, *The Spiritual Exercises of Saint Ignatius: A Translation and Commentary*, ed. George E. Ganss (Chicago: Loyola University Press, 1992), §§ 230-37.

human beings becomes a form of communication. By resituating the conceptual idea of creation out of nothing into a framework of a personal dialogue between God and the human person Ignatius creates a spiritual narrative. The shift of context transforms the idea of creation into an invitation for an encounter-response that blends a conceptual worldview into the stories of each person who makes the *Exercises*. The following description summarizes Ignatius's creation mysticism.

Creation spirituality. God creating establishes a foundational, one could say metaphysical, forum of communication. God is immediately present to all reality. And, given the reflective freedom of human existence described earlier, human existence has the capacity to become aware of God's presence, not directly, but precisely in and through created reality itself. Such is the archeology of the doctrine. When Ignatius deals with creation, however, he personifies God and imagines God personally engaged in the activity of creating itself. God creates, and what God creates becomes a medium or a real symbolic presence of God in the action of creating.[23] The creating action of God may be considered God's communication to reflectively conscious creatures. This transposition in the framework for appreciating creation alters the significance of the analytical idea. The recognition of God in creation, which itself has a narrative before, during, and after, becomes transformed into an interpersonal dialogue and eventually an ongoing conversation with the human community. God is readily available and personally addressing each creature in the act of creating.

The personal story in which one encounters God illustrates God's love for each person and reinforces the idea that creation itself is an outpouring of God's love.[24] God dwells in the world, in each creature, and God makes God's self present to each one. God gives to each one the gift of his or her existence with all its attendant gifts and talents. God communicates to each one his or her identity. God who continuously creates is continually working for the welfare of each single person. Each consideration of creation bends back on the one engaged in it, and the gifts that one has received from God become the media or symbols of intercommunication. Meditation on creation engenders an ontological gratitude that could result in an emotional encounter. But this emotion could hardly be superficial. The consideration is embedded in one of the most profound and central of all spiritual ideas. The

---

23. A symbol is some thing or idea that mediates or makes present something other than itself. For example, human persons present to others their interior selves through their physical gestures. Our bodies are the symbols of our spiritual selves.

24. This paragraph paraphrases the "Contemplation to Attain Love" in Ignatius, *Spiritual Exercises*, §§ 230-37.

dialogue and the wider narrative could also be quite cool and incisive when they draw into themselves the power of the scientific picture of the universe.

In Ignatius's imagination, the doctrine of creation becomes a cosmic principle and framework for God's continuing dialogue with all of humanity. But, more particularly, creation grounds the personal story of each person. When the individual becomes conscious of this, it may generate an explicit dialogue of prayer. Creation allows Ignatius to formulate the seminal principle of "finding God in all things," a formula that weds contemplative contact with God and everyday behavior in the secular world. One who appropriates this creation theology into his or her life becomes a "contemplative in action."

Meister Eckhart recognized how a contemplative spirit could completely envelop action in the world. In his commentary on the story of Martha and Mary in Luke 10:38-42, Mary is the type of the mystic, one captivated by divine truth. Martha is the active type who engages the world, deals with practical matters, and serves others. But Eckhart faults Mary, who may seem to have the higher spirituality, because she is more attached to the pleasure and consolation she is feeling than to service of the Lord. Martha is the ideal because, on the one hand, no one can escape living in the world of creatures and dealing with them, but, on the other hand, Martha did this with such spiritual maturity and degree of union with God that creatures never distracted her from her attachment to God. She dealt with the world from within her complete attachment to God.[25] Eckhart took up the old theme and "not only abandoned the notion of tension-filled oscillation between action and contemplation but also asserted that a new kind of activity performed out of 'a well-exercised ground' was superior to contemplation, at least as ordinarily conceived."[26] In effect, Eckhart develops a this-worldly mysticism as he elevates Martha to one who has so developed her mystical sense that her activity lives within it. She "is able to work undisturbed in the midst of the concerns of the world."[27] In Eckhart's view of Martha, her activity was not a distraction from her contemplation but the fulfillment of it.

In sum, the idea of creation supplies a foundational principle for a narrative spirituality that accommodates the story of each human being.

---

25. See Meister Eckhart, *Meister Eckhart: Teacher and Preacher*, ed. Bernard McGinn (New York: Paulist Press, 1986), Sermon 86.

26. Bernard McGinn, *The Presence of God: A History of Western Christian Mysticism*, vol. 4, *The Harvest of Mysticism in Medieval Germany (1300-1500)* (New York: Crossroad, 2005), 190.

27. McGinn, *Harvest of Mysticism*, 192.

Understanding Sin in Evolutionary Anthropology

Ideas seen earlier about the damaged human condition are reflected in the traditional Christian idea of an original sin that has affected all humanity. The biblical story of creation includes an account of a primeval sin, a mythic story that attends to, if it does not account for, the present situation of moral disarray. It also implicitly exonerates God from responsibility for creating sin by laying the blame on Satan and human freedom. The idea of a primitive sin addresses the question that lies embedded in the massive phenomenon of human sin: how does the evolutionary character of creation affect the way creation spirituality integrates sin into its purview?

The history of ideas has explained the genesis of the Christian doctrine of a primeval sin. The idea of an original sin or fall developed through three principal moments: the Genesis story of Adam and Eve sinning, Paul's discussion of sin in Romans 5, and Augustine's construction of the idea that the acts of the primeval parents affected human nature as such and altered the relationship between human beings and God. The first sin changed the human condition. Augustine affirmed that all were sinful at birth, had a tendency toward sin called concupiscence, and could do nothing for their salvation without prior divine help or assistance (grace).[28]

But Augustine's interpretation of Paul, concluding that all humanity was implicated in the sin of Adam, has been seriously questioned. Moreover, the idea of original sin as stated in its classic literal form has come under severe criticism. Jack Mahoney summarizes the objections to the idea: there is no biblical evidence that the first sin had a universal effect on all people or on human nature as such; no biblical warrant justifies a transmission of the effects of one sin from generation to generation; scripture does not describe a precondition of sin dispelled by baptism; scripture does not teach that concupiscence was a universal effect of a first sin. Finally, death is recognized as an essential biological process that is intrinsic to the existence of all living entities and needs no theological explanation.[29] More generally: "Evolutionary science . . . has rendered the original cosmic perfection, one allegedly debauched by a temporally 'original' sin, obsolete and unbelievable."[30]

The idea of an original sin, however, met a need to understand the damaged moral sphere of human existence. Granted that a fall of the

---

28. Jack Mahoney, *Christianity in Evolution: An Exploration* (Washington, DC: Georgetown University Press, 2011), 51-57.

29. Mahoney, *Christianity in Evolution*, 64.

30. John Haught, *God after Darwin: A Theology of Evolution* (Boulder, CO: Westview Press, 2000), 149.

race makes no sense, is there a way to explain why, prior to the exercise of human freedom, there seems to be a drag on human existence, what Augustine called the curvature of the human spirit in on itself in egoism?

Three distinct approaches help one to understand a certain proclivity to selfishness resident within human existence: the evolutionary, the existential, and the social. Evolutionary biology provides a more empirically based explanation of a certain tendency to sin. The mechanism of evolution requires a selfish impulse to continue existence, and this is written into the world as we know it. "From ants to apes, the animal world is awash in intraspecific [intraspecies] aggression, deceit, theft, exploitation, infanticide and cannibalism."[31] This does not rule out existential impulses or social influences and learned ways of acting. "But even without that legacy of learned behavior, we would still be urged to sin by the genetically programmed selfishness, dating from the dawn of life, that underlies it and gave rise to it."[32] What has been inherited, therefore, has its origins in the very structure of life.

The existential approach to the human condition focuses on the juncture where choice first begins to manifest itself within the process of the development of freedom. As freedom passes from latent potentiality to human act, individuals assert themselves, begin to react autonomously to external stimuli, make decisions, and initiate processes leading to self-determination and a possibility of independence. The exercise of freedom thus has within itself the possibility of asserting the self over against external authority and the moral demands of the welfare of others.[33]

A social explanation of sin turns to the patterns of destructive behavior that have become hardened into cultural and social forms. The social world is constructed of various accepted ways of acting that corrode human values when they do not actually destroy human life. Human beings cannot avoid participation in these social structures. They are embedded in the very languages that human beings learn and speak. Relative to each person, these structures are objective. They stand over against individuals before each one is socialized into them; they defy every individual who seeks to change them. More than this, they fashion and shape individual action into their own image and

---

31. Daryl P. Domning, "Evolution, Evil and Original Sin: Putting the Puzzle Together," *America* (Nov. 12, 2001): 17.

32. Domning, "Evolution," 19.

33. Søren Kierkegaard, *The Sickness unto Death*, in *Fear and Trembling & The Sickness unto Death* (Garden City, NY: Doubleday Anchor Books, 1954); Paul Tillich, *Systematic Theology*, vol. 2, *Existence and the Christ* (Chicago: University of Chicago Press, 1957), 44-59.

likeness. No one can escape social sin because everyone participates in the social mechanisms that injure various victims of society and corrupt the values of all. But all these impulses, existential, social, and biologically inherited, become sinful only when embraced freely to the detriment of self or others.

Where some see a sense of personal sin decreasing in the Western world, the broader perspective on sin that the idea of a universal condition symbolized is more telling. In reality, a sense of sin in its social forms is increasing. This sin is constantly being identified in specific social structures of behavior. Consciousness of this sin, even when only implicit, does not cause personal confusion and anxiety but a general disorientation and a sense of entrapment. It can lead to cynicism and, through cynicism, to the mortal threat to freedom that resides in boredom or indifference. It can sap one's courage and lead a person to doubt the value of good action. Individual good deeds get sucked up into the vortex of social systems that rob any good that the individual accomplishes of any significant effect. A creation spirituality is an antidote to such despair.

An Anthropology of Constructive Action

The discovery of evolution has generated a deep tension at the heart of the human species. Moving forward, the randomness built into reality and life prevents the discernment of any clear lines of purpose in the generation of new species. Yet on a grand scale movement toward greater complexity and expanded forms of consciousness and freedom are perceptible. More personally, human beings direct their lives with a sense of goals: human existence needs and seeks a meaning that is closely associated with purpose. Human beings want creation to be imbued with purpose because they live by it. Can human beings say that the universe is purposeful because some teleology has finally revealed itself within the human species that is spirit of the world?[34] Whether that follows philosophically or not, on the premise that human beings need some coherent structure for their lives, the discussion turns to the way an activist spirituality leads to a creator–creature anthropology in the Christian tradition.

---

34. Human beings can "look out on the world" in two different ways. They can objectively survey the world outside themselves as spectators standing apart from it. Or they can recognize that the world is within themselves because human beings are part of the universe and continuous with its development from the beginning. In this latter scenario, the world is revealed within human consciousness because the human existence is the-world-conscious-of-itself.

Freedom as creativity. God the creator bestowed on human beings the gift of freedom, which, as a real power to fashion new being, carries with it responsibility. Freedom in modernity and postmodernity suggests creativity; it is more than the power to choose; it transcends existentialist commitment; it contains the power to design and effect new forms of being. Through the mechanism of evolution God created this human power. Therefore God desires that it be used. God has confidence in human freedom; God trusts it.[35] God has entrusted creation to human beings not merely as caretakers of a past condition but as co-creators with God of the future. This formula corresponds with the recognition that being is not static but in process, and that human beings were created by God not simply to enjoy creation but, as part of the universe, to work with the processes of evolution and to assume responsibility for its historical movement. Creation of the human is not simply gift; it is also responsibility and task.

An activist anthropology. A creation anthropology integrates contemplation into an activist spirituality. Creation anthropology sets up a tension between mysticism and constructive action, between contemplation and political action for liberation. Spiritualities that have been affected by evolutionary process and historical consciousness strongly react against an anthropology that asserts that the *telos* of human existence lies primarily in pure knowing or mystical contemplation. As Eckhart showed, creation spirituality finds a religious dimension (mysticism) in human action in the world (politics). On a personal level, activist creation spirituality can appeal to the teaching of Jesus. For example, Jesus' parable of the talents (Matt 25:14-30), which forms a part of the explanation of his central message of the rule of God, points to a rationale of creation and a logic of fulfillment that unfolds within the framework of active freedom. Talents, whether they be money or personal gifts, represent something to be used creatively. And in a social context, the fullness of being cannot be construed as an egocentric or individualist desire for wholeness that bypasses the responsibility implicit in being a participant in God's creation of a free human species. The formula for actualizing one's abilities suggests a religious fulfillment (salvation) in which human creativity in the world will find meaning in the context of the destiny of creation itself.

The critical-productive force of creation-faith. Creation-faith also bears within it a critical and productive energy. Creation-faith recognizes

---

35. Edward Schillebeeckx, *Interim Report on the Books Jesus and Christ* (New York: Crossroad, 1981), 106.

the finitude and contingency of created reality; nothing created can be absolutized. It exposes all idolatries: only God is God. Creation-faith thus criticizes theories of history that are either overly pessimistic or overly optimistic, or overly committed to an immovable tradition or to constant change. Created reality balances the contingent and change-able with law and relatively stable pattern. The resulting dynamic tension opens up to human freedom the possibility to fashion a new and better future in history, however tenuous and limited it may be.[36] Creation-faith, then, is sober and balances pessimism with cautious expectation. No theology after the twentieth century can credibly propose that process and human inventiveness necessarily engender moral progress or collective human fulfillment. But Christians share a deep eschatological hope that does not translate into naiveté regard-ing human projects in this world but does energize creativity.

The future as horizon. The doctrine of creation cannot exist without a companion doctrine of the end-time. And no one better than Jürgen Moltmann has formulated the intrinsic role of hope in the Christian response to reality. The biblical origins of Christian faith and the new picture of the universe both require that hope plays a central role in Christian spirituality. The creator God is also a God of the future. This eschatological perspective places God always out in front of history and each person in it. For Moltmann the center and basis of Christian theology are the resurrection of Jesus, because it points forward as a promise of an absolute new future.[37] This view of God is not the view of most people. God is ordinarily the creator and guardian of order in the universe. In this new perspective, God is also a principle of change and a ground motivating people to do new things and to alter the future in the direction of the rule of God. For Christians, the grounds for this hope lie in the resurrection of Jesus: that God raised Jesus into an absolute future for humans and for all reality represents the keystone of the Christian vision. This reorientation of Christianity fits well with the new scientific view of the cosmos, the idea of cre-ation, and a creation spirituality of freedom. Eschatology will be taken up in the last chapter.

---

36. Edward Schillebeeckx, *God Among Us: The Gospel Proclaimed* (New York: Crossroad, 1983), 94, 97-98. See also Philip Kennedy, *Schillebeeckx* (Collegeville, MN: Liturgical Press, 1993), 89-90.

37. "It is only on the ground of the revelation of God in the event of promise constituted by the raising of the crucified Christ that faith must seek and search for the universal and immediate revelation of God in all things and for all." Jürgen Moltmann, *The Theology of Hope* (New York: Harper & Row, 1967), 282.

What Is God?

Up to this point these reflections have moved along on the naïve supposition that all know what the term "God" refers to. But that is clearly not the case. As the new scientific view of the world seeps down and becomes broadly internalized, the natural tendency for anthropomorphism will be embarrassed and the idea of a world impelled by impersonal forces could drain enthusiasm. The finite universe itself is too large for God to be an even bigger person or Father above it all. We need new spontaneous symbols for what we mean by God.

John Haught has approached this issue with a simplicity and a depth that are compelling.[38] His first foray into what we might mean by "God" reaches for metaphors that reflect regions of human consciousness that are the deepest and thus the most able to open up symbols for the place where the reality of God meets us. These generic aspects of our experience are its depth, the future, its freedom, a sense of beauty, and a respect for the truth. God correlates with the source and ground of our being; God is the whither toward which all reality is moving; God is the expansive liberty of unrestricted agency; God is the pure object of human attraction and desire; God is that which guarantees the coherence and consistency of reality itself.

But Haught finds the idea that most ably gathers these signals of God together in Karl Rahner's phrase that depicts God as "incomprehensible mystery." Mystery "functions as the silent horizon that makes all of our experience and knowledge possible in the first place. . . . We go through the course of our lives enabled by the horizon of mystery to think, to inquire, to adventure and discover, but we seldom become explicitly aware of its encompassing presence-in-absence or extend our gratitude to it for giving us the free space in which to live our lives."[39] Mystery makes its appearance not in problems to be solved but at the limits to where we can go. It appears when one finally asks whether there is a point in asking questions at all. What is the ultimate value of freedom? Does truth matter? Mystery appears in a recognition of the limited and contingent character of all problems and questions relative to an infinite horizon. Yet we move toward this mystery. "It is because of our capacity for mystery that we experience the uneasiness and anxiety that provoke us to move beyond the status quo and to seek more intense beauty and more depth of truth. In short, mystery is what makes a truly human life possible in the first place."[40]

---

38. John F. Haught, *What Is God? How to Think about the Divine* (New York and Mahwah, NJ: Paulist Press, 1986).

39. Haught, *What Is God?*, 117.

40. Haught, *What Is God?*, 124.

Christian spirituality will never surrender its personalist language of God; God cannot be less than what the universe has generated in the human. But God is more than "a person," and we have to stay grounded in the essential, expansive empowerment of what God holds out to us. We live embraced by the infinite power of being, which is gracious and loving, and, as a horizon, is always in front of us drawing us forward.

The supposition is that humanity remains opaque. We do not fully understand what it means to be human, nor do we understand the human phenomenon itself. Not only does the depth of humanity leave it unfathomable, but humanity continues to develop in an evolutionary world. The human constantly develops new contexts of extended relationships within itself and with the world in which it continually re-creates itself. But within this complexity Jesus represents the character of the human in its relationship to God. Jesus represents the human both to itself and to God. The idea of "representation" carries various connotations including the revealing, exemplifying, modeling, and leading discussed in this chapter.

Jesus represents as a teacher of divine wisdom. A scriptural paradigm for such representation is found in the prophets, who speak not their own but God's word. But, as Soelle explains, this teacher completely identifies with those being taught in a process analogous to Calvin's view of accommodation but in personalist terms. The true teacher is no mere purveyor of objective information. The teacher totally commits himself or herself to the ones being taught, identifies with them in an educational process that opens up the freedom of the students. "The educational process attains its goal when the pupil achieves identity, when he finds his 'place.' A teacher who does not efface himself, does not remove himself, make himself superfluous, is not a good teacher" (CR,116). In this manner Jesus represents by modeling human existence and offering possibilities for human freedom.

Jesus the representative did not substitute for human freedom. He did not represent humanity in such a total way that human freedom before God loses its defined role; Jesus does not replace human beings. "As our representative, [Jesus] 'runs on before' us to God—he is our forerunner. The correlate of this provisionality of [Jesus] (his 'running on before') is our discipleship (our 'following after')" (CR, 107). If Jesus replaces us and perfectly secures God's grace and our future for us, we vanish as persons (CR, 109). This caution ensures true discipleship and opens the way for the church to take responsible care of the world (CR, 112).

The language of forerunner incorporates the idea found in the Letter to the Hebrews that Jesus was the pioneer. He went ahead, before the many, who are meant to follow his path and reach his destiny (Heb 2:10; 12:2). Jesus does not represent a neutral or objective humanity, but a humanity that is creature of God and called to live a pattern of existence intended by the creator. The idea of representation includes "embodying" in order to show and lead the way.

Jesus' being our representative also entails his being in solidarity with other human beings before God. This means that the effectiveness of Jesus' representation of us cannot be thought of as an automatically effective happening; its success is the result of a long project over time and depends on the assent and the following of disciples, on human freedom and commitment (CR, 123). The point is made by holding Jesus' ministry, cross, and resurrection together and reading them as a single pattern of historical life. If christology exclusively focuses on God's victory in Jesus' resurrection, it contradicts actual history. Christology has to include the ongoing cross, the struggle and suffering of actual history, within which the resurrection is an "anticipatory sign." Hope in the resurrection does not protect people from the sufferings and risks of history (CR, 126). But this is the discussion of the next chapter.

CHAPTER FOUR

The Turn to Jesus of Nazareth

In the Christian view of things, the consideration of creation-faith leads to reflection on Jesus of Nazareth. This and the following two chapters pay special attention to the stories of Jesus' ministry. Drawing those scenarios into this reflection on spirituality helps to keep them closely bound to life. Later chapters will take up an integration into spirituality of Jesus' suffering, death, and resurrection. These chapters thus follow the line of the Christian Creed, but whereas the Creed jumps from "born of the virgin Mary" to "suffered under Pontius Pilate," the aim here is to fill in the gap of Jesus' public ministry that supplies the content for a spirituality of following Jesus. Together these chapters constitute the christological dimension of this essay in Christian spirituality.

But before turning to Jesus of Nazareth, it will be helpful to clarify some of the language that defines the point of view of the chapter. The introduction explained how "spirituality" on the personal level refers to the way people live their lives according to the imperatives of some ultimate concern or commitment. By contrast, "religion" may be understood socially as the cultural or social institution in which a common commitment of faith unites a group. Religion is corporate spirituality, the community where together people share and nurture the responses to their questions of ultimate meaning and live together in that faith. The idea of a seeking spirituality may seem less apparent when religions become established and young people are socialized into a relatively stable religious culture. Searching may seem relaxed when religious meaning constitutes the world as people find it and a particular religion is internalized with culture. But as people enter a postmodern world, with its sense of historicity and a plurality of religions, the searching/seeking character of spirituality and the constant substructure of mystery that characterizes all religion begin to assert themselves. So it seems in developed societies.

Every revelation and religion has some medium or set of symbols and practices that define the form and content of its faith. According to this formula, the logic of Christian faith is christomorphic. This means that, by definition, Christians find their way to God through faith in Jesus of Nazareth, who is acknowledged to be the Messiah or anointed one of God or Christ. The Christian views the world and God through the mediation or the lens of Jesus Christ, who reveals God and God's values for creation. As a religion, Christianity may be described as the organized body of people who are attached to, and the followers of, Jesus as the revelation of God and consequently a salvific way to God. This represents in a large formal way the personal faith of each Christian and the corporate, institutional logic of the religion as such. This chapter looks at the spirituality that constitutes the existential living faith of the institutionally organized religion. It goes beneath the objective socioreligious forms of Christian religion to describe the origins of Christian spirituality beginning with the encounter with Jesus of Nazareth.

This discussion is divided into four parts. The first part locates the discussion in the larger human quest for meaning. The turn to Jesus arises out of the question of meaning and ultimacy. Jesus responds as a public figure who has accrued enormous religious authority across the ages as a revealer of God. The second part explains the distinction of Christian spirituality from the structure of christology, the discipline that reflectively takes up the task of understanding who Jesus Christ is and what he reveals. The third part then focuses attention on Jesus' ministry as that is portrayed in the stories about him in the Gospels; Jesus' ministry constitutes the deepest source of Christian spirituality. As the Gospels portray him, Jesus' person and ministry exhibited a consistent appeal for followers. Thus, the fourth part considers the idea of "following Jesus" as a kind of fundamental spirituality.

Turning to Jesus in Search for God

Why turn to Jesus in a religious search for transcendence? In many ways the creation-faith that was discussed in the last chapter sets up the question of the fundamental logic of Christianity. Creation-faith essentially recognizes a conception of God immediately present to all finite reality, so that all reality subsists within the creating power of God. But in itself creation-faith provides no clear image of the nature of God. God can be described as the ground of being, the pure power of being, the origin and absolute future of finite reality, the infinite source of the coherence and beauty of reality. These various conceptions put words around, or bring to expression, the awesome experience of absolute contingency of being dependent on the source and power of being itself. But to begin to name God more precisely requires appeal to various media of revelation. Finding God in the world always involves a particular communication and story.

A premise for christology maintains that the only way that human consciousness can become aware of God in any explicit or thematic way requires mediation through contact with the finite world. Although God is immediately present to all creation by holding it in being, every human response to that presence that comes to reflective clarity requires language, symbols, metaphors, or analogies drawn from our worldly experience. How else would the human mind be able to assign content or ascribe a character to that which is encountered as transcending all reality? Some religious mediation is necessary for all reflective contact with transcendent reality. No feeling or intuition of transcendent reality will have any definite sense or meaningful reference without some form of language drawn from worldly experience to describe it. Even mysticism, which is often regarded as direct or immediate presence to God, implicitly involves some form of mediation, making it a "mediated immediacy." This means that so-called experience of direct contact with God cannot really escape our bodily existence in time and space; our bank of experience and knowledge always enters into the equation as a bridging filter for our understanding. Jesus, who is often referred to as mediator, on this most fundamental level of religious knowing, functions as a mediator of transcendence that supplies the content of Christian faith.

On this premise, one can discern an elementary pattern that appears within any particular story of spiritual search and discovery. Human beings spontaneously search for some clue to or insight into the ultimacy that correlates with the experience of finitude and dependence. When it is found, it will be a "revelation," not a reasoned truth but a particular gift of insight. This revelation, however, can be found only through a worldly vehicle, some element in and of the world that opens up human subjectivity and communicates to the person or group that is searching for ultimate reality. This sets up an inherent tension between various aspects of revelation. On the one hand, without such a medium the idea of transcendent reality, having no specific content, would remain little more than the object of an ill-defined feeling or surmise. It would lack focus or specific reference. On the other hand, such a medium, as a this-worldly reality, is not itself transcendent and, in the end, while pointing to transcendence, leaves what is transcendent an absolute mystery. This dialectical or tensive dimension of spiritual and religious experience never disappears. As a medium of transcendent reality, a religious symbol both is and is not what it mediates. The revealer both renders ultimate reality present and, at the same time, points to something transcendent and completely other than itself. This means that the medium cognitively lends characteristics to the transcendent reality it mediates even though the symbolized is recognized as transcendently "other." Transcendent reality really reveals itself in a concrete particular situation and vehicle, and yet that reality is recognized as infinitely obscure. Transcendence is always experienced locally, but what is experienced breaks open the confines of its medium and takes on universal relevance. Tensions abound.

This tension is exemplified in Jesus of Nazareth, a local prophet who became a mediator with wide appeal. Although he was a first-century Jew, thanks to the Gospels Jesus as a human being is accessible to all other human beings for their appreciation. Jesus' teaching is not so culturally bound that people of all cultures cannot understand it at some level. It is true that Christians understand Jesus in various ways as being a transcendent figure. But those same Christians hold that, in the words of the classic doctrine, Jesus was truly a human being; he is therefore approachable by all people, at the very least as a religious teacher. Unitarians who do not appreciate Jesus' divinity can still learn from him a way of life. Jews can appreciate that Jesus was in fact a Jew, not a Christian, and that his first followers were Jews and that most Christians continued to be so into the third century. Muslims can revere Jesus as a religious saint and teacher. Hindus can see Jesus as a representative or avatar of God. Buddhists can recognize Jesus as an enlightened teacher. Jesus' moral teaching can move secular humanists. Jesus has become a public figure who can be appreciated by a wide variety of audiences and circumstances. He speaks to all people searching for transcendence.

Jesus and the imagination. This expansion of the reach of Jesus' appeal carries with it some inner imperatives. A narrative searching approach to Jesus' ministry has to stay as close as possible to the plane of history. This should not be taken as slighting the search for transcendence, because this transcendence has to be found in and through the stories of Jesus' actual teaching and ministry. At this point no direct appeal needs to be made to the Christian doctrines about Jesus that developed after his death and resurrection. These doctrines remain there for Christians to appreciate. But the narrative and searching character of this interpretation stays within the boundaries of what the research of the expansive quest for the historical Jesus has been able to achieve over the past decades. The results of this quest are not neutral or objective; they can never escape the variety of human reactions to him that are intrinsic to the texts that represent him. And the person looking for the way Jesus appeared to his contemporaries will always be influenced by the culture he or she brings to the search.

This historical concern raises a pointed question. Today we know that the Gospels were constructed later from memories of Jesus. The stories of the Gospels also reflect the later experience of the communities in which they were composed. A good deal of imagination was used in the construction of these stories in order to make them applicable to life in the nascent communities in their different circumstances. It may seem that this provenance of the Gospel stories prevents the possibility of taking the stories about Jesus as historically representative, and this may seem to undermine a historical approach. There can be little doubt that a historical-critical approach to the Gospels requires a nuanced understanding of the character of the stories about Jesus. The Gospels do not contain directly reported descriptions of events as they actually happened. But the Christian church has been in possession of historical criticism for more than two centuries, so this is not a new problem. The stories about Jesus in the Gospels are products of the authors' and the communities' imaginations because no one can escape that. But they also bear some reference to the way Jesus actually was.

It is possible to come to consensus about certain degrees of historical authenticity relative to many Gospel stories. Various kinds of stories do not imply any historicity, while others contain a more or less historically accurate depiction of the kind of ministry Jesus practiced. It will always be impossible to decide with exactitude the degree of historical authenticity of any story that seems to intend it. But after recognizing these ambiguities, it is still possible to say that the Gospels reveal a good deal of substantial if not detailed knowledge of Jesus of Nazareth.

In sum, everyone who approaches Jesus makes use of the imagination. The imagination refers to a positive and constructive facet of the human mind. Even the methodically careful historian must imaginatively reconstruct the concrete situations in which Jesus' ministry unfolded. The imagination should not be regarded as irresponsible fancy or merely playful fantasizing. Imagination plays the role of constructively projecting on the basis of data possibilities for human life and action. The imagination does not obstruct knowledge; it enables new insight. When the imagination is transposed into our present critical consciousness, it becomes an exercise of intelligent insight and creative freedom. The imagination, when applied to the stories of Jesus, allows one to see new horizons and fashion new possibilities for one's own life into the future.

Following Jesus and the Development of Christology

Following Jesus describes a spirituality. The book by Thomas à Kempis in the fifteenth century entitled *Imitatio Christi* or *The Imitation of Christ* was enormously popular right into the twentieth century and still has influence today. One of the reasons for this is its attempt to capture the essence of being a Christian in the following of Jesus. By contrast, christology is a subdiscipline of Christian theology that provides an understanding of the person of Jesus Christ and his role in the relationship between human beings and God. This discipline has a history that is as long as Christian faith itself. From the beginning, Christian belief has been subjected to critical scrutiny, and christology has always been a contentious enterprise. A discussion of how these two phenomena are related to each other will define more closely the aim of these chapters on Jesus. This can be done in three brief steps. The first characterizes Jesus of Nazareth as a historian might present him; the second describes how followers of Jesus developed interpretations of him that initiated the discipline of christology; the third underlines the relationship between the following of Jesus that generated the christologies and the christologies themselves.

Jesus of Nazareth. Jesus of Nazareth was a Jew who appeared as a teacher, prophet, and healer in Palestine preaching the kingdom of God. His birth is projected back to around the year 7 or 6 B.C.E.; he began his ministry probably in 28 C.E., and it lasted about two years; he was executed in 30 C.E., on the eve of Passover, at the age of thirty-six.[1] Two of the four Gospels include stories of Jesus' birth and infancy, but a majority of critical exegetes would discount the historical character of these accounts: they are stories constructed later to make theological points. Jesus was more probably born in Nazareth than in Bethlehem; many critics believe he most probably had bothers and sisters, as the New Testament asserts. He probably began his ministry as a disciple of, or was at least influenced by, John the Baptizer, and it is generally recognized that Jesus was indeed baptized by John.

New Testament scripture scholars agree that the thematic center of Jesus' message was encapsulated in what he called "the rule of God" or "the kingdom of God." This phrase will be explained more fully in the course of these chapters. But because Jesus is not on record as providing a discursive definition of what the rule of God means, we have to construct it from the many ways Jesus depicted it: in parables,

---

1. Wilfrid J. Harrington, *Jesus Our Brother: The Humanity of the Lord* (New York and Mahwah, NJ: Paulist Press, 2011), 7.

in sayings, in various concrete symbolic actions such as his healings, hospitality at meals, and exorcisms. "If it is by the Spirit of God that I cast out demons," he said, "then the kingdom of God has come upon you" (Mt 12:28). One way of summarizing in a broad but not inaccurate way what Jesus meant by the rule or kingdom of God would be to think of the world according to God's intention, what it would be if everything were in accordance with God's will. The God of Jesus thus appears from one perspective as the creator God who intends a wise ordering of all things. Jesus also depicted God as Father, indeed, a loving Father whom we should address in the responsive language of prayer. Jesus' God exhibits personal concern and care for each of God's creatures.

As to the persona of Jesus, that is, the kind of role or public image in which he presented himself, the titles of teacher, healer, and prophet fairly accurately describe his activities. Each of these roles was part of first-century Jewish culture. Jesus was an itinerant teacher: he went from village to village in Galilee teaching religious and moral wisdom in parables and other pronouncements. Jesus also healed and cast out demons, according to the practice at the time. Jesus was one of many healers in Israel in his day. As a prophet, Jesus challenged a good number of religious behaviors of his Jewish religion. One cannot fully understand his execution without recognizing that he caused conflict and generated enemies, not least among the religious establishment. It is generally agreed that Jesus' sphere of ministry was Israel: he called Judaism to a reform that would make it ready for the approaching rule of God. More will be said of these roles further on.

Sometime around the year 30, at the time of Passover, after he had gone up to Jerusalem, Jesus taught in the temple, where he stirred up some conflict. At some point he was examined by Jewish religious leaders, brought before the Roman governor, and condemned to death and crucified. Historians contest the historical reconstruction of those responsible for his death and their motives.

The development of christology. Sometime after Jesus' death, his disciples regrouped and proclaimed that God had raised Jesus from death. Their experience of Jesus risen from death in and by the power of the creator God was the final impulse needed for the Jesus movement to go forward, and ultimately it developed into the Christian church. Luke's Acts of the Apostles depicts the origins in Jerusalem of what gradually became called the Christian movement, but some scholars are convinced that this movement must have begun in the various communities in Galilee where Jesus conducted the greater part of his ministry.[2] In either case, or both cases, the Easter experience of the disciples marks the key historical event that allowed the Christian movement to go forward.[3] That Jesus was raised by God was understood as Jesus' divine vindication and guarantee of his faithful witness to God. The experience that Jesus is really risen into God's own sphere means that he represents and mediates God's promise of salvation for all. The experience of Jesus risen also explains why the community, then shaped not only by his teaching but also by the memory of him and the experience of his presence among them, began to interpret him in a more exalted manner: the experience of Jesus risen is at the heart of the genesis of christology.

The New Testament contains many different christologies, that is, conceptions of who Jesus is in relation to God and how he mediates God's salvation for humankind. A certain broad development in these christologies can be roughly charted by determining the time and the community that generated the works of the New Testament or the traditions behind passages in any given writing. Beyond the content of these many christologies, the sheer fact of development over time and across relatively different communities and traditions helps to determine the underlying structure of christology. This may be described in New Testament terms as accounting for the hope experienced in Jesus' resurrection (1 Pet 3:15) and responding to the question of exactly who Jesus is (Matt 16:15). The logic and structure of christology appear as the attempt to express or "explain" who Jesus Christ is on the basis of the place he holds in the religious faith of the Christian. Christians experienced the salvation of God mediated in and through Jesus. What does that make of Jesus? Who must he be for him to have that status in one's faith-filled conception of reality? The New Testament provides no single definitive response to this question, but a whole host of christological rationales for the faith of Christians. Whatever conceptions are thought to be the most compelling also have to be interpreted in a way that makes them plausible to people today.

The development of christology did not end with the determination of the New Testament canon. Especially the divinity of Jesus became a major source of contention for centuries. By the second century the language of the Prologue of the Gospel of John had overshadowed

---

2. See Ron Cameron and Merrill P. Miller, "Introduction: Ancient Myths and Modern Theories of Christian Origins," in *Redescribing Christian Origins*, ed. Ron Cameron and Merrill P. Miller, Society of Biblical Literature Symposium Series 28 (Atlanta: Society of Biblical Literature, 2004), 20.

3. The Easter experience refers to what Jesus' followers encountered that enabled them to affirm that God raised Jesus into eternal life. The resurrection refers to what happened to Jesus: he was raised by God from death.

other basic metaphors for conceiving of the divinity of Jesus Christ: "In the beginning was the Word. . . . And the Word became flesh" (John 1:1, 14). In 325 at Nicaea it was determined that the "Word," though distinct from the Father, was strictly divine, of the same nature as the Father, thus making Jesus in whom the Word was present and active a divine figure. This led the way for a doctrine of the trinity since, together with God's Word, God's Spirit too was distinguished from God as Father and became recognized as strictly divine. And later at Chalcedon, in 451, the fourth ecumenical council proposed a compromise formula that sought to protect in the wake of Nicaea the true humanity of Jesus. It said that Jesus Christ was a single person but constituted in two integral natures, together but not confused, human and divine. This formal statement became a classic Christian doctrine, accepted by most Christians, although interpreted theologically in different ways.[4]

The place of following Jesus. During his ministry, Jesus gathered disciples who were gradually initiated into his ways of preaching the rule of God by their lives together. There is no reason to doubt that Jesus did in fact send the disciples out to represent him and to do the things that he did. This group of followers and their following Jesus connect the ministry of Jesus with the continuation of a Jesus movement after his death and resurrection. One can describe with broad but historical accuracy how christology developed out of the following and the ministry of the disciples of Jesus. Christology developed into a discipline out of the process of the earliest followers of Jesus trying to understand what went on in the whole Jesus affair. The initial method of those efforts is plainly written in the pages of the New Testament: the earliest followers consistently appealed to the Hebrew scriptures in an effort to gain clues to what had transpired in the ministry of Jesus, his death, and his resurrection, and hence for understanding his person. They produced a variety of formulas and images.

Becoming attached to Jesus, becoming a follower, and experiencing God (especially God's salvation) being mediated through him and his ministry are the conditions for the possibility of christology. Christology grew out of a spirituality of following Jesus. Following Jesus is the source and basis of christology as a formal discipline. The meaning and the vitality of christology in any age and for any people will

---

4. The doctrine of Chalcedon, the most influential of all christological doctrines, says in technical language that Jesus was both human and divine. It says no more than that, and no less. It offers no explanation. The doctrine had massive theological reasoning supporting its genesis and adoption; but none of the theology forms part of the doctrine. It remains open for and is the subject of different theological interpretations.

be measured against the background of an existential encounter with Jesus.

This analysis clears the way to situate the consideration of Jesus in the pages that follow. They reflect on the following of Jesus that is implicit in the Gospel stories. This is not an exclusive or reductionist analysis; it is not intended as a shortcut to the further development of christology. It is simply a consideration of a spirituality of following Jesus that, in its turn, will give rise to a more formal reflection on Jesus.

Jesus Called to Ministry of the Rule of God

Jesus is a public figure insofar as his ministry has been encapsulated in the four Gospels. But as was said, these Gospels do not provide an intimate portrait of Jesus as an individual. The New Testament offers no physical description of Jesus. And the Gospels do not allow us to penetrate into Jesus' psychological consciousness as one might, for example, if Jesus had written a diary, or if he was the writer of the Gospels. What we have is a third- or fourth-hand portrait of the man based on stories that were handed down and imaginatively embellished for use in preaching and instruction. Jesus, however, does appear rather objectively in his basic teachings. These teachings were profound; they offer a vision of human existence that was passionately held. His teachings and actions thus define him, because he was called to commit himself to them, to live by them, to communicate them to others, and, as it turned out, to die for them.

This approach to Jesus depicts him as a man who experienced a call to ministry. His ministry in turn appeals to a spirituality that, inspired by him, would consist of some form of following him. This description of Jesus is not oriented apologetically to interpret him in ways that provide grounds for claims about his person. Rather, it depicts the story of Jesus, insofar as this can be discerned in the stories about him and the stories he himself told, in a way that allows one to judge what he stands for and offers. It is drawn from the four Gospels. Since the Gospels are collections of stories and do not provide a temporal framework of the events of Jesus' ministry, the chronological markers of his ministry are little more than a beginning and an end with a confused middle. But we can still say a good deal about his ministry and his message.

Different people, when they try to offer an account of Jesus' message, always come up with different portraits even though they are using the same data. This is because Jesus is always being filtered through the one describing him. This presentation of Jesus in his ministry begins with the concrete aspects of his immediate concerns and builds slowly to a bigger and more comprehensive framework for appreciating his vision. It is not meant as a substitute for reading the Gospels.

Jesus' concerns. Because one cannot recover the chronology of Jesus' ministry from the collection of stories that make up the Gospels, we cannot introduce him by starting at the beginning. But we can introduce Jesus by noticing what he cared about in terms of the people he particularly attended to. Chief among those for whom he was consistently concerned were the poor, especially those who were destitute in a generally poor peasant society. The poor are those who have nothing and thus particularly need to have God on their side. "Blessed are you who are poor, for the kingdom of God is yours" (Luke 6:20), Jesus said, promising them liberation by God's power. By contrast, he also warned the wealthy that they had a communitarian and humane responsibility to be concerned with the poor, not to mention the rule of God.

Jesus was also concerned with sinners. "Those who are well do not need a physician, but the sick do. I did not come to call the righteous but sinners" (Mark 2:7). Everyone has personal failings, but public sinners were often branded. People saw a connection between misfortune and moral failure; thus Jesus also attended to those marginalized in society. The point was that he was showing God's compassion for all. And this was manifested by his willingness to join outcasts at table, a dramatic and for some a scandalous sign of solidarity. A good number of stories show that Jesus was attentive to the marginalized place of women in society. Jesus' attitude toward women, given the cultural context, was consistently and remarkably positive. In all, Wilfrid Harrington generalizes: "Jesus always put people first. And his concern was, emphatically, for the vulnerable, the despised, and the outcast. He displayed special regard for those characterized as sinners."[5]

Jesus' social personae. Scholars can close in more tightly on the person of Jesus by paying careful attention to the public roles of teacher, healer, and prophet that were indicated earlier. This refers both to what Jesus did and to how he was perceived in his actions.

The Gospels are quite clear in presenting Jesus as a teacher. By the time the stories of his public teaching and the content of what he taught in parable and aphorism were set down in the New Testament, he was being cast as the new Moses (Matt 17:1-8). But on the ground, the stories of him going around and addressing groups of people in towns and synagogues contain details that fit the pattern of itinerant

---

5. Harrington, *Jesus Our Brother*, 27.

teachers of the same time period. Jesus would have filled a known role as he traveled with a band of followers, with little concern for wealth or title, and taught moral and religious truths of the tradition. This well-known function opens up the imagination to reconstruct with a fair amount of accuracy this aspect of his ministry. The Gospel stories fill in the content of what he taught.

Jesus was also a healer or exorcist. Often the healing consisted in driving out a demon. Jesus could be described as a faith healer, because he often correlated the efficacy of his healing with the power of the faith of the recipient or of prayer. Some of the early stories of Jesus healing involved ritual actions. For example, Mark tells of Jesus healing a man who was deaf and dumb: "He put his finger into the man's ears and, spitting, touched his tongue; then he looked up to heaven and groaned, and said to him, '*Ephphatha!*'—that is, 'Be opened'" (Mark 7:33-34)! Jesus did a good deal of hands-on healing, and we have to think that he gained some renown because of it.[6]

Jesus was recognized as a prophet. A definition of a prophet would include the idea of a social critic. A prophet in the Jewish tradition was one who represented God's word on a particular matter or social situation; the prophet represented God's point of view and valuation of things. Obviously this involved criticism of innumerable customs and social behaviors of the time and warnings about where a course of action might lead. Jesus' prophetic activity did not win him friends among those whom he criticized for not behaving according to the law and the prophets but acting for their own interests. "Woe also to you lawyers! For you load people with burdens hard to bear, and you yourselves do not lift a finger to ease them" (Luke 11:46). Many of the stories of Jesus confronting people in high places, especially in his temple teaching in Jerusalem, explain the conflict surrounding Jesus that ultimately accounted for his execution.

Healer, teacher, or prophet: which one of these most pointedly captures his historical persona? Different exegetes have favored one title over the other two and centered their interpretation there. But it is not necessary to do so. The three roles together and the way they overlap in particular stories help the imagination to reconstruct some of the richness conveyed by the stories about Jesus.

---

6. On the one hand, that Jesus performed what were considered wondrous examples of exorcism and healing is fairly certain historically. On the other hand, what exactly transpired in each Gospel story is impossible to reconstruct historically. There are simply too many variables and unknowns. See John Meier, *A Marginal Jew: Rethinking the Historical Jesus*, vol. 2, *Mentor, Message, and Miracles*, Anchor Bible Reference Library (New York: Doubleday, 1994), part 3.

Jesus' message. Most students of the New Testament find the kernel of Jesus' message in the phrase "the kingdom of God" or "the rule of God." It oversimplifies but does not distort the meaning of this phrase to say that it refers to God's will or intention for the world in contrast to the way it actually is. This can mean that a future rule of God in the end-time will finally put things right; or it may mean that God's presence and power sometimes assert themselves in history itself, usually through some agency. But it is best to think of this as a deliberate ambiguity and that both meanings are generally in play, though either one could be accented in a particular case. Thus, Matthew says that Jesus taught his disciples to pray for the rule of God: "Thy kingdom come. Thy will be done, on earth as it is in heaven" (Matt 6:10).

As indicated earlier, this metaphor of the rule of God came from the idea that God, the creator, was like the king of the universe, so that one could imagine God's concern for the world like the ideal king's concern for the well-being of his people.[7] But this is not just one of the many conceptions that Jesus taught. It functioned more like the overriding vision that drove his whole ministry. It is legitimate to ask how this particular teaching of Jesus or that particular action relates to the rule of God to which he was committed, because for Jesus the rule of God was a comprehensive perspective on things. So, for example, much of Jesus' teaching was communicated in parables, which are noted for sharp endings and reversals of expectation. This usually illustrates how different are human and divine expectations. We say love your family and friends; God says love your enemies. When Jesus said, "The sabbath was made for man, not man for the sabbath" (Mark 2:27), this was radical; it turned on its head much of the basic thinking of the religious establishment and a piety wedded to the law as the expression of God's will. In short, the rule of God was both a vast metaphysical vision of reality depicting the way it should be and is and will be in God's eyes, and also a critical principle that applied to concrete situations and provided leverage for Jesus' religious and moral assessment.

Jesus' representation of God. The primary goal of Jesus' ministry was to represent God and God's rule. And so it is natural to ask how God appears in Jesus' teaching.[8] A few large qualities of God that charac-

---

7. Norman Perrin, *Jesus and the Language of the Kingdom: Symbol and Metaphor in New Testament Interpretation* (Philadelphia: Fortress Press, 1976), 16-20. In the chapter that follows I will appeal to a deeper association of the rule of God with God's will as expressed in God's law that resonates in the Jewish imagination with Torah.

8. This question gets complicated with a moment's reflection. How could one possibly sum up Jesus' teaching about God? The complexity deepens because, during

terize Jesus' teaching about and modeling of God are drawn from the Gospel stories.

God of course is God, creator of heaven and earth. Even though Jesus never actually refers to God as creator in the Gospels, he refers to God's sovereign vigilance over the world. "Look at the birds of the air: they neither sow nor reap nor gather into barns, and yet your heavenly Father feeds them. Are you not of more value than they" (Matt 6:26)? But this transcendent one is also personal: Jesus referred to God as father to mark God's care, compassion, and loving forgiveness, not God's patriarchy. This God, too, is pure love, not because Jesus actually described God in the same language that the writings of John do, but because of God's absolute concern for the ones least respected in life. God, then, is savior: as such God bestows a depth of significance on human existence itself that is purely gratuitous and unexpected on the surface of things. As the ground of this meaningful coherence, God establishes justice and criteria for judgment. God is the one who sustains and holds out to human consciousness a moral substance and imperative inherent in being itself.

When they are added up, the Gospel stories about Jesus offer in relatively straightforward language a profound vision of reality: God, the world, and human life in relation to God and in society. They offer a substantial vision of reality and outlook on human existence.

Following Jesus

Jesus had disciples during his ministry. Jesus called people to join his cause, to follow him. This section relates to the last as a response does to an appeal. It shows the way in which an understanding of Jesus depends on an existential engagement with his message. The assessment of the person who is unmoved by Jesus' teaching will be different from that of the follower. The interpretations will be as different as a genuine prophet is from a deluded disturber of the peace. Comparing these judgments shows that an appreciation of Jesus involves more than an objective analysis of historical data. The appeal that Jesus made during his ministry and still makes now does not address reason through argument but appeals to the whole person by offering a meaningful vision of life that calls for commitment. The story of Jesus, then, offers a way of life that is intended to win followers.

The idea of conversion provides an entrée into understanding what following Jesus entails. Conversion was a central theme in the preaching of John the Baptist: "Repent, for the kingdom of heaven is at hand"

---

the course of the Jesus movement after Jesus' death and resurrection, followers began to recognize Jesus himself as a kind of icon or living parable of the rule of God.

(Matt 3:2). "Repent" translates the Greek verb meaning to undergo change of mind or disposition. But the measure of real change is less psychological and more in terms of lifestyle, a person's way of behaving, his or her story. A narrative method looks at the story of Jesus for insights into how he impacted the lives of his followers and could do so again today. On the one hand, the Gospels portray Jesus preaching and acting. On the other hand, the follower is one who internalizes Jesus' words and actions, and these change his or her life accordingly.

Three stories in the Gospels form an imaginative unit that tells of Jesus being inaugurated into his ministry, explaining his message of the rule of God, and seeking disciples to join his cause. There are different versions of these stories in the four Gospels, and only in Luke, who has all three, do these distinct incidents form parts of a single but discontinuous literary narrative. And regardless of whether these events happened as described, it is clear that Jesus began his ministry, explained his "vision," and recruited disciples. The stories then have some broad historical verisimilitude.[9]

Jesus commissioned (Luke 3:21-22). Luke's account of Jesus being baptized is very brief; it simply says that Jesus was baptized by John. But it surrounds the affirmation with symbols that offer a later theological commentary indicating that this baptism was actually a commissioning by God. But, aside from the theology, exegetes largely agree that historically Jesus was indeed baptized by the ascetic preacher John, and that Jesus was associated with him for some period of time before striking out on his own. In any case, the story represents Jesus' commitment and the inauguration of his ministry.

Jesus describes his program (Luke 4:14-30). This second vignette is an imaginative masterpiece. Jesus returns to his hometown, Nazareth, with a reputation already gained. Called upon to read in the synagogue, he is presented with some lines from the Prophet Isaiah (especially Isa 61:1-2 and 58:6). The text speaks of one anointed by the Spirit of God to proclaim good news to the poor, freedom to captives, sight to the blind, liberty to the oppressed, and a jubilee year of remission of

---

9. Recall what was said earlier about the imagination. These stories about Jesus were written down decades after Jesus' appearance. Those who wrote them down and those who edited them used memory and imagination in their composition. Those who read them today gain an understanding of them that is assisted by the imagination. Even exegetes who decide that they are more or less historically accurate use their imaginations. A narrative approach that explicitly engages the imagination also signals that the correspondence of these stories to the actual unfolding of events, however real that connection might be, can only be very broadly construed.

debts. "And he closed the book, and gave it back to the attendant, and sat down; and the eyes of all in the synagogue were fixed on him. And he began to say to them, 'Today this scripture has been fulfilled in your hearing'" (Luke 4:20-21). Sorting out what Jesus said from Luke's later interpretation of him, which was inspired by Isaiah, requires careful nuance and cannot be adjudicated here. What the story does communicate with power is that Jesus appeared within a religious tradition, that he preached the rule of God, and that he acted it out with healings, teaching, and prophetic critique. This story represents Jesus introducing his message at the start of his ministry.

Jesus solicits followers (Luke 5:1-11). A number of stories depict Jesus recruiting disciples. This story of Luke is a combination of two stories to gain dramatic effect. It begins with Jesus preaching to people on the shore of the lake while seated in a boat of fishermen. After he spoke, he asked the fishermen to move their boats further out and drop their nets; when they did, they caught a huge load of fish. Three of the fishermen were so overwhelmed by the event and presumably Jesus' teaching that "they left everything and followed him" (Luke 5:11).

These stories feed the imagination and fill in an abstract conception of Jesus beginning his ministry. He was called, and he nurtured that calling with an affiliation with John the Baptizer. His baptism symbolizes the inauguration of his own ministry. Like a political campaigner, Jesus had to establish his message in traditional terms; he had to articulate the character of the rule of God that was pressing in on him and on Israel. As he moved forward in his ministry he attracted followers who associated themselves with him in different capacities.

The logic of following. This phrase refers to what it means, or to what is going on, when a person becomes a follower of Jesus. This could be described in several ways. For example, today it may mean that a person enters the church. Since the church is composed of the followers of Jesus, one becomes such a follower by joining the group. Or it may mean that a person believes Jesus' or the church's teachings. While not denying the coherence of these conceptions, the phrase "following Jesus" bears a closer analogy to Jesus' original followers and has an explicit reference to Jesus that carries one deeper into the significance of his ministry.

Speaking descriptively, all the stories of Jesus choosing or gaining followers occur when Jesus meets people, invites them, or so influences them that they are drawn into his orbit. Two lives or two stories intersect, and the life and vision of Jesus resonate with a religious authority that attracts the other. This process continues over time not only because of the community that keeps the tradition alive, but also literarily through the Gospel stories. What philosophers call a fusion of horizon, which describes how literary ideas of one period in a tradition can become relevant to another, may be called a fusion of narratives in the appropriation of Jesus into a person's life in today's world. Persons enter the stories of Jesus and to the best of their ability appreciate them from the inside as past events. They allow the stories, and the whole story to which the many vignettes give rise, to converge and reverberate with their own lives in a way that releases possibilities for present existence and the future.[10] Because Jesus was a human being, he can be imitated. People can imaginatively *try on* his teachings and values, reckon their potential within the parameters of the social, cultural, and personal possibilities of their own lives, and then *try them out*: put them into action—in a wide variety of ways. For example, today the love of the Samaritan for the victim along the road to Jericho may best be shown by making the road safe and establishing a just social system that eliminates the need for banditry.

Following Jesus describes a spirituality, that is, a way of life governed by an ultimate concern that centers one's life and energies, and acts as a coordinator or measure of one's identity. Spirituality really points to the center of gravity or deep commitment that organizes a person's behavior. When Jesus has a decisive influence on one's way of life, whether through his literary person or through the Christian community, one becomes a follower of Jesus. Obviously the phrase "following Jesus" becomes more literally accurate and actually deeper when the relationship to Jesus of Nazareth as he is represented in the Gospels becomes more explicit and overt.

In sum, Jesus of Nazareth was a teacher, healer, and a prophet in first-century Palestine. From that beginning, through his iconization in the Gospels, he has become a public figure for the whole human race. He responds to the religious question and solicits followers according the capacity of each.

* * *

---

10. Paul Ricoeur is convinced that a story of the past can communicate an authoritative truth to the present, but not in terms of a one-to-one correspondence to the things located in the horizon of one's actual world. Rather, one learns existential possibilities for living, ideals that can project a new future for the self. The world designated by the stories of Jesus is not simply there objectively, but is there as intentionally construed, and participation in it is projected into the immediate future. The reference that the text points to "is a *proposed world* which I could inhabit and wherein I could project one of my ownmost possibilities." Paul Ricoeur, "The Hermeneutical Function of Distanciation," in *Hermeneutics and the Human Sciences*, ed. J. B. Thompson (Cambridge: Cambridge University Press, 1981), 142.

We began this chapter with the premise that the only way human beings have of finding and relating to transcendent reality lies through some historical mediation. This premise is postmodern; it undermines the universal rationalist kind of thinking of modernity. This premise sets the ground rules for all religion and all existential being-in-relation-with-God. We may think that one may break free of religious mediation, but every abandonment of one form of mediation is reliant on another. This gives an appeal to Jesus an initial plausibility. We can transcend our particular viewpoints by entry into dialogue with others, but we cannot escape them. Everyone lives by faith.

In the turn to Jesus, his identity may appear to be lying right on the surface of the Gospel narratives. Modern critical approaches to scripture have complicated this perception considerably. They show that the Gospels both do and do not represent Jesus simply as he was historically, that the New Testament texts were imaginatively constructed but still give a substantially accurate "portrait" of Jesus, and that people are allowed to use their own imaginations in their interpretations of him. In fact one cannot do otherwise.

Behind all christologies, both those of the New Testament and the later theological and dogmatic christologies of the churches, lies the narrative of Jesus of Nazareth. The primary datum to which one turns when one turns to Jesus of Nazareth for transcendent spiritual meaning is his story. A person who engages the story of Jesus receives something from it. Entering the story of Jesus then engenders active engagement; it is difficult to remain passive and not react. The Jesus story issues a summons to direct our histories along a path analogous to his. Jesus does not only offer a salvation to simply take; he also shows a direction of life that promises salvation in the future.[11]

These two basic insights were appreciated by the Reformers when they broke free of thinking from above by turning to the scriptures, particularly the New Testament. One stresses passivity and reception, and the other active response, but these are inseparable. On the one hand, Luther captured the interpersonal existential character of faith's attachment to Jesus. What transpires between Christ and the believer when he or she clings to Jesus Christ in faith is frequently referred to as the "wonderful exchange." What is ours becomes his, and what is his becomes ours. That is, Christ takes on our sin as his justice becomes ours.[12] This liberation can be appropriated analogously today. The

---

11. This should not be read as a hard distinction but as a matter of focus or emphasis. One cannot erect a clear boundary or division between these two aspects of an appropriation of Jesus Christ.

12. Luther writes: "Accordingly the believing soul can boast of and glory in whatever Christ has as though it were his own, and whatever the soul has Christ

more one is drawn into the leadership of Jesus, the more one is transformed by a power from outside oneself that does not submerge the self but enhances it. The more people go out of themselves and enter into the logic of Jesus' life and ministry, the more they may internalize a sense of being commissioned by a transcendent power, be caught up in a mission to expend their talents for a self-transcending cause in history, and join a movement with similar goals. For the seeker this does not give instant salvation, but it points one's life in a meaningful and meaning-giving direction.

On the other hand, Calvin captured the activist character of following Jesus. His own re-presentation of Luther's early emphasis on justification by faith by his coupling of sanctification with justification leads in a more spontaneous way toward an activist spirituality.[13] Calvin's spirituality, especially as it is represented in the *Institutes*, looks toward an alignment of the will of the Christian with the will of God, generally in the world, and specifically in his or her individual case. Calvin's is a spirituality of participation in God's cause in the world and concretely in each society.

---

claims as his own." "The Freedom of a Christian," in *Martin Luther: Selections from His Writings*, ed. John Dillenberger (Garden City, NY: Anchor Books, 1961), 60. Luther also writes: "And this is that mystery which is rich in divine grace: wherein, by a wonderful exchange, our sins are no longer ours but Christ's: and the righteousness of Christ is ours." Martin Luther, "Psalm 22," *Select Works of Martin Luther, Vol. IV, Commentary of Martin Luther on the First Twenty-Two Psalms*, trans. Henry Cole (London: T. Bensley, 1826), 369.

13. In his *Institutes* John Calvin places a certain stress on sanctification, that is, growth in holiness through an active, ethical Christian life, by commenting on this element prior to considering justification, which is in a logical sense prior to but inseparable from sanctification. *Institutes*, III. chaps. 3, 6-10. Other elements of Calvin's theology converge in a way that justifies describing his spirituality as activist. See Roger Haight, *Christian Community in History*, vol. 2, *Comparative Ecclesiology* (New York: Continuum, 2005), 118-42.

CHAPTER FIVE

God in Jesus' Ministry

The number of books introducing Jesus of Nazareth on a popular and a scholarly level that are published each year is astonishing. During the last two centuries, Christians have shown great interest in the way Jesus appeared to his contemporaries in his public ministry. It would be strange if Christians were not interested in the historical figure who determined the basic contours of Christian faith.

The canonical and some of the noncanonical Gospels provide the main sources for describing the ministry of Jesus of Nazareth. But these limited sources do not preclude substantial differences among the historical interpretations. The context and intention of the interpreter and the variations within the sources themselves help account for multiple portraits of Jesus. Because they were composed some time after Jesus' death and resurrection in different communities with different traditions and concerns, each Gospel has a distinctive point of view. There is no single correct telling of the story of Jesus; in fact the story itself lacks a definite chronology. We have a commonly accepted historical starting point in Jesus' baptism by John and a definite historical ending in Jesus' execution in Jerusalem, but not much certainty about the order of events in between.

Most presentations of Jesus' ministry operate within the framework of certain goals. Three points will help to define the distinctive approach of this chapter. First, this chapter pays attention to a distinction between the way Jesus appeared to his contemporaries and the way he was later appreciated as Messiah by the emerging Christian community. This distinction is too delicate for its boundaries to be absolutized. But there are instances where it is clear that the way Jesus was later portrayed adds much to the way Jesus actually appeared. For example, critical exegetes tend to agree that, when Jesus predicts that he will be rejected, killed, and "after three days rise again" (Mark 8:31), this fairly exact knowledge of things was added by those who knew them after the event. On the basis of this distinction, the account that follows is attentive to the degree to which the actions of Jesus seem historically plausible.

Second, every interpretation of Jesus will be influenced by a pre-vailing interest and a distinctive aspect of Jesus' person and ministry. The point of view of this chapter can be illustrated by contrast to an alternative. It is generally agreed among exegetes and historians that the primary object or content of Jesus' ministry centered on the rule of God rather than himself. Thus the maxim: Jesus did not preach him-self but the rule of God. Yet many, if not most, of the presentations of Jesus of Nazareth aim precisely at producing a portrait of him. The subtitle of Gerhard Lohfink's *Jesus of Nazareth* illustrates the point: *What He Wanted, Who He Was*.[1] In other words, attention is focused on the identity of Jesus as this can be discerned in his teaching and ministry. By contrast, the focus of this chapter more pointedly rests on the content of Jesus' message of the rule of God and the image or conception of God that is implied there. This preoccupation does not impugn in any way the other, and the two foci cannot be completely separated from each other. But the difference should be noted. This chapter is less interested in the claims about Jesus of the early church and more interested in what he communicated historically about God, even though both of these interests are important. The question here is: Who is the God reflected in the narrative of Jesus' ministry and in his teachings about the rule of God?

Third, it may be important to underline the role of the imagination in this narrative approach to Jesus' teaching on God. Human beings cannot understand or think about reality without an accompany-ing imagination. The stories about Jesus that were remembered and assembled into the Gospel narratives were imaginatively constructed all around: by those who first told them, by those who wrote them down, and by those who edited them into the Gospels. And people who read them today reimagine the scenarios in their own way. This inescapable role of a constructive imagination makes a retrieval of Jesus in the stories about him a highly creative enterprise. The differ-ent positions of exegetes on precise historical conclusions all involve complex imaginative frameworks that are operative in their thinking. For those who believe that there is only one true interpretation of Jesus of Nazareth, this diversity is a problem. For others who are comfort-able with pluralism, the situation is a boon.

The movement from a consideration of Jesus' ministry to a char-acterization of the God he reveals moves through three stages. The

---

1. Collegeville, MN: Liturgical Press, 2012. Lohfink does not carefully attend to the distinction between Jesus' historical appearance and the interpretations that came later, unless they are obvious. It is important to note that exegetes differ among themselves both in theory and in practice on this issue.

first stage considers various stories about Jesus in the Gospels that illustrate some of the principal characteristics of his ministry and the prominent qualities of God that are directly addressed or implied in it. The process is highly selective and hardly a substitute for reading the four Gospels. The second stage analyzes the way the mind may work as it translates stories about Jesus mediating the rule of God to a description of the God who is implicit in it. The third completes the transition by offering an inevitably anthropomorphic portrait of God that emerges from Jesus' ministry.

Stories of God in Jesus' Ministry

The four Gospels assemble a whole host of stories about Jesus as he performed his ministry of the rule of God. Jesus' idea of God is embedded in the notion of "the rule of God," a conception that formed the controlling idea guiding his ministry.[2] The best way to get an idea of the character of God that Jesus communicated would be to read and reread the chapters of the Gospels and allow those stories, especially the stories that Jesus himself told portraying the rule of God, to make an impression on the imagination. This would allow Jesus to determine the reader's idea of God and short-circuit the tendency to measure what Jesus says about God by our own convictions. Since a purely analytical account of "Jesus' idea of God" would subvert the New Testament narrative, the lead section of this chapter offers six Gospel narratives, recounted in an imaginative way, as a basis for the move from story to reflective appreciation.[3] The six stories roughly illustrate Jesus operating as a healer, a teacher, and a prophet; they also highlight a particular aspect of the God whose rule is being announced. These stories provide sources from which to extrapolate the "portrait" of God that follows.

Jesus defines his mission (Luke 4:16-30). This is the story of Jesus returning home to Nazareth, where he was raised, after he has been baptized and has begun his public ministry. He has already gained a certain notice in Galilee as one who taught in the synagogues of the towns

---

2. Jacques Schlosser, *Le Dieu de Jésus: Étude exégétique*, Lectio Divina 129 (Paris: Éditions du Cerf, 1987), 1.

3. I retell these stories and insert commentary from exegetes along the way, rather than simply cite the texts, in order to fill in some blank spots that would have been known in Jesus' time and to draw out some imaginative aspects. Many of the Gospel stories have been honed into the schematic units to which readers of the Bible have become accustomed. But they were produced by the imagination and provoke an imaginative reception. Telling the story in a somewhat fuller way is meant to stimulate the imagination.

with the power of God's Spirit. But Luke uses this story as a kind of overture to Jesus' whole ministry, for it shows him setting out a large programmatic framework for his ministry. From the very beginning, therefore, the story has a fairly dramatic context in which the newly arrived prophet and public figure is someone whom many people already know along with his family.[4]

Jesus went to the synagogue on the Sabbath where the service included reading a section of the scripture from the Prophets. Jesus stood up to read, and he was given the book of the prophet Isaiah. He opened the scroll and found one of the four passages that describe the suffering servant of God. The figure of the suffering servant has been the subject of many interpretations. It could be a messianic messenger or it could be Israel itself personified. In any case, in Luke's telling the words that Jesus read are a compilation of verses that promise the appearance of a figure who will be empowered by God's Spirit to preach good news to the poor, a release to those in debtors' prison, liberty to those who are oppressed, and a Jubilee year that cancels debts to jump-start new social beginnings.

When Jesus sat down, all in the synagogue had their eyes fixed on him, expecting him to comment on the text. And he did. He said, "Today this scripture has been fulfilled in your hearing" (Luke 4:21). Now it is not exactly certain whether this was a personal claim that he was the figure to whom Isaiah was referring, or whether this scripture was being fulfilled in Galilee and more generally among God's people at this very time. In other words, Jesus may have been identifying with a larger movement of God's rule beginning to make itself manifest in Israel. In either case, the moment was still dramatic and the claim arresting.

Generally the first impression of those in the synagogue was positive: "all spoke well of him, and wondered at the gracious words" he spoke (Luke 4:22). But gradually the mood changed as they measured the vision against the familiarity of the one announcing it; this was Joseph's son. The scene changed to one of debate, in which Jesus accused his townspeople of little faith, and they grew angry enough to drive him out of his hometown.

This story is unforgettable for several reasons. It has Jesus declaring his fundamental commitment to a rule of God that spells liberation especially to the poor and physically and socially marginalized. It definitely pertains to this world. Everyone understood him because he

---

4. Mark and Matthew have the essentially the same story of Jesus returning to his home country occurring later in his ministry. These versions do not include the dramatic action of Jesus reading from Isaiah (Mark 6:1-6; Matt 13:53-58). This indicates that this is probably a Lucan interpolation.

referred to a standard feature of the tradition: God's rule is coming. He did not promise something far off but announced that it was happening now. The scope of the declaration and the particular familiarity of this herald prevented any of those present from hearing it. Jesus had to prove his assertion with a marvelous sign, or get out. This would become a pattern.

A day in Jesus' ministry (Mark 1:21-39). This passage early in Mark's Gospel describes what can be imagined as a typical day of Jesus' ministry. Although it transpires in one place, Capernaum, over a period of about twenty-four hours, Mark may have created the story by stringing typical incidents together. Thus it shows well how one can imagine with a fair degree of general accuracy what Jesus' ministry looked like. Mark lays out the narrative in five panels.

Having arrived in Capernaum, Jesus went to the synagogue on the Sabbath and was invited to teach there. He taught with authority, and people marveled at it. While he was there, a man possessed by an "unclean" spirit recognized him as a holy representative of God. But Jesus silenced him and ordered the spirit out of the man. Jesus' teaching authority was thus compounded by a demonstration of his command over evil spirits. This power in teaching and healing became the basis of his fame in Galilee.

On leaving the synagogue, Jesus went with Andrew, James, and John to the house of Simon, also called Peter, where he would stay that evening. Simon's mother-in-law was sick and lay prostrate with a fever. Jesus went to her, took her hand, helped her to stand, and in the process she was healed, and she offered them hospitality. The scenario unfolds as simply and naturally as that.

After sunset on the Sabbath, when people could help those who were disabled to go out and about, it was as if the whole town appeared at the door of Simon's house. This scene shows Jesus reaching out to the whole community in the way he did earlier in the day. "He cured many who were sick with various diseases, and he drove out many demons" (Mark 1:34). In other stories Mark tells of Jesus healing with ritual gestures.

Early the next morning, before dawn, Jesus left the house to be alone in an isolated place in order to pray. Jesus undoubtedly knew the Psalms by heart, so he always had them with him.[5]

Then Simon and the others went out looking for him, because a good number of people were asking for Jesus. But rather than go back, Jesus told them that he wanted to push on to other towns to do what

---

5. Lohfink, *Jesus of Nazareth,* 167.

he had done in Capernaum. He said this was what he was meant to do. "So he went into their synagogues, preaching and driving out demons throughout the whole of Galilee" (Mark 1:39).

This story leaves strong visual impressions rather than a record of the content of Jesus' teaching. Whether Jesus is speaking or healing with a touch, the reaction is amazement or astonishment at an authority that fixes attention and performs wondrous deeds. Jesus does not do this by his own innate power: the Spirit of God is at work in him, and this is the rule of God being mediated by him. The story shows Jesus channeling the power of a God of life in a world of sickness and death.

Jesus as teacher: the Lord's Prayer (Matt 6:5-13). Both Matthew and Luke tell the story of Jesus teaching people how to pray by using a formula that has come to be known as the "Lord's Prayer." The two versions of the prayer are close to each other. But Matthew's prayer has a whole phrase that does not appear in Luke's: "your will be done, on earth as in heaven." Many think that Luke's version is the more authentic, because it is easier to add words to a received tradition than to cut them. Also, the two stories offer different imaginative scenarios: Luke has Jesus teaching his disciples in an intimate setting after one of them asked him to teach them to pray; Matthew presents Jesus teaching a crowd how to pray publicly in his Sermon on the Mount. Both stories encourage an analysis of the content of the prayer that Jesus himself taught, and Matthew's additional phrase makes something explicit that is important.

The prayer begins by calling upon God as Father. It presents four petitions or direct requests to God on behalf of the community that prays: "Give us today our daily bread; and forgive us our debts, as we forgive our debtors; and do not subject us to the final test, but deliver us from the evil one" (Matt 6:11-13). The prayer also expresses two or three wishes or hopes: "hallowed be your name, your kingdom come, your will be done, on earth as in heaven" (Matt 6:9-10). The last two wishes provide an occasion to expand on what Jesus means by the rule of God.

These two desires, that the rule of God come and that God's will be done on earth, are in some ways synonymous. Together the phrases reflect fundamental qualities of the rule of God. The rule of God represents God's will for God's people, the way the world and society should be and would be if God's intentions were respected. God reigns as king, lover of justice, who will judge the world.[6] "The proclamation

---

6. This is the message of Psalms 93, 95-99, praising God as king of the universe.

of the reign of God coming now is the definitive historical realization of what has always been before Israel's eyes and what it sought to live in the Torah: for Israel there can be only this *one* God and he must become Lord of one's whole life, of every hour of the day of all spheres of life."[7] The second phrase underlines that God's rule "is a historical will: it is manifested in God's actions in his people in the midst of this history."[8]

The rule of God also has a comprehensive character that elicits a total response. It calls forth an unconditional commitment. One cannot serve two masters (Matt 6:24), and nothing should compete with the rule of God. It appeals to one's inner being. Jesus' parable of the poor widow shows her giving the substance of her worldly possessions to the rule of God (Mark 12:41-44). Jesus himself represents such a radical response: he left family, embraced celibacy, became an itinerant teacher, preached a rule of God that interrupted social expectations, and was killed for it. God's rule is something that draws us out of ourselves, "so that this desire for God and God's cause is greater than all our human self-centeredness."[9]

The rule of God on earth as it is in heaven points to its fullness up ahead. In the absolute future that is promised by God's rule there is nothing but the fullness of being: abundant overflowing potential. "The joy of the *eschaton* has begun. God's banquet with his people Israel, which is to expand into a banquet for all nations, is now beginning. Jesus is so sure that the reign of God will now become reality in the form of an abundant banquet that he calls the poor and hungry hearers blessed."[10]

God as a loving father (Luke 15:11-32). The Lord's Prayer communicates God's authority and love: one does not petition a mean-spirited God. But Jesus develops the character of God's fatherly love more fully in the story called "The Prodigal Son." God's personal love for each individual finds a classic expression in this parable.

The story unfolds in three acts. In the first, the younger of two sons asks his father for his share of the family inheritance, leaves home, squanders his wealth in self-indulgence, and all but destroys himself. He wishes he could eat with the pigs. But he repents and decides to return home. Act 2 has the father spotting the returning son at a distance, as if he were watching for him. He unconditionally welcomes

7. Lohfink, *Jesus of Nazareth*, 174.

8. Lohfink, *Jesus of Nazareth*, 175.

9. Lohfink, *Jesus of Nazareth*, 235.

10. Lohfink, *Jesus of Nazareth*, 242. See Isa 25:6-8 for the source of this theology.

him back and even has an extravagant banquet prepared for him. Act 3 shows the older brother feeling resentment. His constant commitment, all the more faithful by contrast, seems to be taken for granted and unacknowledged. But the father reassures him and explains the implications of their steady relationship.

This story is a simple narrative that depicts God as a father of unbounded and excessive love. But the light of this parable penetrates deeply into the human condition as such and illumines individual lives. The quality of the father, who for Jesus symbolizes God, controls the whole story. God as loving father stands in contrast, but not in contradiction, with the power and might of the creator of the universe. The story implies that God's infinite love surpasses and incorporates into itself God's sheer power as the creator of the universe. The meaning of "father" becomes fixed as an unconditional personal love directed to individual persons; every person is the offspring of this father. The injury to the father and the family inflicted by the younger son dramatizes by contrast the unconditional love of the God. There is no unforgivable sin for the repentant.

The effects of God's love differ greatly from person to person, and the story illustrates a distinct outcome in each of the two sons. In the case of the younger son, the father's love transforms death into life. Jesus, speaking through the father, plainly states the point twice: "this son of mine was dead and is alive again; he was lost and is found!" This affirms fairly exactly that God's love sustains life and, in the end, guarantees it. God wants life; God loves life into being. God abhors death; God transforms death into life by the power of love. Love is the basis of life; without it death has the last word. Thus, the value of life itself rests on the power of the creator taking the form of love.

In the case of the older brother, the same love of the father works in a different way. In dialogue with his consistent fidelity, this love transforms inequality into equality. This effect of love goes beyond reconciliation, beyond the acceptance that heals relationships. This love communicates to the beloved the very qualities of being that are possessed by the lover. "Son, you are always with me, and all that is mine is yours." The excess or superabundance of this love creates a bond between the two that makes them as one within a relationship of complete openness and mutual sharing. Don't resent the excess of love when it rescues another; rejoice in the status of beloved companion already yours. It seems hard to take in the excess of God's love reflected in Jesus' ministry.

God as judge (Luke 16:19-31). Jesus communicates a portrait of a God who loves human beings unconditionally, but this saving love always includes God's judgment.[11] The injustice of the world provokes this judgment. Three distinct dimensions of the religious life of his time prompted Jesus' prophetic critique in the name of the rule of God.

On the personal level Jesus' criticism of religious observance implied a judgment of what God valued. His criticism of religious observance was sharp and clear: "The sabbath was made for humankind, and not humankind for the sabbath" (Mark 2:27). This meant that religion "is to serve men and women; men and women are not to be enslaved by religion."[12] He accused religious leaders of imposing superfluous religious obligations on the people. "Woe to you lawyers also! for you load men with burdens hard to bear" (Luke 11:46). He attacked an empty, rote, external religious observance that lacked subjective substance. "Now you Pharisees cleanse the outside of the cup and of the dish, but inside you are full of extortion and wickedness" (Luke 11:39).

Jesus warns of God's judgment against the whole of Israel because of social conditions. The poor are not being attended to, and people lack repentance; they do not reach out to the poor and oppressed. This forces a crisis and the need of a decision for or against the rule of God. To repent and accept God's rule spells blessing, or the rule of God will go to others because the banquet will be filled.[13]

Jesus taught that God's justice pervades the universe, and it will be served in the end. This comes through in the story of the Rich Man and Lazarus in Luke 16. While the rich man lived in splendor, Lazarus, who camped at his door, was poor, sickly, and hungry. When Lazarus died, he was carried to "the bosom of Abraham," a place of everlasting comfort, while the rich man died into a place of suffering and torment. When the rich man appealed to Abraham for pity, he was told that no one could reach across these two final states. The finality of things was sealed in justice. Thus, Abraham told him that in life he had his blessings and Lazarus did not; "now he is comforted here, whereas you are tormented" (Luke 16:25).

The realism of this story may make it seem dark; but Jesus' warning against God's judgment is essentially positive. It presupposes a basic trust in a moral universe that recognizes how "a world that would not be judged in this sense would be a world without hope, without purpose, and without dignity."[14] Jesus' teaching about God's judgment is an announcement of the principle of coherent meaning that affirms the legitimacy of basic trust. Judgment recognizes injustice and evildoing

---

11. Schlosser, *Le Dieu de Jésus,* 263.

12. Wilfrid J. Harrington, *Jesus Our Brother: The Humanity of the Lord* (New York and Mahwah, NJ: Paulist Press, 2011), 56.

13. Lohfink, *Jesus of Nazareth,* 158-62.

14. Lohfink, *Jesus of Nazareth,* 163.

for what they are. It illumines their ugliness in the light of the absolute values of God. It says that "history will reveal its own meaning. The masks will fall; the veils will be torn away; the self-deceptions will be removed."[15] In sum, Jesus' prophecy simply unveils God's judgment, which is carried by the rule of God's love in the face of human wretchedness and all those who wittingly perpetrate it.

Communicating God through action (Matt 9:9-13). Jesus was not a theologian who presented a teaching about God that was analytically organized and systematically presented. One has to approach his representation of God from a variety of different angles. Another entrée is found in some of his overt actions. It is clear that he made statements through symbolic actions. Thus, one can determine something about Jesus' notion of God from his attitudes toward the law, his positions toward sinners, and his relationship to the Pharisees as these appear in some of his actions.[16]

The Gospels facilitate this move. Jesus told parables to make a point. But the earliest Jesus movement also told stories about Jesus in such a way that they made him into a parable of God. This means that the Gospels offer more than the verbal teachings of Jesus about God. They also tell stories about his typical behaviors that throw light on the God whose rule guided his ministry.

A good example of this is the story of Jesus publicly eating with tax collectors and sinners. After Matthew, a tax collector, responded to Jesus' invitation to be a disciple, Jesus went to his house for a dinner and "many tax collectors and sinners came and sat with Jesus and his disciples" (Matt 9:10). The Pharisees noticed this and did not understand it. Jesus explained his actions: "Those who are well do not need a physician, but the sick do. Go and learn the meaning of the words, 'I desire mercy, not sacrifice.' I did not come to call the righteous but sinners" (Matt 9:12-13). Regardless of whether the words are authentically those of Jesus, on internal evidence they sum up neatly the pattern of his ministry and thus his idea of God.

The point of this story is made in the paraphrase of God's word in the prophets. But it exceeds the example. The consistent pattern of Jesus' ministry communicates a message and a reality at the same time. The healings, the teachings, and the sharp critiques form parts of a larger concrete association with people in need. Through the actions of his ministry Jesus reveals the character of God. He translates the rule of God into action. One can read the nature of God in

15. Lohfink, *Jesus of Nazareth*, 163.
16. Schlosser, *Le Dieu de Jésus*, 16.

Jesus' actions. Jesus' ministry, as a way of life according to the rule of God, reveals and makes present in a particular way the rule of God. In his ministry Jesus reveals God by translating the rule of God into action.[17] In response to the question, "What is God like?" the Gospel stories respond, "God is like Jesus."[18]

God reaches out to the marginalized: the sinners, tax collectors, the diseased, those who have no future. God appears as the basis of hope for meaning in a situation that offers no hope. Jesus reveals God as "the one who gives the future to those to whom no future can, from the worldly point of view, be promised."[19] Jesus' ministry was an appeal to relate to this God who in turn interacts with history and individual lives.

From Narrative toward Theology

How does one move from reading a story to spiritual reflection? A story and a more analytical reflection leading to an affirmation are different genres of discourse. They relate to each other somewhat like the writings of Flannery O'Connor and Thomas Aquinas. People tell the story of a religious conversion like that of Augustine or Ignatius of Loyola and talk about God on the basis of their testimony to an "intervention" of grace in those lives. The transition is told narratively on the basis of the religious experience and testimony of those figures. The basis of meaningful interpretation lies embedded in the story and is distinct from the narrative itself. This raises the question: How should one understand the relation between the two ways of thinking, the one focused on physical events occurring in this world, the other describing a vision of transcendent reality that arises from the story?

This esoteric theological problem has direct relevance to anyone who picks up the New Testament and reads one of the stories about Jesus. Those who have faith do not see any problem because they read the story from inside that conviction. But explaining what goes on in that "reading with faith" will clarify a distinct human experience. The key to it lies in the imagination.

---

17. Edward Schillebeeckx, "The 'God of Jesus' and the 'Jesus of God,'" in Schillebeeckx, *The Language of Faith: Essays on Jesus, Theology and the Church* (Maryknoll, NY: Orbis Books, 1995), 101.

18. Juan Luis Segundo, *The Christ of the Ignatian Exercises,* Jesus of Nazareth Yesterday and Today 4 (Maryknoll, NY: Orbis Books, 1987), 22-26.

19. Schillebeeckx, "The 'God of Jesus' and the 'Jesus of God,'" 102. Of course, that is ultimately everyone, but some more dramatically than others. It is good to add here that this God is the God of all; and the salvation held out is to human existence collectively. There is no private salvation over against others.

What follows is a relatively brief response to a large question in four points that describe a process that happens quite spontaneously. These points are not chronological steps but dimensions of an experience that, when isolated, may clarify it. Together they expand Paul Ricoeur's aphorism: "The symbol gives rise to thought."[20] The question here is how the imagination travels from historical interpretation of Jesus in the direction of a reflective language about God. The four points show how a dynamic metaphor or symbol forces one to think.

Parable as the model. Paul Ricoeur takes the parable as the model for understanding how one moves from a story to a metaphorical imagination that seeks to understand God. Analysis of how that works in the parables of Jesus uses Jesus' own practice to throw light on the whole narrative of the Bible. The common description of Jesus' ministry as a parable of God helps to reinforce this step. It rests on the supposition already described that Jesus reveals God not just by his words but also by other phases of his public life of ministry.

The immediate benefit gained by this move consists in its ability to show how imagination has a role in this whole process. For example, the parable of the Prodigal Son proposes that the father's behavior opens up to our imagination the outsized forgiving and welcoming love of God. As an imaginative construct, the story is not a report on a historical event. But it tells a story that possesses enough historical plausibility to reveal the way things could be. It is realistic.

Emphasizing that narratives are constructed by the imagination explicitly blurs the distinction between narratives that represent historical events and narratives that are fictional. "Blurring" does not mean "wiping out" a legitimate distinction. In some circumstances it is important. But it is not crucial in this discussion. What has to be emphasized here is that all narratives require imagination for their construction. Whether a story is historically accurate or a piece of pure fiction, or somewhere in between, where the story represents historical reality but not in its details, in each case the imagination plays an important role.

This places the focus of this discussion within the human person, within the human subject. The transition from appreciating a story to reflective understanding happens within human subjectivity. This is not a subjectivity cut off from an outside world and reflecting only on itself without any reference to things outside the self. Nevertheless, subjectivity refers to a person's interior processes. This point is quite

---

20. Paul Ricoeur, *The Symbolism of Evil* (Boston: Beacon Press, 1969), 348. I borrow much of what is said here from Paul Ricoeur, *Figuring the Sacred: Religion, Narrative, and Imagination* (Minneapolis: Fortress Press, 1995).

important. The transition from story toward theology is not objective in the sense of empirical; it happens within human experience. An example of trying to understand the transition *objectively* is found in the argument for the divinity of Jesus from miracle. Jesus performed miracles; only God can reverse the processes of nature; therefore Jesus is divine. This argument simply does not work today for many reasons of which most people are aware.[21] By contrast, the move toward theology from story can be made only on the basis of some experience in the person who engages the story. Engagement with the story in an existential seeking of transcendence provides the premise for the reflective movement toward theology.

Parable, as narrative metaphor, appeals to the imagination. A parable is a narrative metaphor. And a metaphor is an implicit comparison of something to something else. As a comparison, the metaphor shifts one's attention from the subject matter to the other thing, usually quite different; and the comparison, on the basis of some similarity, reveals a new facet of the subject matter, sometimes in dramatic ways. Alice is a summer storm; Harry is a zombie before his coffee; God is the father of a prodigal son; God is a landowner who, after hiring people throughout the day, pays the last hired who only worked an hour or two the same as the first who worked all day, out of pure gratuitous (and unjust?) generosity (Matt 20:1-16).

The role of the imagination stands out in all these examples. The more penetrating the creative imagination that sees inner similarities with something really different, and the more succinctly and clearly one can articulate this in words, the more metaphors hit home and penetrate. They communicate something in a really new way and open up new possibilities of understanding the subject matter. As narrative metaphors, parables hold out a direction for my life and, in order to be plausible, human existence generally. Their narrative structure gives parables the dynamism that comes with dealing with human action. They proffer goals for our action into the future. This narrative dimension, in contrast with a purely descriptive analysis, appeals to human desires and the will; it suggests objects for existential engagement. The two parables of Jesus just referred to are not analytical descriptions of strict justice; they do not illustrate a measured legal response to a situation; his Semitic excess and exaggeration appeals to constructive pos-

---

21. Several factors render this reasoning incorrect. Usually we do not know in any exact detail the history that lies behind the miracle stories. Sometimes the miracles are not historical but are meant to make a theological point. The argument rests on a conception of miracle as contrary to the laws of nature that was not intended by the stories. Most exegetes take all this for granted today.

sibilities that by social standards may seem impossible: turn the other cheek, be generous in a way that seems unjust, love your enemies. They lay bare this new world, a world that can penetrate into human minds and hearts only by way of the imagination because it does not represent actual social norms.

The passage toward theology occurs in an acceptance of Jesus as God's representative. The fact that Jesus' parables are about the kingdom of God and implicitly about the God whose set of values and will are being described moves the stories about Jesus in the direction of reflective spirituality. Jesus' parables describe how God acts: such is the rule of God. The human imagination in turn construes the actor in the action. Jesus' parables, because they are stories and as such dynamic narrative metaphors, tell how God acts, and from the action one discerns the character of the actor. The subject matter of Jesus' parables is mostly the rule of God, what God wills, how the world would be according to God's will, and the directions of God's impulses in regard to human subjects. God acts as the father of a prodigal son; God acts like the over-generous employer; God heals and judges; God is the sovereign concerned about his or her people. Since God is the way God acts, one imagines God as the one who acts as the story indicates. God remains absolute mystery, but through the narrative the imagination ascends to form an image of God.

From the parables one can extend this idea to the four Gospels on the formula that Jesus may be considered the parable of God. This is the hinge on which turns Ricoeur's view of how Jesus becomes the revelation of God. He explains this transition with an appeal to the views of American theologian H. Richard Niebuhr on revelation.[22] Revelation refers to a moment or event in one's life or a longtime conviction in which one is overpowered by an image. This could be anchored in a story, an event, a person, or a place that gives rise to the vision. In the light of this image all other events of one's life, both personal and social, become intelligible. It is a decisive enlightenment that provides the imaginative framework for the whole of one's life.[23] In the case of Christian revelation, one's appreciation of Jesus as God's representa-

---

22. Paul Ricoeur, "Toward a Narrative Theology: Its Necessity, Its Resources, Its Difficulties," in *Figuring the Sacred*, 236-48.

23. H. Richard Niebuhr defines revelation as "that part of our inner history which illuminates the rest of it and which is itself intelligible." He goes on to say that Christians relate to "Jesus Christ, in whom we see the righteousness of God, his power and wisdom. But from that special occasion we also derive the concepts which make possible the elucidation of all the events in our history. Revelation means this intelligible event which makes all other events intelligible." Niebuhr, *The Meaning of Revelation* (New York: Macmillan, 1962), 93.

tive and the story of Jesus as the parable of God mark such a turning point. Recall that this happens in human subjectivity, to some and not others, for faith is always a function of grace and freedom. But this process is not rare: all human beings, insofar as they have a coherent view of reality and life in it, have some central and controlling image drawn from their history to guide them. From the Christian perspective, one can almost define Christianity and being a Christian in terms of Jesus providing the images for understanding ultimate reality. The world, history, and the universe make sense when viewed through the lens of Jesus: his ministry, his destiny, his person.

Narrative imagination is accompanied by descriptive metaphorical imagination. One further step completes the transition from story to a reflective spirituality in a direction moving toward theology. Up to this point the emphasis has fallen on how Christianity's basic notions of God are drawn from images and symbols that are embedded in narratives. This is so because the primary revelatory medium for Christianity is Jesus, and Jesus is presented to us in the Gospels through narrative. But can the imagination break out of a narrative mode? Can it move from experience to reflection on experience? It can, following the axiom of Ricoeur that symbols give rise to thought. Imagination can stop the narrative flow and do a still life for analysis. Consider the painting of a face, a landscape, or a fruit bowl. Stillness satisfies a need for thought, depth, clarity, and quiet contemplation as distinct from restless movement, as from a train one stops the endless flow of scenery with a photo and later contemplates its beauty. "One needs more clarity than stories can give us, and also a little rest. The kind of pure spatial articulation we find in painting and sculpture, with all movement suspended, gratifies this deep need. Also in meditation and in theoretical endeavors we are a little less completely at the mercy of our own temporality."[24] We cannot be satisfied with only a series of images flashing by; we need a descriptive metaphorical imagination to stop action, contemplate, study, analyze, and understand.

This leads directly to an accurate description of spiritual reflection. It consists of speaking of God on the basis of a metaphorical imaginative representation of God gleaned from Jesus' narrative portrayal of God. There are, of course, many distinct tasks and methods of such reflection. The more analytical reflection becomes, the more it approaches the discipline of theology. Theology consists in second-order reflection on the religious experience expressed in primary met-

---

24. Stephen Crites, "The Narrative Quality of Experience," *Journal of the American Academy of Religion* 39 (1971): 297-303, who draws the point from Augustine (308).

aphorical religious language, like the stories of Jesus and the stories about Jesus that portray him as an agent of God. This reflection or reasoning engages the status of the mediator or symbol (Jesus), what it reveals (God), and the self and humanity in relation to these. What or who must Jesus be in order to explain the situation in which I find myself, namely, one whose relation to God has been mediated by Jesus the parable of God? This is a theological question provoked by the story of Jesus. This makes theology second-order reflection on the religious experience elicited by narratives and based throughout on the creative metaphorical imagination. It is the thought about ultimate truth to which symbols give rise.

The imagination has been underrated in Christian theology and perhaps in human understanding generally. The imagination here does not refer only to fictional fancy, but more pointedly to the realistic creativity of human freedom in its understanding of reality. All human beings have a native artistic dimension that they alone uniquely possess. It lies embedded somewhere between a person's individuality and his or her creativity. Each person brings his or her personal story and an interpretive power to the task of understanding the world and the ultimate reality that embraces it. In the end, the salvation that Jesus offers is his revelation of a God who draws forward people's freedom and imagination for the constructive task of living life into the future.

What Jesus Reveals of God

The question of what Jesus reveals of God will always remain partly open because it includes an interpretation of what Jesus' ministry yields and what each person takes away from it. Once the imagination becomes involved, the specific historical circumstances of each individual person are drawn into the mix. Right from the start the project becomes wrapped in constructive creativity: God, who as ultimate reality transcends the finite order of creation, can only be understood through imaginative constructs drawn from human experience. Thomas Aquinas, relying on an earlier tradition, provided a formula for recognizing the tentativeness of our predicates for God. We know God in a threefold, tension-filled way: we can affirm qualities of God from our experience of this world; but we have to deny that they apply to God in the precise way they are understood by us because God infinitely exceeds finitude itself, let alone our conditioned grasp of it; and yet we may be confident that, precisely in negating the finite meaning, we recognize the transcendent One, and we make contact with God because God embraces us.[25]

---

25. Thomas Aquinas, *Summa Theologiae*, q.13, aa. 2-3. The things we say of God

In trying to digest the ways in which Jesus mediates to our understanding a conception of the character of God, it is not a good principle to think against the grain of the Judaism in which he was formed. Not only should one expect a connection between Jesus and his own tradition, but also such continuity serves as a principle for sound interpretation. There is evidence that Jesus had internalized verbally much of the Hebrew scriptures.[26] Relative to the Sermon on the Mount, often considered to be a distinctive body of teaching, Gerhard Lohfink says: "There is not a single statement there that does not have an Old Testament background."[27] Jesus neither simply repeated Old Testament teaching nor inserted completely new content into it, but sifted the tradition through his own voice for his own time in order to bring it forward with new light.[28]

The formula is perennial. Understanding the past at any given time always and inescapably involves interpretation, a drawing of meaning into a present-day context. And so it is today. No two people will be impressed by Jesus or the God he represents in exactly the same way. But rather than prevent conversation, historical context promotes it. The five pointers to the God whom Jesus communicates to us that follow are a commentary on some of the stories in the first part of this chapter and should be understood as topics for an open conversation.

God is transcendent. The transcendence of God is built into Jesus' conception of God's rule. Lohfink shows that the deep logic of God's kingly rule is reflected in the Psalms that extol God as king (Psalms 93, 95-99). It rests less on an analogy with the Jewish kings projected on God and more on a sense of the creator God's being Lord of the universe. The rule of God is grounded in Torah, the absolute transcendence of God that elicits an absolute loyalty on the part of God's people. "I am the Lord your God" (Exod 20:2). No other God, nothing at all, supersedes God. We do not project God's transcendence; it interrupts and makes its claims on us.

A searching spirituality does not have to emphasize the transcendence of God. Transcendence is the very object of the search. It is

---

"are denied of God for the reason that what the name signifies does not belong to Him [God] in the ordinary sense of its signification, but in a more eminent way." ST, q. 13, ad 2. Important in this traditional conception is the tension between these elements. The "higher" release of meaning is enabled precisely by the negation of the initial predicate. The tension may be called "dialectical" because it is unrelieved; it cannot be escaped.

26. Lohfink, *Jesus of Nazareth,* 167: "Thus we can take it as given that Jesus would have known crucial passages from the Torah and the prophets by heart, and probably all the psalms and some parts of the Wisdom literature as well."

27. Lohfink, *Jesus of Nazareth,* 187.

28. Lohfink, *Jesus of Nazareth,* 187-88.

important to note that that searching never really ceases because, as transcendent, God remains infinite incomprehensible mystery even when God finds us. This seems to be compounded today because we live in a larger physical universe than that of Jesus. From one perspective, the size of the universe does not affect the logical contrast between the finite and the infinite, between creation and the creator. But when human imagination is factored in, the unimaginable age and size of this universe and possibly others seem exponentially to expand the creator's infinite transcendence. In fact, God's transcendence may take on negative overtones: many are convinced that the experience of an all-encompassing and benevolent ordering power seems remote from our little world. But the infinite transcendence of God includes God's freedom from physical determination and entails God's immanence to finite reality as analyzed in the chapter on creation out of nothing. Those who experience God's closeness can point to many signals of God's presence. The question is whether consideration of Jesus' ministry can awaken this sense that God's transcendence is such that it entails God's presence within the world. To that question the Christian answers yes.

God is personal. The very language of God includes the idea that God is personal. The personal character of God was completely taken for granted in Jesus' ministry. He related to God spontaneously as the transcendent father in heaven: he prayed to God; he taught others to do the same; he conversed with God; and he used the Psalms as his language.

This personal familiarity with God and God's nearness is not reinforced by the post-Enlightenment culture of the West. It sounds anthropomorphic even when it is chastened by its analogical structure and symbolic functioning. But as we have seen in the consideration of evolutionary creation, it is difficult to imagine a ground or source for being that is less than that which its creative power has generated. The very idea of a creative power and a sustaining support of being that includes human existence seems to entail personhood within itself. We cannot analytically think of God as *a person,* for that immediately signifies anthropomorphic containment of self-consciousness such as we know within ourselves. God is not a person, but God encompasses the intelligence and freedom of personhood.

Such considerations arise out of a conception of the universe recently transformed by science. In no way do they establish either God or God's personhood. But they do open up a receptive space for Jesus' revelation of God. Jesus does not offer an idea of a personal God in order to assuage human suffering; God is not there in order to save human beings, thus making God a function of human need. That is projection. By contrast, Jesus presented God as he understood God in the anthropomorphic terms of the tradition. But that tradition knew that God transcended its language. For Jesus it was simply the case that this personal God holds out a power of salvation because the universe in which he lived was suffused with God's personal presence. The power of the rule of God, creator of the universe, includes within itself intelligence and love.

God is love. In his first letter, John says straight out that "God is love" (1 John 4:8). We do not have any record of Jesus making such a metaphysical-sounding statement. But Jesus' ministry can be described as making the idea of God's love an actual force in people's lives. Jesus taught consistently and in many different ways that the essential character of God was a personal benevolence toward creation, an active overflowing love for the world. Whether Jesus actually interpreted himself in the words of Isaiah as in the scene from Luke's Gospel, or whether the early Jesus movement recognized him as just such a figure, he communicated a message that God's rule, God's cause, was the flourishing of humankind.

Jesus' authenticity lay in the correspondence between his words and his active ministry. What he said he actualized in his actions. His "typical day" of healing people, his standing up for those who were burdened by religious requirements, his table fellowship with those on the margins of society, and his outgoing receptiveness of people can be considered concrete mediations of God's concern and love for the world. The portrait of Jesus that is presented in the Gospels offers a transparency of the rule of God, and that rule is precisely a rule of outgoing love: the love of the creator. Jesus offered as a model for that love an ideal father, whose love was simply unconditional: it knew no boundaries.

This infinite loving embrace of God has a universal scope that reaches out to each individual. The awesome infinity of God, which usually suggests the sheer power of being, becomes transformed into personal solicitude for particulars, for the details in the lives of individuals. "Why, even the hairs of your head are all numbered" (Luke 12:7). This is a stunning religious idea when it is appropriated in an existential experience. God's love cannot be subdivided or diminished in its scope; it is subject neither to division nor to competitiveness; each one is loved as though there were no others. Not only is the universe supported by power and guided by intelligence; it is embraced by the love and concern of God.

God is just and the ground of justice. One of the deepest drives written into the very character of human existence is a desire for justice. It is an essential ingredient of freedom itself that is constituted relationally with the world and other human beings, and it demands fairness with respect to the self and implicitly all others. An evolutionary world does not provide justice; the intrinsic social constitution of each person does not ensure justice but consistently thwarts it; justice is not a quality inherent in the world as we know it. It is not the case that we can take God's love and justice for granted and then interrogate them in the face of reality. Rather, God's love and offer of justice challenge the world as it is. God's offer of love filtered through justice only begins to make sense when we recognize what appears to be their absence.

Jesus the prophet expressed God's justice and righteous anger at situations and incidents of injustice that diminished human lives. He could not remain silent when Israelite religion was used to bind human freedom rather than release it. Jesus stood for God's justice in history and promised it for all in God's future. But in this world he stood for those who needed a spokesperson and a mediator of God's love and justice. The God of Jesus supplies the grounds for moral outrage at what some human beings do to others, and at the unjust situations we are all willing to tolerate. Jesus' prophetic outlook urges reaction against injustice and hope for an absolute kingdom of God that is always coming because its presence is only fragmentary. In the end, the absolute future is where one has to look for a general condition of justice and a final reconciliation between God's justice and mercy.

God guarantees meaning. This proposal has a metaphysical character; it promises transcendent meaning in an absolute future. This is not the way that Jesus communicated this offer. He did it with his healings, which turned sickness into health and released freedom for the potential of new commitments. New coherent meaning was also extended in the spiritual sphere of sin and guilt: Jesus promised and mediated God's forgiveness to sinners. He offered God's acceptance to those gripped by shame and paralyzed by guilt, and this bestowed a new freedom that was unimaginable from within the former state. On the level of social relationships, he reached out to various groups of people that were systemically marginalized. He symbolically dramatized God's values by his own reaching out to persons against whom society discriminated. These basic values and utopian social ideals that affirm individual human worth and dignity are held out as God's values and as God's promises. God's "promise" symbolizes ultimacy. It signifies the metaphysical character of God and the solidity of God's intentions for humanity and the world.

This list of God's qualities and this analytical account of Jesus' ministry so reduce Christian experience to conventional language that it may embarrassingly negate the potential power of these very experiences. It is meant to point to what the human imagination might look for in the ministry of Jesus and to shape a receptive expectation of what one might find in Jesus' representation of God. But we should also look at how Jesus represents human existence.

CHAPTER SIX

The Human in Jesus' Ministry

The previous chapter moved from narrative toward reflective spirituality. Consideration of some of the stories of Jesus in which he portrayed the rule of God enabled speech about God. The stories allow one to "stop action" and imaginatively consider the character of God contained in the stories. The chapter developed a characterization of God in symbolic terms drawn from the Jesus story.

This chapter moves from narrative toward anthropology. It rests on the premise that reflection on Jesus, spirituality, and ethics are interdependent; they mutually influence each other in such a way that development in any one of the three spheres can and does provoke revisions in the others.[1] The very recognition of God engages human existence. Because of the character of God, especially as creator, God is entailed in being human; the relationship defines the nature of human existence. The Gospel stories about Jesus present him teaching or modeling how human existence stands before God. After a presentation of stories, which offer salient instructions about what it means to be human, the discussion turns to some ethical implications of the stories. Is it possible to distill certain moral dispositions highlighted by the stories of Jesus that may be described as fundamental to being a follower of Jesus or even a human person? The chapter ends with a consideration of Jesus as "representative." "Representation" provides a functional way of summing up the place of Jesus in the spirituality of a Christian.

What Jesus Proposes about Human Beings

The Gospels are collections of stories about Jesus and his ministry. What Jesus called the rule of God designates a center of gravity and a pervasive motif that give these stories an internal consistency. The rule of God was the driving concern of Jesus' ministry. The previous

---

1. Lisa Sowle Cahill, "Christology, Ethics, and Spirituality," in *Thinking of Christ: Proclamation, Explanation, Meaning,* ed. Tatha Wiley (New York and London: Continuum, 2003), 193.

chapter proposed a series of stories that helped put in focus the character of the God that Jesus implicitly stood for. The stories in this chapter direct attention to what the rule of God implicitly affirms about human existence. What characteristics of the human are either presupposed or summoned forth by the rule of God that Jesus preached and acted out?

This straightforward procedure raises a question. Since these stories are enlisted to define something fundamental for Christian self-understanding, why are these particular stories chosen rather than seven or ten or twenty others? No apparently objective response to this question would satisfy everyone. Even after one reads all four canonical Gospels and others that are not canonical, some principle or other will govern one's interpretation of Jesus' teaching, healing, criticizing the religious practices of his day, and acting dramatically. The stories chosen here selectively represent a variety of human qualities and ideals that Jesus' preaching calls forth from human freedom. Human beings are dependent on God, related personally to God, bearing an inherent dignity, in possession of unique talents and responsibilities, in a purposeful existence that binds them spontaneously to religion and society.

Dependent on God (Mark 12:28-34). In this story, a scribe enters a discussion that Jesus is having with some Sadducees, and he asks what is the greatest commandment of all. It was common enough in Jesus' time to try to reduce the prescriptions of Torah to some comprehensive obligation. Jesus cites Deuteronomy 6:5, that one should love God with one's whole being, and he adds a second from Leviticus 19:18, "you shall love your neighbor as yourself." Jesus and the scribe agree that this is the very heart of Jewish religion. But why is this the case?

One way of describing the condition that supports this response is the absolute dependence of human existence in being on God. People today consciously live within the framework of the scientific story of creation. The scientific narrative demonstrates human dependence on the elements of nature. The slow upward climb of life through so many species to human existence moved through complex random stages. Independently of science the biblical story of creation cuts through empirical naturalism to the power source of being itself. Arising out of the existential theater of the human experience of dependence, it proposes that God is creator acting within the whole process. That existential encounter is depicted in terms of prayer in Psalm 104; it speaks of God expansively fixing reality on its foundations. In Psalm 29 the manifestations of nature's power become the voice of God's rule over all reality.

Jesus did not have to teach that God is creator; it had become the foundational stone of his tradition. Translated into a current idiom, he understood that human existence, as a species and as manifested in each individual person, is absolutely dependent in its continuous existence on God.

Each person can reach some appreciation of this in experiences that correlate with biblical teaching. Through introspection, people can arrive at a point where they have to acknowledge consciously that their actual coming to be was not and is not within their power, and that we continually survive on the surface of an abyss of non-being or extinction. Each one can imagine his or her own extinction through an inevitable death. But what is true of the individual also applies to the species. The story of evolutionary creation unfolds within contingency. Each individual is a part of and lives with other humans the story of our corporate, serendipitous coming to be and dying. This transpires in what appears as a nanosecond against the background of the time and space of the universe.

This level of reflection yields the groundwork of equality and solidarity that characterizes human beings. This tends to be ignored, because each person has a self-consciousness that can look out upon the world and other people as objects. But each person is a part of something larger than self: a conscious part of the world; a member of the human species; a participant in several communities. The religious experience of being created entails contingency, finitude, temporality, struggle to exist, and final death. Yet people act out of an implicit premise that "being" is good. My existence is good. The ground of such basic trust is God the creator. Hence the two commandments.

Related personally to God (Matt 6:25-33). This passage is part of Jesus' Sermon on the Mount, a representative collection of Jesus' teachings gathered together by Matthew. The essential message counsels against anxiety over things ephemeral or beyond one's control. God knows what each one needs, and God provides. "But seek first the rule of God and God's righteousness and all these things will be given to you besides" (Matt 6:33).

The meaning of the text jumps out when contrasted with the objective "size" and power of the creator of the universe: God is personal and has a personal love for each creature. This infinite love has no boundaries, cannot be divided, attends to everyone in a noncompetitive way, and envelops each person in a personal relationship of love. "The closest thing to a definition of God in the Old Testament appears in Exodus 34:6: 'A God merciful and gracious, slow to anger, and abounding in steadfast love and faithfulness.'"[2] Jesus builds on that tradition.

This personal relationship completely transforms an understanding of human existence within an impersonal universe. Being dependent on a transcendent power is one thing. Positing that this power is personal automatically suffuses the universe with intentionality. The transition from objective impersonal power, blind force, and random energy to intelligent spirit does not alter a single finite phenomenon; but it utterly transforms the whole of reality by injecting into it subjectivity and personhood. The whole universe becomes part of and subsists within something larger than itself that is intelligent and purposeful.

This relationship of human being to a personal God allows what may be called a critical anthropomorphism in our speech. Traditional language speaks of God as a person even though doing so promotes false expectations. Earlier chapters indicated that God does not act directly as a finite agent in the finite world. The relationship of the love of God for human existence does not mean that God interrupts finite process or supplants human freedom. No one understood Jesus to be saying that they did not have to work because God was provident. But when creation shows its impersonal and ruthless face, people instinctively address God as "a person." In the combat between species, in the violence of life's struggle, and amid the destruction of natural disasters, the relationship to a personal sustainer of being provides a ground for basic trust that being is good and life is going somewhere. God's love in the end subverts the negativity of existence.

Being related to a personal ground of being, therefore, bestows a moral dimension to reality. The negative side of the great commandment states that nothing finite can take God's place. Every person or power that usurps the role of God becomes exposed by God's love. No earthly agent can maintain authority when it undermines the flourishing of human beings that is willed by God's love.

Each one bearing inherent dignity (Luke 10:29-37). Jesus told the story of the Good Samaritan in response to a lawyer who asked who is my neighbor that I should love as myself. A man traveling from Jerusalem to Jericho, presumably a Jew, was mugged and left by the side of the road for dead. Two temple officials passed him by, offering no help, but a Samaritan, an enemy of Jews, or at least an outsider, stopped and went out of his way to care for him. The lawyer had to agree that the

---

2. Daniel J. Harrington, in Daniel J. Harrington and James F. Keenan, *Jesus and Virtue Ethics: Building Bridges between New Testament Studies and Moral Theology* (Lanham, MD: Rowman & Littlefield, 2002), 81.

Samaritan had acted like a neighbor. Jesus said "Go and do likewise" (Luke 10:37). The story refers to the second great commandment and gives it a social interpretation that touches everyone.

This story is revolutionary for those who divide moral responsibility into pockets and limit their solidarity to the groups in which they participate and self-identify: family, kinship, tribe, nation, class, race, gender. Jesus' teaching says there are no boundaries of human solidarity and responsibility. God's personal love as a presence within and for all humankind gives each individual being an inherent value, an ontological value, which exceeds estimated human worth. The love of the creator effectively bestows on each person an infinite value.

This explains Jesus' and God's preferential love for the poor and those who are marginalized in society on the basis of race or gender or sexual orientation or social condition or anything else. It explains Jesus' prophetic critiques of his religion and his society. Just as physical healing historicizes the rule of God in the lives of individuals and restores their position in society, so too rearranging relationships of power in society according to justice manifests the rule of God.[3]

The story of the Good Samaritan finds an echo in Jesus' teaching of the golden rule. He said, "Do to others as you would have them do to you" (Luke 6:31). This teaching of Jesus is found in many religions, and Immanuel Kant formulated it as a "categorical imperative," an inherent moral demand written into being human.[4] Kant recognized that what Jesus was teaching was not a pragmatic principle of self-protection, and not an external command, but the principle of the inviolability of an autonomous person existing from the hands of the creator, accompanied by the creator's love, and in solidarity with all others.

The universality of the moral imperative grounded in the human condition means that it extends to enemies. Jesus said, "love your enemies, do good to those who hate you, bless those who curse you, pray for those who mistreat you" (Luke 6:27-28). This absolute command crosses all social boundaries. Love as Jesus means it, however, does not correspond to the spontaneous affective attraction that essentially controls use of the term today. It more closely reflects the way one treats or actively relates to others; the meaning is closer to "respect" than emotional desire to be close. But this only makes it plausible

---

3. Lisa Sowle Cahill, *Global Justice, Christology and Christian Ethics,* New Studies in Christian Ethics 30 (New York: Cambridge University Press, 2013), 115.

4. Immanuel Kant, *Fundamental Principles of the Metaphysic of Morals,* trans. T. K. Abbott (Buffalo: Prometheus Books, 1988), 21-65. In this work Kant formulates the "categorical imperative" in three different ways, but each of them reflects a universal respect for the intrinsic value of other human beings as the core of morality.

and not less difficult to appropriate and follow the radicalism of the anthropology of the rule of God.

With talents and responsibility (Matt 25:14-30). This parable of Jesus goes directly to human existence and a spiritual life. A wealthy man, preparing to leave on a journey, entrusts sums of money to his servants. He gives different amounts of his money to each one. Two use the money for trade and double it; the third buries the money and preserves it intact. On his return the man praises the entrepreneurship of the two and rewards them, but he berates the third for inaction and condemns him to punishment.

This story offers a framework for understanding human existence today. Talents refer both to a sum of money and to personal endowments, abilities, or gifts. Each person is a unique package of talents given by the sources of life itself. They are entrusted to us. They define individuality and yet are not quite fully our own without accompanying responsibilities.

These capacities should be used and not protected; they are potentialities for the exercise of freedom. The one who gives them is looking for increase. This seems to be central because the one who failed is chastised for not making the effort. People who do not use their gifts lose them and themselves as well. The parable supports an activist spirituality.

The gifts are not equal; all endowments are individual and diverse. As gifts, they justify neither pride nor a sense of inferiority. Resentment, because one's gifts are comparatively moderate, cannot be used as an excuse for inactivity. The vast array of different gifts, most of which are ordinary, and none of which are merited, can be used for something appropriate. Equality lies in a proportional correspondence between the gift and an expected outcome. Hence the truism: we do the best with what we have.

The cause of the inaction of one servant in Jesus' story is fear, a paralyzing fear of not succeeding and an attempt to cover it over by playing it safe and guarding the investment. This seems to make some sense. How about the case of one who works the money and fails? Did the master celebrate initiative or success? The case is not explicitly covered in the story, but it reminds us that no one knows the future and that the use of freedom is by definition a risk.

This is a parable about the rule of God and the commitment of one's talents to it. This brings to the surface a basic issue of freedom today: does one act for the development of one's talents or for the building up of the rule of God in the human community? Individualism conceives of the purpose of community, society, and government as enhancing possibilities for the freedom of individuals. Social idealism invites individuals to commit to the service of the common good of the community. In many Western societies and cultures these sets of values compete with each other in strident, exclusive terms. No intrinsic reason demands this. The rule of God gathers individuals and society in one embrace. Jesus sought followers on the basis of one sure paradox: the more people actively contribute to the common good, the more their individuality is enhanced.

Living with purpose (Luke 10:1-12, 16). This story tells of Jesus sending seventy-two disciples ahead of him to visit the towns where he would pass on his way to Jerusalem. He gives them instructions on how to move about and behave: travel light; offer peace to each village; stay where you are offered residence; do what I have been doing, teaching and healing; and declare that the rule of God is at hand for them. "Whoever listens to you listens to me" (Luke 10:16).

It may not be obvious why this story responds to the question of the purpose of human existence. But Jesus did not respond to this metaphysical question in metaphysical terms. One has to ask the question of his mission as it appears in a ministry bound up with the rule of God.

The rule of God counters sin but not human existence; on the contrary, the rule of God is *for* human flourishing and fulfillment. Sometimes a preoccupation with moral failure skews the rule of God into laws or negative commandments that restrict human freedom and curtail genuine human striving. The object of Jesus' ministry, by contrast, is positive. It offers a vision of where human existence is headed and what it is for. Jesus' ministry of the rule of God *is* his revelation of the purpose of human existence.

Jesus shares his ministry with his followers. "Here they are called to do what Jesus does in his ministry and to share actively in his mission from God."[5] Jesus reveals the purpose of human existence in and through his own mission and ministry: "to proclaim liberty to captives and recovery of sight to the blind, to let the oppressed go free" (Luke 4:18). This is what human beings are called to do. The ultimate goal lies in fulfillment in the end of days.

But is it possible to hold up Jesus' ministry as a model for human existence as such? Jesus was radical. He left home and family; set out on his own as an itinerant teacher, healer, and prophet; did not marry; and preached a consistently critical message of the rule of God. "Jesus does not live for himself but is totally and exclusively surrendered to

---

5. D. Harrington, *Jesus and Virtue Ethics*, 51.

the cause of God."[6] He had close disciples, but they were limited, and not all his followers were disciples in the same sense. This story is not the story of everyone.

And yet the essence of Jesus' mission lies in his concrete dedication to his ministry. He did not talk abstractly about the purpose of human existence but lived it in a radical way. What one finds in Jesus' ministry, then, is not just any manifestation of the purpose of human existence, but an essential type or radical set of ideals that assumes many different forms in his followers. Human beings are called to be agents of God's values in this world in service of one another. The second part of this chapter will describe how Jesus' single fundamental commitment to the rule of God can provide a basis for a set of moral dispositions in which all can participate.

Related to religion (Mark 2:23-28). One Sabbath, while Jesus was walking through grain fields, his disciples plucked the ears of grain and ate them. But some Pharisees interpreted this as an infraction of Sabbath law, because it was unlawful eating or working, and they let Jesus know. Jesus, however, defended his followers. He cited the example of David, who did something far more unlawful when he and his men were hungry and in need. Then he made the point with a ringing maxim: "The Sabbath was made for men and women, not men and women for the Sabbath" (Mark 2:27).

It is difficult to be quite sure why what Jesus' disciples were doing was unlawful: what exact law was being ignored and by whose interpretation? But those questions seem insignificant when compared with the clarity of the humanitarian interpretation of religious law that the story communicates. Jesus did not offer this critique of legalism and formalistic religious observance from outside Judaism. He was an upholder of the law. But nothing set him more at odds with the official leadership of the Judaism of his day than this straightforward conviction that formal institutional religious custom and practice are for the flourishing of men and women, and not the other way around.[7] Jesus' authority for this view was the rule of God.

One should notice the distinction between spirituality, as an existential commitment to the rule of God, and religion, as socially and institutionally patterned behavior, that lies beneath this critique. More important still is how the distinction functions. It does not consist in the difference between individuality and social conformity: the prayer

---

6. Gerhard Lohfink, *Jesus of Nazareth: What He Wanted, Who He Was* (Collegeville, MN: Liturgical Press, 2012), 236.

7. Wilfrid J. Harrington, *Jesus Our Brother: The Humanity of the Lord* (New York and Mahwah, NJ: Paulist Press, 2010), 54-59.

of a gathered community is authentic spirituality for each individual who participates in it, and the idea of a private Jewish or Christian spirituality set off from a community in principle is self-contradictory. No intrinsic antithesis divides an individual from the communities to which he or she belongs. But objective institutions grow out of, express, and are always accountable to the community of persons who created them in the beginning and continue to sustain them. Religious institutions express the personal and corporate spirituality of the members; they live on the basis of a community's encounter with the Spirit of God. Some serious tensions can arise when either members or the leaders of institutions lose the inspiration of the rule of God.

No religious institution, no law, and no ritual observance bears religious authority of itself or by itself. Objective forms always serve the inner existential relationship of individuals to God, especially individuals who together form a community. Religious institutions, offices, laws, and prescribed rituals are functional, not "merely" functional because we cannot do without them, but "really" functional when they express and mediate God's rule for human salvation. In Judaism and in Christianity, that functionality has the goal of channeling the will of God (Torah) and the rule of God (God's will in this world and in the absolute future) and making it effective for the flourishing of humankind.

Related to society (Mark 12:13-17). Jesus met a good deal of resistance while he was preaching in Jerusalem before his arrest and execution. This story tells of a discussion with two groups with views opposed to each other seeking to embarrass him. Those loyal to the Herod family would look kindly on the Romans who supported them in power; Pharisees are here depicted as chafing under Roman occupation and rule. They asked Jesus whether it was lawful to pay taxes to Caesar. "No" would make him an enemy of Rome; "Yes" would alienate him from the people. Jesus asked them to produce a Roman coin bearing an image of Caesar. The fact that they had one placed them inside the Roman system. Then he responded with his famous answer to the question: "Repay to Caesar what belongs to Caesar and to God what belongs to God" (Mark 12:17). The brilliant ambiguity of the response answered each side with no specifics.

Daniel J. Harrington shows clearly that one finds "no uniform teaching about 'church and state' in the New Testament."[8] Some passages affirm that the Roman Empire's authority comes from God and should be obeyed; other writings reflect pure resistance to an evil sys-

---

8. D. Harrington, *Jesus and Virtue Ethics*, 116.

tem; and still others, like this story, reflect suspicion and caution. All the teaching is so responsive to particular issues that it yields no general principles. The history of Christianity presents so many different Christian churches, in so many different periods and places, dealing with so many different societies, political cultures, governments, and nation states that it would be impossible to sort out anything more than obvious generalizations.

Yet it seems important to reflect on how a Christian anthropology, reflected in a spirituality of commitment to the rule of God as preached by Jesus, positions a person and a community relative to the public sphere. The term "society" refers to general social patterns and includes the government and authority of the nation-state. The point of the topic is to decouple Christian spirituality from a private relationship with God and to show its relevance for society.

Christian anthropology and spirituality stimulate two reactions to society, the one negative and the other positive. Whatever in the public order is repressive of authentic human life or freedom should be resisted; and whatever in the public order promotes human flourishing of all should be promoted by Christian participation. Such general terms resolve very little in terms of specific public strategies and programs, because they merely identify the objects of discussion. But, in principle, they prohibit buying religious freedom at the cost of ignoring systemic human degradation. And they supply some norms for the debate. The rule of God preached by Jesus criticizes public policies that damage or ignore the interests of large groups of people. It encourages participation in programs that reduce human suffering and promote humane values. As Lohfink emphasizes, "the kingdom of God is primarily and above all on earth."[9] The rule of God pushed into the future has no bite; it loses all its explosive power.[10]

Human existence, in sum, exists within the embracing power of the love of a personal God. God has given this form of being a reflective consciousness, an inherent dignity, freedom, a set of talents appropriate to each one, and the broad lines of purpose for existence. That purpose may be formulated in several ways that always include the flourishing of the human community. Religion and society in their various forms are meant to facilitate this arduous and complicated task. Can this view of humanity, culled from the stories about Jesus, generate ethical guidelines for living?

---

9. Lohfink, *Jesus of Nazareth*, 25.
10. Lohfink, *Jesus of Nazareth*, 39.

Jesus as a Source for Ethics

Jesus expressed his relationship to God in a ministry of the rule of God. As the Gospels present it, Jesus' ministry communicated a conception of God and a conception of human existence. This raises the question of whether one can discern an ethics within Jesus' representation of the rule of God. One also has to ask whether such an ethics can have some normative purchase on human existence today. The responses to both questions require interpretation. This section proposes an ethical interpretation of Jesus by using the idea of fundamental moral attitudes as a bridge for an application to life today and giving some examples of them.[11]

Analogical interpretation. A method for an ethical interpretation of historical narratives can be found in an analogical imagination. Things are analogous when they are partly different and partly the same. An analogical imagination lies in the ability of the human mind to grasp the similar within or across differences. Analogy provides a way of understanding how we learn and communicate. We move from the familiar to the less familiar; total difference between references across cultures prevents communication. William C. Spohn has shown that "if new experiences bore no resemblance whatsoever to familiar ones, they would be unintelligible. There would be no bridges from the actually known to what is not yet clear."[12] He continues, "We understand others by analogy with our own experience."[13] As David Tracy puts it, "We understand one another, if at all, only through analogy. Who you are I know only by knowing what event, what focal meaning, you actually live by. And that I know only if I too have sensed some analogous guide in my own life."[14]

The structure of analogical communication, recognizing similarity within difference, lies in a proportional relationship. In the mathematical proportion, 2:4 :: 8:16, the sameness does not obtain between 2 and 8, or between 4 and 16. It exists in the relationship of 2/4 to 8/16.

---

11. Glen Harold Stassen (*A Thicker Jesus: Incarnational Discipleship in a Secular Age* [Louisville: Westminster John Knox Press, 2012]) provides a good example from an evangelical perspective of a social ethics drawn from a historicist interpretation of Jesus. What is needed is a "thick, historically-embodied, realistic understanding of Jesus Christ as revealing God's character and thus providing norms for guiding our lives" (p. 16).

12. William C. Spohn, *Go and Do Likewise: Jesus and Ethics* (New York: Continuum, 1999), 54.

13. Spohn, *Go and Do Likewise,* 58.

14. David Tracy, *The Analogical Imagination: Christian Theology and the Culture of Pluralism* (New York: Crossroad, 1981), 454-55.

The two different fractions have equal value. In simple fractions such as these the imagination immediately sees the proportional equality. The task of making the match in situations of life, personal or social, is more complex but shares a similar structure. This structure can be described as follows:

$$\frac{\text{NT text}}{\text{Its world}} = \frac{\text{Christian understanding today}}{\text{Our world}}^{15}$$

The key to analogy is the imagination: the imagination in this case enables one to intuit the similarity within the difference. Thus, Jesus told stories, parables, in order to provide models for people's lives. After the story of the Good Samaritan, which illustrated how to be a good neighbor, Jesus says, "Go and do likewise." The "likewise" is not always easy to imagine, but that is exactly what is called for: how to imagine analogous behavior that is partly different but proportionately the same in our own situation.

Appreciation of how an implied "ethics" of Jesus can be relevant for a present context and situation involves a hermeneutical theory or a description of the process of interpretation. This engages two different imaginative frameworks, that of the text or person of the past and that of the interpreter. An imaginative framework is the vision of reality that constitutes the world of the text. Another imaginative framework accompanies a person or community reading the text, and it supplies the apperceptive background for interpreting it. "It is a basic horizon or framework within which everything else is apprehended. It works as the presuppositions of the 'Newtonian universe' did for scientists before the advent of relativity theory."[16] There is a normative function operating in all this. "Metaphorical frameworks exercise a normative role because they rule in certain dispositions and rule out others. They make some actions seem appropriate and others inappropriate."[17]

The movement from one framework to another involves several adjustments.[18] The process begins with the interpreter who is inquir-

---

15. Spohn, *Go and Do Likewise*, 55. See also Edward Schillebeeckx, *Church: The Human Story of God* (New York: Crossroad, 1990), 42.

16. Spohn, *Go and Do Likewise*, 66. Spohn thus aligns an imaginative framework with the idea of a paradigm that has been useful in various disciplines. A paradigm is the set of presuppositions and methods that provide a coherent field or matrix within which practitioners of a common task go about their standard business. The concept is drawn from an essay in the philosophy of science by Thomas S. Kuhn, *The Structure of Scientific Revolutions* (Chicago: University of Chicago Press, 1965).

17. Spohn, *Go and Do Likewise*, 69. I use the phrase "imaginative framework" with the same sense that Spohn assigns to "metaphorical framework."

18. These "steps" are elements of a single process and are distinguished here only for analytical clarity.

ing into the past for meaning. The interpreter thus brings questions that have arisen within his or her worldview and imaginative framework. The interpreter considers the source from which the answer is sought, that is, the person or text or event of the past. But this requires some study of the past context in order to understand the meaning found in a situation different from that of the interpreter. What human response to the world do these texts, or this person, or these events bring to public expression? In a final move interpretation brings the meaning forward, and, in a comparison of imaginative frameworks (past and present), seeks the best expression of the contextual meaning of the past for the present situation.[19] This process produces an understanding that is roughly proportional or analogous to what is contained in the sources.

Is there a way to make this abstract structure of interpretation more concrete and focused on moral responsibility? One way of doing this walks from interpretation theory across the bridge of fundamental moral attitudes into a description of the relevance of Jesus for the present world.

Fundamental moral attitudes. One can reflect on the ethical implications of Jesus' ministry in more than one way.[20] In this analysis, I draw upon the category of a "fundamental moral attitude" from the work of Dietrich von Hildebrand, a prominent Christian phenomenologist who flourished in the mid-twentieth century.[21] As a phenomenolo-

---

19. This is a schematic version of the interpretation theory of Hans-Georg Gadamer, in which I have substituted the idea of an "imaginative framework" for his notion of a "horizon" (Gadamer, *Truth and Method* [London and New York: Continuum, 2004]). While this preserves the creative role of the imagination in the process, "horizon" highlights that which both surrounds and remains out in front of the interpreter, always receding in relation to the advances of understanding, and thus preserving the mystery of the transcendent object of interpretation and the searching character of human reflection.

20. The social gospellers reconstructed Jesus' "principles," which could be applied analogously to current historical situations. This could be workable today with a more sophisticated hermeneutical background theory. See Francis Greenwood Peabody, *Jesus Christ and the Social Question: An Examination of the Teaching of Jesus in Its Relation to Some of the Problems of Modern Social Life* (New York: Macmillan, 1900); Walter Rauschenbusch, *Social Principles of Jesus* (New York: Association Press, 1916). The efforts of D. Harrington and Keenan to work with the "virtues" taught, exemplified, and nourished by Jesus is also viable. See D. Harrington and Keenan, *Jesus and Virtue Ethics*. Working with fundamental moral attitudes is itself analogous to these other approaches.

21. Von Hildebrand's major work in value theory is *Christian Ethics* (New York: David McKay, 1953). His value theory is operative in a host of other works, but he addresses directly the category employed here in *Fundamental Moral Attitudes* (New York: Longmans, Green, 1950).

gist in the tradition of Edmund Husserl, he developed a theory of values akin to the work of Max Scheler. He employed value language in extensive ethical reflection. His thinking has a philosophical base, but he readily applied it to Christian ethics and spirituality. This category of fundamental moral attitudes offers a way of understanding how Jesus can influence moral behavior and ethical reflection without a complex ethical theory or formal system.

Fundamental moral attitudes need to be situated in von Hildebrand's larger theory of values. A value is a distinct objective quality of a being or a social relationship. Value refers to an in-itself goodness of a being as distinct from agreeableness or usefulness.[22] These values are not constituted by valuation but are intuited, grasped, or understood as being constituted by an importance in themselves. There are different kinds of values: ontological values qualify the being of a thing; moral values appeal to a moral response; aesthetic values have their own distinct character.

Values appeal to a response on the part of human subjectivity. A value response does not create a value but discovers and corresponds to the intrinsic appeal of the value itself. Perception of values requires an open subjectivity that transcends the self and enters into or engages the value. Value recognition begins with a realistic cognitive act of perception where the object governs consciousness of it. Perception promotes an affective response, a resonating with the value that exceeds passive reception. And this leads in its turn to a value-response, an act of self-transcendence that recognizes the intrinsic beauty, or moral quality, or inherent authenticity of a value. One can see at this point how the objective appeal of values and value-response are correlative and reinforce each other.

Fundamental attitudes of openness are required for value discernment. For example, von Hildebrand describes the fundamental moral attitude of "reverence" for the dignity of being.[23] This reverence, as distinct from a pragmatic attitude, allows the world to reveal itself with its accompanying values. This openness of the human subject becomes set in an "attitude in which the depth of things is open to a person, an inner readiness to fully receive and penetrate the essential beheld by our spiritual eyes."[24] In sum, the perception and response to values require a subjective disposition. Various closed subjective

---

22. Von Hildebrand, *Christian Ethics*, 64-71.

23. Von Hildebrand describes reverence in his short book *Fundamental Moral Attitudes* on pages 1-15. He goes on to describe four more fundamental moral attitudes that enable human subjectivity to appreciate the world of values.

24. Dietrich von Hildebrand, *Liturgy and Personality* (New York: Longmans, Green, 1943), 112.

attitudes, such as egocentrism, pride, or aggressiveness, can create a barrier between a person and values, while openness allows values to appear in consciousness and affect people in accordance with their objective, in-itself goodness and nobility.

The analysis that follows considers the ministry of Jesus of Nazareth as a parable representing fundamental moral attitudes. In other words, Jesus is not only a parable of God but also of human existence standing before God. This means that he displays fundamental human attitudes that enable perceptions that can in their turn be important for the development of ethics.

Fundamental moral attitudes drawn from Jesus' ministry. These fundamental moral attitudes are not drawn from the consciousness of Jesus but are products of an interpretation of his ministry. They correlate loosely with the various facets of his roles as prophet, teacher, and healer. Together they broadly describe a rudimentary profile of moral dispositions guiding Christian behavior in a spirituality of following Jesus. This is where Christian ethical norms find their grounding.

Openness to transcendence. The rule of God appeals to hope. Hope refers to a fundamentally positive openness to being as a process moving through time. It relates to the future with confidence. It may be described as basic trust in being itself in the face of inevitable negativities. Because being itself is historical and always moving toward a future, some Christian theologians believe that hope more accurately names Christian faith itself.[25] Hope has to be near the center of a searching narrative spirituality. This fundamental moral attitude prevents the Christian community or individuals from looking backward out of fear; hope acts as a resource for courage to move forward as illustrated by the story of talents. Hope includes a sense of commitment and a desire to serve. A person enters the future by action. The impetus to do something, to create, to give, to contribute to the world is a latent potential in human freedom to which Jesus and his message of the rule of God appeal.

Gratitude, lament, and irony. These three distinguishable moral attitudes can be grouped together around human dependence on God. They acknowledge the gratuitous character of being and one's own particular existence. Gratitude names a fundamental moral attitude that accompanies a spiritual recognition of God and God's support of

---

25. For example, Jürgen Moltmann, *The Theology of Hope: On the Ground and the Implications of a Christian Eschatology* (New York: Harper & Row, 1967). Moltmann grounds Christian hope in the resurrection of Jesus. The next chapter will show how hope as a prior disposition enables recognition of Jesus' resurrection.

creation. Great suffering can and too often does kill this response, but it does not have to. Gratitude can absorb suffering in lament, another basic disposition. Lament belongs to those who know themselves and their world realistically before God. As a general response, it mourns what could have been by measuring the amount of suffering in the world against human potential aided by God's grace. Thus, Jerusalem mourned after the Babylonians leveled everything: "How lonely sits the city that was full of people" (Lam 1:1). But lament can be a positive, constructive social response when it motivates creative reaction against negativity. Standing before God should provoke a sense of irony out of the contrast between actual finite being and the infinite being of the creator God. God's love should enable one to retrieve a sense of value in the face of the vastness of being and in the face of adversity. The creator's love makes all finite being surprisingly important, in itself, because God's creating it establishes its ontological value.

A deep desire for interruption and reversal. This moral disposition isolates the dialectical character of standing before God that was just described. It is built upon frustration at more of the same. In many instances in his ministry, Jesus' teaching and prophetic critique cut across the standard behavior of the time, either of the culture or of certain groups within it, and pulled human expectations up short. Jesus announced God's values, which frequently confronted routine, challenged human values, and showed a radically new way of being in the world. The prophetic ministry of Jesus correlates with what has been described as a negative experience of contrast, a recognition that something is wrong, which in turn elicits a forceful moral impetus to actions that negate the negativity and right the wrong. The prophet breaks open things taken for granted and names evil as evil. This fundamental moral anticipation of the interruptive character of God's rule has played a major role in the development of a Christian theology of the Word throughout the twentieth century. It supports the idea of Jesus Christ as representative and revealer of God. A dialectical imagination recognizes the distance between the world's status quo and what should and could be with God's grace.[26] This fundamental desire for change mirrors Jesus' moral impatience.

---

26. An analogical imagination, which searches for continuity between the world and God, and a dialectical imagination, which remains struck by the distance of God relative to human existence, should not be considered alternatives. Neither has precedence over the other; the two have to be held together in tension. For a fuller discussion of these two relationships to God, see Tracy, *Analogical Imagination*, passim.

A sense of responsibility and agency relative to God's values. The sense of judgment that accompanies recognition of God as revealed in Jesus has to be accompanied by a sentiment that seems to be its polar opposite. God created human beings, and God said that they are good. In a historicized world, this ontological goodness gets translated into a conviction that God trusts human beings and has entrusted the world to humans by giving them intelligence and freedom. This sense of responsibility was felt deeply during the period of the Enlightenment as a sense of autonomy. Primitive conceptions of God depicted God over against human existence and human beings in competition with their creator. A completely different vision of reality emerges out of the ministry of Jesus: God's cause is the cause of human existence and its flourishing. And that flourishing works through freedom's agency and its new role in creation itself. Jesus sent his associates out to do what he did. This fundamental moral attitude can provide a platform for deep commitment to an active spirituality. If God's judgment reveals human sin, then God's forgiveness frees the human spirit into creativity in pursuit of actualizing God's values for humanity in history.

An experienced tension between self-seeking and self-transcendence. This theme too runs parallel with a sense of interruption and reversal, and it qualifies the moral disposition toward service. The tension reflects Jesus' teaching about "blessing" and "woe," promise of fulfillment and threat of total ruin, success and failure. But the key to these alternatives in Jesus' teaching reverses common human striving. Seeking to fill up the self with the world that surrounds us is exposed when Jesus proposes expending the self in service of other people or social goals outside the self. Here again one faces alternatives between two absolutely basic moral dispositions that govern one's relationship to the world. Jesus issues a summons, for it is more than an invitation, to the higher moral attitude of self-transcendence displayed in the many facets of his ministry. Openness to self-transcending values lies close to appropriation of the rule of God.

Love and mercy. How often in the course of Christian tradition has the Christian ethic been summarized as an ethic of love? Jesus himself seems to have accepted the summary of the Law and the Prophets in the twofold commandment of love of God and the love of neighbor common in his day (Matt 22:37-40).[27] Ideally, this basic moral attitude, described as love and mercy, will enable a positive response to

---

27. D. Harrington and Keenan, *Jesus and Virtue Ethics*, 77-79.

the prescriptions of the law and facilitate the fidelity to God urged by the prophets. Such a love resonates in Jesus' own ministry, and love easily slides into mercy, on the supposition that the two can be distinguished. Love and mercy are not just principles of personal ethics but inner dispositions that open the human subject up to the needs of people in society. Few have made the case more strongly than Jon Sobrino that mercy gets right at the heart of the ministry of Jesus and the revelation of God implicit in it.[28] Love and mercy thus become fundamental moral attitudes of the follower of Jesus.

Noncompetitive solidarity. The idea of a noncompetitive attitude toward others appears in Jesus' relationships and his spiritual and moral teaching as portrayed in the Gospels. But it may be that this basic moral attitude stands out because of the need for it in today's world. Jesus seemed not to have a sense of rivalry with other healers: Luke has Jesus say "he that is not against you is for you" (Luke 9:50). But there are deeper grounds for this moral attitude in a common creator of all. With his commandment to love enemies, Jesus is pushing ethics beyond the boundaries of kinship, tribe, culture, and nation into a universal human domain. Today it reaches out more widely in ecological concern. On this large scale, noncompetitiveness does not forbid struggle and emulation in a common cause. It urges basic respect and reverence for the other and guards against the natural impulses that lead from competition to hatred. A sense of solidarity with others describes this noncompetitiveness positively.

Desire for inclusion and reconciliation. Few things are more needed in a world teeming with people who are interacting more and more closely across innumerable frontiers of difference and alienation. In this world, where people are being thrust together without their seeking it, and frequently against their will, the world desperately needs a fundamental desire for mutual recognition, reconciliation, and inclusion. The rule of God reconciles; it draws people in; it aims at creating a community based on justice. This cuts directly against the actual social grain and, as a general social condition, it seem impossible to hope for justice and reconciliation. The principal actors in the great wars of the twentieth century were civilized Christians fighting among themselves: a sobering fact that forces ethical realism. Nevertheless, the promise of reconciliation and the charge to strive for it have to be central moral ideals for Christians.

---

28. See Jon Sobrino, *The Principle of Mercy: Taking the Crucified People from the Cross* (Maryknoll, NY: Orbis Books, 1994).

These fundamental moral attitudes add up to a lofty spirituality. Enumerating these fundamental moral attitudes helps to draw out distinctive moral values embedded in Jesus' ministry. They enable a positive response to the solicitation of the rule of God. One cannot, of course, just adopt these dispositions or put them on. But continual immersion in the Gospel stories of Jesus may increase familiarity with them and a desire to internalize them.

Jesus the Representative

The efforts in the previous chapter and this one to interpret the spiritual and anthropological implications of Jesus' ministry lead to what may be called a functional christology. An important distinction will help clarify what "functional christology" means.

There is a difference between discussing the impact that Jesus had upon the people who were influenced by him and, extrapolating from this, discussing the essential character of Jesus' being. The first is a wide-ranging conversation about the influence of Jesus of Nazareth on the formation and continuing appreciation of the Christian message; the second is a narrow discussion of Jesus' divinity and humanity. In the first open sense, christology refers to the way Christians relate to God through Jesus, and this has implications across the span of Christian life. But in the second, theological sense, christology refers to the very specific question of the character of the person Jesus Christ, especially as he relates to other human beings and to God. This "formal christological question" is narrowly defined. Its classical model is the doctrine of the Council of Chalcedon that Jesus Christ is a single person who is constituted in two natures or kinds of being, human and divine. This includes questions about Jesus Christ's status in being. Was he a human being like all others? Was he essentially God manifested in the integral form of a human being? Was he both of these at the same time? And, if so, how can the constitution of such a one be understood and characterized? These questions and their answers arise out of the existential influence that Jesus had and still has on people. But their answers demand metaphysical language in order to clarify the position Jesus holds in the context of a comprehensive understanding of reality.

A "functional christology" describes how Jesus functions in people's lives; it is positioned at the threshold of formal christology narrowly defined; functional christology obviously has a bearing on the questions of Jesus' humanity and divinity, but it does not engage those issues in the language of metaphysics. Limited to analyzing what Jesus does and how people react, a functional christology stops short of an analysis within a context of a metaphysical worldview. Functional christology does not include or substitute for a "metaphysical" christology. Rather it provides the existential presuppositions upon which classical or formal christology builds.[29]

The functional christological formula adopted here can be stated in the phrase, "Christ the representative." It refers to a "representational christology." The presentation of this christology is drawn from Dorothee Soelle,[30] but the language is not uncommon and has other supporters. This christology operates at more than one level: it describes what is going on in the ministry of Jesus, but it is also open to a metaphysical construal. It thus functions at a practical communicative level and at the same time can be used as a basis for interpreting the doctrine of Chalcedon of the humanity and divinity of Jesus. This christology also contains within itself a suggestion in the term "representing" for a theory of redemption or salvation. Proposing this language at this point in the discussion, however, does not reach that far; it remains on the functional level. The key benefit of the language of representation lies in its ability to drive reflection on the ministry of Jesus to a deeper level of its meaningfulness for human existence as such while stopping short of metaphysical and doctrinal christology. It is thus appropriate for a spirituality moving toward theology.

Soelle presents Jesus Christ as representative of God and of human beings before God, thus obliquely reflecting the Chalcedonian formula concerning the humanity and divinity of Jesus. In each case she signals three things: representation does not mean replacement, so that Jesus does not substitute for God's freedom or our freedom; yet Jesus identifies with both humanity from God's side and with God from the human side; and in both cases Jesus depends on God in representing God to us and he exhibits his humanity in his representation of us.

---

29. For example, people said that Jesus is savior out of their experience of "being saved." They said he was divine, because he saved and only God can save. Still further questions engage the meaning of salvation, divinity, and their explanations. In these examples the logic moves from the functional, through analysis, to more metaphysical conclusions.

30. Dorothee Soelle, *Christ the Representative* (Philadelphia: Fortress Press, 1967), 99-152. This work is cited in the text as CR. The concept of "representation" is a theological construct. It has many analogies with metaphors used in the New Testament, where Jesus is mediator or go-between from God to us and intercessor and advocate before God on our behalf. See Edward Schillebeeckx, *Christ: The Experience of Jesus as Lord* (New York: Seabury Press, 1980), 490-92. While the texts of Soelle inspire the following account of a representative christology, I have felt free to interpret and adapt her description so that what follows is an approximate rather than an exact presentation of her views. Also, Soelle tends to use the term "Christ" in an indiscriminate and general way as a name rather than a title. When she is obviously referring to Jesus of Nazareth, I substitute in brackets [the name] "Jesus" for [the title] "Christ."

These enigmatic formulas will become clearer in what follows. They recapitulate in the language of representation what Jesus did in his ministry and how he functions in the later Christian community.

Jesus as representative of God. The idea that Jesus represents God among human beings addresses one side of the christological equation, that Jesus is a divine figure. Soelle does not understand this doctrine through an analysis of the metaphysical concepts used in the patristic period to interpret the Jesus of the Gospels. She uses dynamic functional terms. The earlier suggestion that Jesus can be considered "a parable of God" sets a framework within which Soelle may be understood.[31]

Soelle lays down the principle that every understanding of how God is represented in Jesus has to be attentive to the culture in which it is communicated. Today's culture demands a searching christology. Traditional theological reflection on Jesus' representation of God presupposed recognition of the existence of God. In a modern or postmodern context of the absence of God, representation of God takes on a new meaning: it is now responding to the question of where God is and how God may be recognized. To ignore this cultural situation "is to remain a prisoner within the private sphere of individual religious attitudes and experiences" (CR, 131). Today God's seeming absence requires that God be represented or mediated. In Soelle's view, Jesus represented this absent God by being the man for others. To be God is to be the creator, lover, and protector of human beings. Jesus assumed this role, and left it to be continued by his followers.

Jesus identified with God by assuming two functions: he proclaimed the message of God, and he played the role of God in history. For most moderns the world is disenchanted. The theology of creation supports this: what God created is not God but has a God-given autonomous identity. The world is not God. In a world where God does not appear, God needs to be mediated, symbolized, represented. "Because God does not intervene to establish his cause, [Jesus] appears in his place. He comforts those whom, up to now, God has left in the lurch, he heals those who do not understand God, feeds those whom God allows to go hungry. But he does all of this as one who identifies himself with the absent God. All representation begins with the representative's identification of himself with those he represents."[32]

---

31. The English words "represent," "representative," and "representation" have multiple meanings. This plurality releases suggestive power on the imagination and increases its usefulness in christological understanding.

32. CR, 137. "[Jesus] takes the part of God in the world, plays this role which without him would remain unfulfilled. His identification with God takes place, so to

Being the ambassador or *porte-parole* of God and taking on the active role of God in history do not mean that Jesus was identical with or a replacement of God. As Soelle puts it, "[Jesus] at the same time preserved the difference between him and God. He only represents God. He does not replace him. It would be a mistake to interpret incarnation as God's complete self-emptying into human form. This would mean that we had already had all there was to have from God and nothing remained to look for from him" (CR, 138).

It follows that Jesus remains dependent upon God, and what God promises has not been completed by Jesus. "[Jesus'] identification with God, his claim on God, remains non-identity. For only non-identity leaves an open future. If [Jesus] were identical with God, we would have nothing further to expect, except Jesus" (CR, 143). Because Jesus plays the role of but is not identical with God, there is more to come; a future of "more" lies out in front of humanity.

What is it in the end that allows one to recognize in Jesus this representation of God? Or how does Soelle begin to explain what being the representative of God consists of? Increasingly in her later essays Soelle emphasized Jesus' divine power in his being a "man for others," borrowing the phrase of Dietrich Bonhoeffer. "He was the man-for-others because he was the man of God and knew himself to be so borne up by God that he did not fall out of God, not even when he felt himself abandoned by God."[33] This "man for others" begins to function as an equivalent of the Chalcedonian formula: he was a human being whose "for others" consisted in the power of God in him "because God is for others the God of love."[34] This insight implicitly depends on a doctrine of grace in the Augustinian sense of *auxilium Dei* or divine empowerment. In other words, Jesus was the loving, self-transcendent representative of God not on the basis of his own power but on the basis of God's presence within him.

Jesus as representative of human existence. Jesus is our representative before God. This thesis corresponds to Jesus' humanity in the doctrine of the two natures of Jesus Christ. Soelle develops this not by analyzing "natures" but by showing how Jesus fulfilled this aspect of the role of representation. Besides representing us to God, Jesus reveals human existence to itself.

---

speak, behind the ontological problem of God's being . . . and makes that problem anachronistic, since God is present in [Jesus'] playing of his part, though no longer as the directly experienced God." CR, 140-41.

33. Dorothee Soelle, "Christ, the Man for Others," in Soelle, *Theology for Skeptics: Reflections on God* (Minneapolis: Fortress Press, 1995), 96.

34. Soelle, "Christ, the Man for Others," 96.

CHAPTER SEVEN

Jesus' Death and Resurrection

The death of Jesus and his resurrection from death lie at the heart of Christianity. Christian religion has been built on these two events and the salvation they carry.[1] Frequently Jesus' death and resurrection are considered distinct and treated separately. Chronologically they are sequential and may seem as separable as death and life. Because of this difference, some views of how Jesus accomplished human salvation fix neatly on Jesus' suffering and death and thus elevate the cross as the central symbol of Christian faith. Other views of salvation focus attention on Jesus' resurrection, his victory over death, as the core of Christian faith. Besides these two extremes, other views alternate between them in various accents, and still others may raise up Jesus' ministry as exemplary and salvific. Thus, while many agree that Jesus' death and resurrection are central to Christian faith, these events are cluttered with diverse theological interpretations.

In keeping with a seeking spirituality, this discussion will approach these religiously charged topics from a historical perspective. This does not mean limiting what can be said by an empirical or naturalist premise. It means being attentive to the historical genesis and development of religious encounter and interpretation. The first part discusses this historical approach to the story of Jesus' arrest, suffering, and execution prior to possibilities for theological interpretations of it. The second and third parts discuss the experience of the disciples that Jesus was raised by God from death and the nature of Jesus' resurrection that is the content of that experience. Then in part four, the chapter traces some of the many interpretations of these events as bearing salvation. From the many different conceptions of how Jesus saves, the chapter offers a constructive proposal that takes today's Western culture into account.

---

1. I use the term "salvation" as a general category that has many specifications of what exactly the term means, how it was accomplished, and what it entails. This will be noted in the course of the chapter.

A Historical Approach to Jesus' Death

We begin this consideration of Jesus' suffering and death from a historical perspective. "Historical" suggests a distinction between a level of facticity and elaborated meanings drawn from those events or read into them. While such a clean distinction can never be realized because all knowledge is also interpretation, the distinction still alerts those approaching this subject matter to the degree that spiritual appropriation is at work in the passion narratives. The idea that we can reconstruct the "history" of Jesus' passion and death seems to promise too much. We know less about the actual details about Jesus' suffering and death than is usually imagined, but what we do know is sufficient for various theological interpretations of it.

Different views of historical-critical method. With the rise of critical-historical methods of examining the Bible, the story of Jesus' passion and death has spawned significantly different ways of understanding what is going on in the texts and of how to appropriate them. The debate is frequently cast in terms of the relationship between history and theology. In this tension history may be understood as a reconstructive attempt to determine how texts were written, the meaning that they represented when they were written, and, in the case of narratives, how they relate to what happened. Theology has to do with what the texts propose for understanding the relationship between God and human beings and their meaning in the context of the faith of the church.

These two distinct aspects of one story become intimately involved with each other in the events of the passion narrative. This can be illustrated dramatically by further distinguishing the question involved in the two approaches. Paul Capetz writes, "I understand a historical question about a text to be descriptive and explanatory in nature: What is being said and why?"[2] A further historical question may be whether a series of events actually occurred in the way it is narrated, that is, the question of historical authenticity. "By contrast a theological question is hermeneutical and normative in nature: How is the claim made by the text to be understood today and is it true?"[3] Because the events of the passion of Jesus were appropriated by interpretation from the very moment of their transpiring, and because the legacy of those interpretations defines the very meaning of Christian faith for so many, it

---

2. Paul Capetz, "Theology and the Historical-Critical Study of the Bible," *Harvard Theological Review* 104 (2011): 467.

3. Capetz, "Historical-Critical Study of the Bible," 467.

becomes clear that one has to have some framework for appreciating the very character of the narrative itself.

Within the tension between a critical-historical and a theological interpretation of the passion narratives lies the question of the degree to which the passion narratives of the four Gospels correspond to what happened in a historical sense, that is, what was or could have been witnessed. The question is this: To what extent do the scenes that make up the passion narratives correspond to what happened historically? The answer to this question has to do with the quality of one's faith conviction and how it indirectly influences but does not determine its object. On the supposition that empirical events do not of themselves generate faith in transcendent matters, and at the same time granting to Jesus of Nazareth the role of mediating Christian faith in God, how should one read the relationship of the historical and theological dimensions of the passion narratives?

It will be helpful to illustrate further how different imaginative frameworks for understanding this relationship between theological and historical data may come to bear on an appreciation of the passion narratives of the four Gospels. What follows is an oversimplified typology that makes a useful point by illustrating differences in the way this relationship may be construed. At one extreme, the passion narratives record things as they happened; at an opposite extreme, the passion narratives have very little historical value; and middle positions hold the two together in tension with each other.

First, a conservative theological stance insists on the historicity of the passion narratives. Negatively, this theological position fears a reductionism of the story and the doctrines within them that have been communicated by God to historical explanation, historical context, and merely human experience. One cannot reduce the meaning of religious texts to historical determinations. Positively, therefore, this position will stress the normativity of the theological meaning that has consistently defined the faith of the church. And to ensure that the witness of scripture is true, this position values as well the integrity of the historical witness. It will not allow historical criticism to relativize the truth of the word of God or to isolate it from the historical narrative.

On the opposite side of the tension, a careful critical-historical examination of the textual traditions of the four passion narratives shows that theological interpretations of what happened to Jesus are drawn from the Jewish scriptures, and they virtually dictate the form and to some extent the very content of the scenes that make it up. John Dominic Crossan, a representative of this view, calls the process of writing a historicization of prophecy. "The individual units, general sequences, and overall frames of the passion-resurrection stories are so linked to prophetic fulfillment that the removal of that fulfillment leaves nothing but the barest facts."[4] In this view one cannot trust that any of the texts of the passion narratives report events as they happened; from the very beginning Jesus' death was being read within a framework of fulfilled prophecy.

Middle positions may vary greatly among themselves, but they share some measure of distinguishing but holding together historical and theological accents and not allowing either one to virtually cancel out the other. Raymond E. Brown exemplifies this position even though Crossan characterizes Brown's stance as "history remembered" and as antithetical to his own.[5] But Brown also admits to considerable amounts of interpolation into the texts on the part of the communities that composed the stories; they injected their later theological interpretations into the scenes. In general, the Gospels "are distillations of earlier Christian preaching and teaching about Jesus."[6] The passion narratives are certainly not the result of the memory of modern reporters but expressions of faith in stories that are "heavily scripturally reflective, kerygmatically oriented, and theologically organized."[7]

Four principles running through Brown's commentary and analysis of the passion narratives may help to define a centrist position. The first is that Mark's passion narrative, which Matthew and Luke knew, was probably based on a prior tradition of stories that reached back more closely to the events. It is more likely that John's passion narrative was influenced by a pre-Gospel tradition similar to Mark's than by Mark's Gospel itself. The second principle qualifies the first: the existence of a prior tradition does not necessarily entail historical authenticity; any number of details may be interpretive additions after the events. Third, it does not seem logical to presume that only the followers of Jesus, after his death and resurrection, actively interpreted Jesus' actions in the light of the scriptures. It must be presumed that

---

4. John Dominic Crossan, *The Birth of Christianity: Discovering What Happened in the Years Immediately after the Execution of Jesus* (San Francisco: HarperSanFrancisco, 1998), 521.

5. Crossan, *Birth of Christianity,* 520-21. Brown accepts the designation. The early followers of Jesus "did remember basic items in sequence about the death of Jesus." Raymond E. Brown, *The Death of the Messiah: From Gethsemane to the Grave. A Commentary on the Passion Narratives in the Four Gospels,* 2 vols., Anchor Bible Reference Library (New York: Doubleday, 1994), 1:17.

6. Brown, *Death of the Messiah,* 1:13.

7. Brown, *Death of the Messiah,* 1:22. I have placed Brown in the middle of two extremes because he recognizes that the scenes of the passion narrative and the details in them do not all share the same probability of historical authenticity. But there remains plenty of room within this center for "right" and "left" leaning interpretation.

Jesus himself did a fair amount of self-reflection in the light of his tradition before and during his ministry. Finally, each stage of the passion story needs to be weighed for meaning and historical authenticity: one global judgment does not apply to all scenes or details.

The deeper implications of a historical approach. The historical is particular and contingent. It happens. Contingency means that the historical has not been choreographed or predetermined by God; it cannot be completely rationalized, because it flows out of human decisions responding to the situations that had fallen into place at a particular moment. Much of historical reconstruction relies on sources that do not explain the motives of the actors; they remain unknown. Frequently reconstructions hinge on hypotheses that actors were operating on the basis of a certain set of premises and for certain goals, so that different perceptions of intentionality issue in different meanings of behavior and events. Historical reconstruction of the final days of Jesus works within a framework of conjecture about the motives of the crowds in Jerusalem, of the various sets of religious leaders, individually or as groups, and of the leadership of the occupying Roman authority that controlled order in the city. Relative to Jesus, a historical approach works on the premise that Jesus was not acting out a part or scripted role. Even if he modeled his ministry on the prophets, his responses were not programmed ahead of time. Because Jesus was a human being like us, he did not know the future but had to act on ordinary signs for discerning the consequences of events and his behavior. Historically conscious exegetes are more or less unanimous that the texts of the New Testament do not allow us to enter into the psychology of Jesus. In this way, a first approach to Jesus' suffering and death on the level of the historical suggests severe limits to our knowledge.

The assumption of a historical point of departure for a later spiritual and then theological consideration of Jesus' suffering and death entails some further corollaries. Depending on the stringency of the criteria that various historical investigations of the passion narratives employ, they will generate more or less "data" that may be considered authentically historical and that will be judged on the basis of more or less probability. In other words, historical reconstruction does not operate mechanically but on plausible inductions based on various appreciations of evidence by interpreters, who themselves have dispositions inclining them in this or that direction. This account of appreciating "the historical" in the matter of Jesus' death simply reflects some of the consequences of the shift to critical-historical methods in the study of the Bible that is commonly accepted today. But relative to naïve approaches to the passion narratives it describes a revolution. Prior to the adoption of a historical approach to the story of Jesus' passion, events seemed to prove a deep metaphysical and religious meaning that was unfolding in them because they fulfilled scriptural foreshadowing or prophecy. From a historical viewpoint, the same fulfillments, recognized after the fact and in the interpretive writing, call their exact historicity into question. In other words, prophetic fulfillment from a historical viewpoint makes the passion narratives appear more like a long narrative interpretation constructed on the basis of scriptural texts than a series of actual events.

At the same time, however, the passion narratives of the four Gospels refer to a basic story that has a high degree of historical plausibility. One can recognize a basic series of events, distinct from the details, that enjoys historical coherence. For example, even though the dialogue between Jesus and Pilate may not be historical, it is plausible that Jesus was brought before Pilate. Such a historical approach encourages a distinction between what is less or more important, or what is not important at all, for understanding the events behind Christianity's central symbol. Things that are products of a creative imagination but historically implausible have to be understood for what they are. For example, is it ultimately important who was finally responsible for the death of Jesus or the degree of participation in it? This question has proved resistant to any exact answer that transcends bias and enjoys unanimity. At the same time, the amount of energy that has gone into the effort to resolve it seems confused: it implicitly attributes metaphysical value to a question of fact whose answer is also indeterminable. A critical-historical approach to the passion of Jesus helps clear away a lot of historical and theological underbrush.

The story of Jesus' death.[8] Jesus was in Jerusalem at the time of Passover. It is not clear whether this was the first time he brought his ministry there, or how long he was in Jerusalem. Far more important is the fact that this time he antagonized those in authority, principally the religious leaders and more specifically the temple officials. This element of conflict in Jesus' ministry, testified to in various stories, not least his preaching in the temple precincts, offers some explanation of why he was apprehended. Jesus' ministry generated conflict. The timetables of the four accounts of the passion are not exactly synchronized, nor do they agree in a number of details. But the time of the arrest was on or near the feast of Passover, the day before the beginning of the

---

8. This narrative of the passion of Jesus follows the scheme laid out by Raymond Brown in his *Death of the Messiah*, beginning with the prayer and arrest of Jesus in Gethsemane.

Sabbath. Mark, Matthew, and Luke tell how Jesus and his disciples ate a Passover meal together in Jerusalem. The story is told in a way that suggests that Jesus knows what is to follow.

After the meal Jesus and his followers went to the Mount of Olives and a place called Gethsemane, where Jesus is depicted as praying to God in the face of his possible death. He was apprehended there in a plot that involved the Jewish Sanhedrin and Judas, one of Jesus' twelve closest associates. He was brought that night to the Sanhedrin, the court made up of priests and other religious officials and over which the high priest presided. There followed an interrogation or a trial in which Jesus was accused of blasphemy. Much about this scene is contested: Mark, Matthew, and John have it that night, Luke the next morning. It is not clear whether it was a formal proceeding, or exactly what Jesus said or did that amounted to blasphemy and merited death. It is relatively certain, however, that at some time prior to Jesus' arrest the Sanhedrin planned to neutralize his influence.

The next morning the religious officials had Jesus brought to Pontius Pilate, the Roman prefect or governor who was in Jerusalem during the time of the religious festival. This scene too involves many details that are interpreted differently. Was Pilate acting according to Roman law or standards in questioning Jesus? Is the dialogue or interchange between Jesus and Pilate, especially in its developed form in John's Gospel, historically authentic? In Luke's account, on learning that Jesus was a Galilean and knowing that Herod Antipas, the ruler of that region, was in the city, Pilate sent him to Herod. Brown believes that this is a Lucan addition that is not historical but was used to add Herod's voice to Pilate's sentiment that Jesus did not deserve to die. Theologically one can see the forces of injustice closing in on the righteous prophet.

In the course of these proceedings, Pilate appears as one who is not convinced that Jesus merited death. The main charge against Jesus relayed to Pilate was that he was claiming to be a king, but it is not clear what warranted the charge or how Pilate was able to process it. Was it connected with Jesus as Messiah or with his preaching the kingdom of God? At one point Pilate seeks to buy off the crowd by offering to free either Jesus or a convicted evildoer, Barabbas, according to a custom honoring the Jewish feast. But the crowd chooses the release of Barabbas. Did this happen, or is this a literary device to underline the forces of evil marshaled against Jesus, another instance of dramatized theology? In the end, Pilate condemned Jesus to death by crucifixion and, as part of that intentionally dehumanizing ordeal, to an initial scourging. Throughout these scenes Pilate is portrayed as indecisive and reluctant relative to Jesus' guilt, but in the end as yielding to the pressure of the leaders and the crowds at hand.

Jesus was then led off to be crucified on a hill called Golgotha outside the city wall of that time. The tradition used by Mark and John said that a certain Cyrenian named Simon was forced to help Jesus carry the crossbar of the cross. At Golgotha, Jesus was crucified with two other men who were executed that day. The inscription of the charge against Jesus attached to the cross read "The King of the Jews" (Mark 15:26). The scene of Jesus' crucifixion is accompanied by a number of details: Jesus was twice offered wine to drink; his clothes were divided among the executioners; he was mocked by passersby, by Jewish leaders, and by some soldiers; and he spoke a number of times before dying. When he died, there were a number of natural phenomena, such as an earthquake and an eclipse, which marked his death. Some of these details are literary commentary; others may relate back to unfolding events. According to the tradition used by Mark and John, Jesus died that afternoon and was buried before sunset and the beginning of Sabbath. To the best of Brown's reckoning, Jesus died on April 7, 30 C.E. at the approximate age of thirty-six.[9]

It is not certain what motives guided a certain Joseph of Arimathea, who was a member of the Sanhedrin, to offer a new grave for Jesus not far from the place of execution. The end of the passion story describes women who saw where Jesus was buried. This serves as a bridge to their being the first witnesses to the empty tomb.

The significance of Jesus' death. What is spiritually important and significant in this story? The ability to formulate these things requires fixed interest in the story and a sense for the question it raises. Jesus brought to a focus the attention of the crowds and aroused the religious hopes of many. Nothing would have been remembered were this not the case. For those who were completely captivated by Jesus and his message, his death could have caused something like a religious trauma, for several reasons. First of all, Jesus is presented as a victim of injustice and violence at the hands of the same people who were expected to uphold and guarantee justice and peace. Whether it was Jewish leaders or Roman authorities or some cooperation between them, and whatever the conflict that arose around his person and teaching, Jesus' execution seems completely out of proportion to his message. Jesus is portrayed as the incarnation of innocent goodness: his violent, torturous, and dehumanizing execution creates a dramatic contrast. Such innocent suffering constitutes an attack on meaning itself. The

9. Brown, *Death of the Messiah*, 1376.

prevalence of such violence against human beings, along with its consistency and impunity, does not mitigate the negative experience of contrast with basic human values: it is wrong and evil.

Encountering events of innocent suffering can be disorienting. Jesus' crucifixion could undermine the basic trust in the coherence and value of human existence of anyone who appreciated Jesus' message. Something like this seemed to have happened: the expectations of Jesus' disciples were crushed. Nowhere is this better expressed than by the Lucan understatement: "We had hoped . . ." (Luke 24:21). In other words, the "cross" here does not mean something detached from concrete history, some free-floating meaning like self-negation, or confused lack of meaning. It refers to this real event that blatantly contradicted the message that Jesus taught of a loving and provident God who cares for God's creatures and with whom Jesus seemed to exhibit some authoritative familiarity. The people who internalized that message were scandalized.

Jesus' real death on a real cross thus concentrates in an actual real but also symbolic event a challenge to the human spirit that transcends its particularity. The challenge is precise: can one, and if so, on what grounds, reappropriate an ultimate meaning to human life that transcends the regular rhythms of violence and injustice? Are cynicism and stoicism reasonable appraisals of human existence that are no less justified than confidence and hope in coherent meaning? Are we condemned deep down to look upon human nature with a kind of contemptuous mistrust? Are there grounds for any trust in human motivation or expectation of self-transcendence? Should "seize the day" be translated into a metaphysical pragmatism, and life be leveled out and buried by time? The passion narratives follow Jesus' ministry and so bring it to a climactic end. The symbol of the cross, that real event, contains in its densest form a challenge to the coherence of human existence itself. This story happened at the end of Jesus' life; the same challenge can be experienced by anyone who remembers it today.

Finally, the cross is important because this historical event challenges the idea of God. It is another story of Job, of innocent suffering that calls the Jewish conceptions of God that were in place into question. All stories of innocent suffering do the same thing. This one is particularly jarring because the events seem so sharply to conflict with the very message that Jesus preached.[10]

---

10. This negative character of the story of Jesus' execution provides a good example of how history should chasten enthusiastic Christian exclamations of the cross being a sign of God's love for human beings. Such language seems to have lost its historical moorings.

These important features of this history of the end of Jesus' ministry are not esoteric; they lie on the surface. But they have deep humanistic roots. These facets are the negative side of the religious question, the place where spirituality's relationship to transcendence is challenged. This is what is at stake in the Easter experience.

The Easter Experience

Jesus' life on earth in the ordinary empirical sense ends with his death. The narrative historical approach directs focused attention on Jesus up to this point. Now historical attention shifts to the disciples, to how they reacted to Jesus' death, and to how they came to experience him alive by God's power and with God. This first approach to the resurrection of Jesus through the experience of the disciples puts the subject matter for the discussion within the ken of disciples of Jesus today; it also makes it available to anyone who approaches Jesus for the first time.

The before and the after of the Easter experience. The New Testament has no story or description of Jesus' resurrection itself. Nor does it identify or represent any witness to "the event" of the resurrection. This makes sense because the resurrection should be understood not as an empirical event of history but precisely as Jesus being drawn into the life of God, the infinite and transcendent one. Resurrection is not a historical event but a transcendent event.

Stepping back from the several narrative incidents surrounding Jesus' resurrection as portrayed by the New Testament, one thing stands out: the dramatic contrast between an initial despair and confusion among the disciples that are readily understandable and, somewhat later, the confidence among them that Jesus had been and was raised by God. So strong was this conviction that it enabled and empowered a Jesus movement that bore witness to the Nazarene as now risen and vindicated by God. The question of an "Easter experience" fits into this contrast and asks what it was that caused the radical turnaround and continued to hold the disciples together as a group.[11]

The spontaneous response to this question appears on the surface of the resurrection accounts: the empty tomb and the appearances of

---

11. An "Easter experience," a category drawn from the writings of Edward Schillebeeckx, refers to the experience had by the disciples that enabled them to arrive at the conviction that Jesus was risen. The object of that experience was that Jesus was in fact or really raised by God to new life. There is no question here of reducing the objectivity of the resurrection to the experience of the disciples. See Schillebeeckx, *Jesus: An Experiment in Christology* (New York: Seabury Press, 1979), 379-97. Note that the theory of the Easter experience proffered here does not correspond exactly to that of Schillebeeckx.

Jesus. Jesus is risen because the tomb was empty, an angel told them that he had risen, and the disciples saw him alive. These responses to the question of the Easter experience still retain their power and legitimacy on a popular imaginative level, because they directly communicate the point: Jesus is risen. But critical examination of the scriptures shows the degree to which these stories, when they are read as historical accounts, contain inconsistencies and incredible elements that show in turn their symbolic character.[12] While these stories state that Jesus is alive, they do not describe external events as they unfolded empirically, but tell stories that themselves bear witness to the fact that Jesus is risen. The particular language of an empty tomb and apparitions almost seems to be based on an implied physicalism that cannot understand, because it cannot imagine, a reality that cannot be represented in some physical form. Even if the material form is ethereal and, like the wind, made of a substance that is thin and volatile, it has to find a place in one's imagination. In this context, spirit, as a negation of matter and physicality, would appear incomprehensible because it is unimaginable. The only way the authors of the New Testament, or more generally the early Christians, could affirm the reality of Jesus' resurrection was to portray it in some physical or material way.

The question of the Easter experience in theology is thus speculative. Whatever position a theologian holds, he or she will have to defend it on a critical level with speculative arguments. And the most speculative arguments of all are those that take the appearance narratives at face value as historical. What kind of experiences were these? What kind of object presented itself to the disciples? What was the quality of Jesus' being there? Were these revelatory hallucinations? Such questions are still entertained by many, while others, exhausted, resort to the phrase that "somehow" Jesus physically appeared to the disciples as a real identifiable self. But the term "somehow" communicates nothing. By contrast, what follows offers a narrative account of the Easter experience in broad communitarian terms and then proposes a more analytical reflection.

A narrative of this community experience. Luke's Gospel contains the story of how Jesus appeared to two disciples while they were walking from

---

12. Those who mistakenly understand symbols as a weak form of language and communication, indicated by the phrase "only a symbol," will not be convinced by this proposal. It would be a digression to make the case that spiritual language about transcendent reality is necessarily symbolic. In any case, the term "symbol" as it is used here represents a strong vehicle of communicating transcendent truths that cannot be expressed in any other way. These stories are like sacraments that represent and mediate spiritual truths through two concrete images used in description and narrative.

Jerusalem to a town called Emmaus (Luke 24:13-35). This story, one of the most beautiful in the New Testament, shows the careful, almost encoded, character of several of Luke's narratives and speeches. The story can be read in various ways, as the history of biblical interpretation readily attests. But the comparison of two distinct levels of interpretation highlights a way of understanding the Easter experience as a communitarian event.

The first level of interpretation consists of the obvious surface meaning of the events as they unfold: on the first day of the week after Jesus' crucifixion two disciples leave Jerusalem bound for Emmaus. They are speaking of all the things that happened to Jesus. They meet Jesus along the way, but do not recognize him. Jesus enters into their conversation; he draws out their reactions to the events; he then proceeds to explain how all that happened followed the logic of the scriptures. Toward the end of the day Jesus stays with them for a meal, which is depicted by Luke as a eucharistic meal, and the disciples recognize Jesus in the breaking of the bread. Jesus then vanishes from sight and the disciples immediately return to Jerusalem to communicate the basic message of the story that the Lord is risen.

The same story can also be read allegorically as a story that was developed later and presents an account of an extended Easter experience of the followers of Jesus. The story is really about how the group of disciples, loosely but as a whole, came to the recognition over a more or less protracted period of time that Jesus was raised by God from death. This view of the story gives it a somewhat stronger historical authenticity, because the events of the story depict in very general but realistic terms stages through which the community would have moved to arrive at this conclusion of faith. In this view the Easter experience is less an individual's experience and more a community's group experience.

The narrative clearly marks the stages of the developing conviction. The initial stage consists of the questioning confusion and near despair caused by abruptness and finality of Jesus' execution. "But we had hoped . . ." (Luke 24:21). One has to reckon that the disciples of Jesus could not refrain from talking about it. A second dimension of the story is contained in Jesus appearing unrecognized to the disciples and eliciting their discussion. One can imagine endless conversation and discussion among the disciples in their effort to figure out what had happened. Although Jesus' presence to the disciples is presented supernaturally, it represents their still vivid memory of his ministry. A third and very important factor in the story lies in the interpretation by means of the application of scriptural texts to the events, and the discovery of a deep logic to the whole Jesus affair. This has a factual reference: the New Testament testifies to the searching exegesis of prophecy and fulfillment by which the earliest disciples began to put the pieces together. A fourth dimension of the story, equally important for understanding the Easter experience, is implied by the nonrecognition of Jesus at first and their sudden recognition of him and his disappearance. This signals that God is an implied actor in the story; this whole story unfolds under the canopy of the revealing presence and grace of God. Then, fifth, the meal at which the disciples suddenly recognize Jesus turns out to be a eucharistic meal, and Jesus' being alive and present become "known to them in the breaking of the bread" (Luke 24:35). This more than suggests that a shared meal of disciples was a scene for the recognition that Jesus is risen. The conclusion of the story, then, follows as a result of the story: Jesus has been raised by God.

On this level the story does not unfold in a day; it represents a more or less extended period during which Jesus' resurrection was revealed to the earliest groups of his disciples. Although the stages of the story's unfolding appear formal and abstract, they refer directly and plausibly to the actual unfolding of events. In other words, this interpretation provides a concrete historical reference not to the resurrection but to the Easter experience by which the disciples were able to appropriate the resurrection of Jesus.

An Analytical Theory of the Easter Experience

Narrative gives rise to analysis. What follows supplies an interpretation of the elements that contributed to the coming to faith in Jesus' resurrection. This too has a hypothetical character; no single understanding of the epistemology behind the affirmation of the resurrection is accepted by all. But all reflective believers in the resurrection in fact operate on the basis of some motives. Such an analysis, then, bears some importance for a reflective appropriation of the content of one's faith. In this proposal, four elements help to explain the Christian affirmation of Jesus' resurrection: it is elicited out of hope; it is partially mediated on the basis of Jesus' ministry but requires the impulse of God's Spirit or grace, so that the appearance stories of the Gospels are expressions of faith rather than objective motives.

1. Faith and hope. One way of bringing out the intelligibility of an affirmation is to show its continuity with the way we understand human existence as such, how it resonates with our self-understanding. It has been stipulated earlier that affirmations about transcendent reality can be made only on the basis of faith; if they were empirical and demonstrable they would not be matters of faith. Relative to the

resurrection, the dimension of hope within that faith plays an important role. Hope is one of the fundamental moral attitudes that can be
learned from Jesus' teaching.

Hope refers to a human attitude much deeper than looking forward
to a future empirical event, for something to happen. It refers rather to
a positive acceptance by the human spirit of being in the world. Karl
Rahner looks on hope as the openness of the human subject to being
itself. It implies receptiveness to all forms of being because reality
itself is not hostile but good.[13] Edward Schillebeeckx associates hope
with the "basic trust" discussed in chapter 3, a conviction that existence itself and thus the future can be approached with confidence.[14]
Once this elementary aspect of human existence itself is factored in, it
becomes apparent that faith in the resurrection of Jesus is much more
than an acknowledgment of an objective fact or piece of empirical or
even transcendent "data." Our own being, through the disposition
of hope, is engaged in the trust and commitment to the character of
reality that Jesus' being raised implies. Faith-hope in Jesus' resurrection simultaneously entails hope in our own, by the same logic and
in the same measure. In this way, expanding one's horizon, faith, and
hope in Jesus' resurrection stretch outward to encompass being itself.
This faith-hope becomes a fundamental moral attitude of positive confidence in the character of reality. The resurrection of Jesus signals
God's fidelity as the ground of this trust.

2. Jesus' ministry as an external witness. We are working on the premise established in an earlier chapter that faith, to have content, has to
have a historical mediation that supplies its content and specifies its
object. Some theologians think that that mediation was the appearances of Jesus or the angel at the empty tomb that said Jesus was risen;
others think that Jesus himself, during his earthly ministry and in
his preaching and wonder-working, supplied sufficient evidence for
belief in the resurrection. But neither of these positions succeeds: one
is supernaturalistic, and the other does not add up to belief in Jesus'
resurrection.

But there is a way of thinking of Jesus during his ministry as providing a historical mediation for the *revelation* of his resurrection after his
death: first, by considering the content of his ministry and, second, by
reflecting on his person. Jesus' message, in the many ways it was deliv-

---

13. Karl Rahner, "On the Theology of Hope," in his *Theological Investigations*,
vol. 10 (New York: Herder & Herder, 1973), 242-59. This theme of hope and Rahner's
contribution to understanding the depths from which it comes will be revisited in
chapter 9 in the consideration of eschatology.

14. Edward Schillebeeckx, "Secularization and Christian Belief in God," in his *God,
the Future of Man* (New York: Sheed & Ward, 1968), 74.

ered, stressed the goodness of God. It spoke of and dramatized God's loving and saving intent; it underlined the fidelity of God. Through his parables, those that he told and the symbolic actions he performed, Jesus represented God's faithful commitment to the flourishing and fulfillment of human existence. Along with and through these behaviors Jesus exhibited what Günther Bornkamm called Jesus' authority.[15] This refers to a quality of his person that, through his overt actions, elicited a response that allowed him to sway hearts and minds. Jesus' authority is that which caused his disciples to remember him. And this memory of him is precisely what urged the disciples to experience *his* resurrection as distinct from resurrection in general. On the one hand, then, the memory of Jesus in his ministry provides the primary referent of the Christian belief in resurrection, that is, the resurrection of Jesus. On the other hand, we understand that the resurrection of Jesus bears reference to the creator God, the God of life for all people, and thus is a promise of each person's resurrection.

3. *An initiative from God as Spirit.* The third element of this theory of the nature of resurrection faith consists of an initiative of God's revelatory grace, or the Spirit of God, as an ultimate cause of this religious experience. This element is drawn from spiritual reflection on this affirmation of faith that refuses either a rationalistic explanation for this belief or a purely fideistic conception that takes it to be a purely gratuitous assertion without reasonable motives. It can be argued that all truly religious experience carries with it a dimension of external gratuity: the experience of transcendence and of God cannot be controlled; it comes to us, so that we are subject to it, rather than the maker of it. But reflective reasoning encourages rather than rules out following such interior movements. These themes from the philosophy and psychology of religion appear in the theological tradition as the experience of dependence on God, God's initiative in the human response of faith, and God's sovereignty and not manipulability by human wishes. In short, just as the resurrection of Jesus is God's doing, and it could not be otherwise, so too the coming to an awareness of it and commitment to it are the product of God's revelatory working within us. No one is ever going to prove the resurrection of Jesus to someone who is not open to entertaining the possibility.[16]

4. *Objective expressions of resurrection faith-hope.* This point has already been made, at least implicitly. The stories of the empty tomb

---

15. Günther Bornkamm, *Jesus of Nazareth* (New York: Harper & Brothers, 1960), 60-61.

16. One of the problems with accepting the apparition stories as reports on empirical events is that such an interpretation removes the Easter experience from the sphere of faith.

and the appearances of Jesus were written after the Easter experience, and their point is to communicate the message that Jesus is risen. When they are taken too literally as descriptive of historical events as they happened, they become a trap that associates resurrection with a resuscitated corpse and radically limits the range of religious experience and the meaning of resurrection itself. Literalism reduces the Easter experience of Jesus' resurrection to naive religious stories. By contrast, these four elements, when taken together, correlate neatly with the exegetical and social interpretation of the story of the disciples on the road to a eucharistic encounter at Emmaus. They also accord historically with the Christian spiritual conviction that Jesus of Nazareth was raised by God from death. Jesus, like a second Adam, represents the promise of God for humanity's future.

The Resurrection

The Easter experience yields the conviction that Jesus is risen; Jesus of Nazareth being alive with his proper identity names the content of the Easter experience. What can be said about Jesus risen? One cannot respond to that question with the kind of language that describes empirical events: Jesus was raised into God's sphere of being in an utterly new and transcendent way. It might be better to call what follows a meditation or a descriptive account of how Jesus' resurrection completely transcends our power of knowledge but impresses itself upon us to reorient life into the future.

The content of the Easter experience. Modern theology has provided many alternatives to the content of resurrection faith that is proposed here. For example, many theologians hold that the memory, power, and consequent influence of Jesus lives on in the Christian community. This allows one to say that Jesus is risen, but the meaning of the affirmation has been significantly changed, enough to allow the simultaneous affirmation that the actual person, Jesus, was not raised. In other words, the autonomous identity of Jesus ended in his death so that what lived on is not him but people's memory of him. Similarly, reducing the resurrection to the concept that Jesus lives on in the memory of God allows one equally to admit the finality and decisiveness of his death. These formulas preserve the language but in an ambiguous way that some people might regard as duplicitous. They are not so intended. They represent bona fide interpretations of the resurrection. But in contrast to these alternatives, the position espoused here is that the individual Jesus of Nazareth was raised from the state of death by God.

The resurrection was and is a transcendent reality. That is, it cannot be conceived of as an event of history and must be approached as a transcendent mystery about God and God's dealing with human beings after their death. The point of the doctrine of the resurrection of the body is not that Jesus' corpse was vaporized or snatched up and put somewhere, but that Jesus in his personal, individual identity was assumed into God's life. The nearest analogy we have to the historical side of the resurrection is the concurrent belief that other human beings are, like Jesus, resurrected in his name. And yet we affirm that their real bodies remain buried on earth to decompose. Resurrection is not about corpses reawakening.

The credibility of any understanding of the resurrection runs into a number of obstacles that make it appear as wishful thinking or mere projection. One always has to be aware that deep human desires are driving such beliefs, but this does not in any way necessitate a reduction of what is affirmed to self-interest. In fact some theologians exploit the spontaneous tendency to survive as a sign, if not an argument, that points from nature to the reality of such a goal. But a real problem that directly confronts the resurrection runs deeper and lies entailed in the fact that the only human life we know is the physical, tangible life of a body. Science repeatedly underscores the way the human spirit depends in its being and functions on being embedded in physicality and bodiliness. We cannot conceive of mind without brain or, more generally, the human outside the world and history. As Aristotle conceived it long ago, our physicality gives us our individual identity. How is it even imaginable that the human spirit could be raised without the body?

The role of imagination in resurrection faith-hope. The resurrection is beyond human knowledge and conceptualization, but there must be some way that the human mind can begin to think about it. A consideration of how the imagination functions in resurrection faith and hope, especially its strengths and limitations, helps to clarify the logic of a resurrection faith.

The workings of the human mind that we tend to associate with imagination include a considerable range of activities, but three functions of the imagination can help explain its role in resurrection faith and hope. The imagination mediates the knowledge that human beings draw from the world. We observe with our senses and, attending to that data, find intelligible patterns within it. This integrating role of the imagination closely ties human knowledge to the physical world. The imagination also stores images, and the memory preserves them. Memory and imagination together describe the bank of knowledge wherein each human being carries his or her experience in forms that can be readily drawn upon to measure new experiences by comparison and contrast. Finally, the imagination is creative. For example, by putting images together it creates a new being in the mind that can then be fashioned by the hands. In the last few centuries we have come to realize the enormous collective power and scope of this creative power that has its fundamental moorings in the imagination. If human freedom can be described as creative energy, the imagination is its dynamo.

Sorting out the different ways in which the imagination feeds into faith-hope in the resurrection helps clarify faith's logic. The imagination vaguely constructs a future out of the present. Resurrection means life after death, the extension of one's being into an infinitely open future by the power of God. The imagination can strengthen the plausibility of such a future by turning to the story of creation, which is also unimaginable because of its sheer size and complexity, but which is attested to by the scientific account of why one exists in the present moment. The scope of the "God of power and might" appears to the imagination paradoxically as "finite unlimitedness." But when the imagination is applied to the actual event of resurrection or the state of being of a resurrected human person like Jesus or ourselves, the imagination can turn against us. The imagination's connection with body and matter automatically draws the transcendent reality of the resurrection and the resurrected into the sphere of this world; the imagination transforms them into a mere projection of this world rather than a transformation of what is resurrected into a new *transcendent* form. At bottom, resurrection faith requires a symbolic imagination that does not literalize imaginative conceptions of it but allows them to stimulate the infinite openness of human hope.

How faith-hope affirms the resurrection. How then does this combined power of faith and hope affirm the resurrection, if the imagination will not cleanly or literally carry it forward? On what basis do Christians and perhaps others affirm the reality of the continuation of human being within God despite the projective character of imaginative descriptions? The answer to this question can only be drawn from the Easter experience itself and its constitutive elements. These elements merge to form the existential dynamics of revelation that are stimulated by scripture. The ultimate logic rests on the conviction that what Jesus communicated of God by the words and the actions that constituted his person is true. God is as Jesus reveals God to be and makes present by his symbolic or sacramental representation. Being in contact with God in and through Jesus is salvation now and in the future. One so encounters God, the creator of heaven and earth, in Jesus' representation that Jesus in turn constitutes the promise of God of an absolute future. In the liturgical tradition this basic faith-hope is celebrated by saying that God is the Alpha and the Omega of reality and thus human existence. God is the author and finisher of life.

A Theory of Salvation for Our Time

Paul, we saw, did not exaggerate the significance of Jesus' resurrection for Christian faith: there is a correlation between Jesus' real resurrection, that of others, and the resurrection of each one (1 Cor 15:12-17). That view can be nuanced in different directions, but the Easter experience was the turning point that provided the transcendent religious motivation behind the Jesus movement. The Easter experience generated the message that Jesus is risen, and this message reverberated through the disciples of Jesus and shaped them into a movement. On this premise the focus now falls on the relevance of the resurrection for Jesus and humankind.

The significance of the resurrection for Jesus. The resurrection was Jesus' vindication. His ministry seemed to end in failure; his execution as a criminal negated for many the ideas of Jesus being Messiah that existed prior to it.[17] The religious experience that he lived on in God's power, expressed in the straightforward language of "He is risen," changed everything. Now the Jesus affair and the whole scenario that made up his story had to be reexamined and reinterpreted. Everything was turned upside down again and righted.

The resurrection of Jesus meant that Jesus had a special relationship with God. In the course of the first century that relationship would be described in many different ways: the origin and the development of what we call christology formally began with the Easter experience and is based on the affirmation of Jesus' resurrection. Tracing

---

17. All do not accept this view. Gerhard Lohfink imagines Jesus appropriating to himself the role of the suffering servant in Isaiah. "Jesus listened to the fourth Servant Song among all the many voices and used it to interpret the true role of God and his own life" (*Jesus of Nazareth* [Collegeville, MN: Liturgical Press, 2012], 187; see also 174). Daniel Boyarin too builds a case for Jesus' messianic consciousness around Jesus' internalization of the Book of Daniel's image of a divine Son of Man coming to restore Israel (Dan 7:13-14). Jesus also linked this self-understanding with an appropriation of Isaiah's suffering servant. He writes, "we find a Jesus who sees himself, imagines himself, and presents himself as entirely fulfilling the messianic expectation already in place to the effect that the 'Son of Man must suffer many things'" (*The Jewish Gospels: The Story of the Jewish Christ* [New York: New Press, 2012], 142). Both authors resist the idea that the events of Jesus' death gave rise to these later interpretations.

this development as best one can through the writings of the New Testament shows the probing, searching character of these first efforts at christology. The process demonstrates how this deep conviction of spirituality can generate many different "explanations" of Jesus' person and what he did. But the important thing appears in looking at this effort in the other direction: all these christologies offer testimonies to belief in the resurrection of Jesus and to the Easter experience that generated it. All of them express the sense of being saved by God through Jesus.

The resurrection thus reveals the character of God. God is the God of life and not death, as Jon Sobrino writes so eloquently.[18] In the face of our world and all the evidence it provides that death has the upper hand, the resurrection asserts in the clearest possible way that God saves. It will be shown further on that his suffering could not be construed as salvific apart from Jesus' resurrection. Here the logic is analogous: the power of the saving love of God appears in the contrast between Jesus' resurrection and the kind of death he endured. All other aspects of Christian faith yield in importance to this central appreciation of God: God is the guarantor of meaning and life that overcomes even death itself.

The significance of the resurrection for all. The distinction between the significance of Jesus' resurrection for him and for us is thin at best, but it provides a way of organizing the discussion. Here attention turns to the various ways in which Jesus' resurrection impacts the lives of all who embrace him, first in objective terms and then in the existential ways it comes to bear on the Christian life.

Jesus offers a response to the religious question, and the resurrection ratifies that response. The religious question, recall, asks most fundamentally about the reason for existence: existence itself and mine in the middle of it. Jesus responds to that question with the characteristics of the rule of God and his service to them, and the resurrection adds to the formula that all of this will be saved from the jaws of death and extinction. Meaning, value, and finally life emerge out of the universal pattern of death.

This resurrection is what makes Jesus the Second or Final Adam. Paul saw him as the new prototype of the human because in him life is lived through the full cycle of the worst possible death of an innocent and dehumanizing execution. The vindication of that life bathes all

---

18. For example, Jon Sobrino, *Where Is God? Earthquakes, Terrorism, Barbarity, and Hope* (Maryknoll, NY: Orbis Books, 2004), 126-37.

human existence in the light of hope. Paraphrasing an ancient Christian Creed, for us and for our salvation Jesus is the New Adam.

As the Second Adam, Jesus provides a broad model for understanding who God is and what human existence will become by God's power. Salvation here responds to the equally secular and spiritual question of the nature of ultimate reality and human existence in relation to it. Jesus mediates salvation by revealing God. In so doing he also represents an understanding of human existence in relation to God. Anyone can enter into this pattern of understanding, discover the meaning and destiny of their lives, and live according to these convictions.[19]

The pluralism of views of salvation. The sheer fact that there are so many different views of what Jesus did for human salvation and of his person in the New Testament raises the question of how Christians should think about these issues today. The question is complicated because the solution cannot simply reside in choosing one from the many; all of them are expressed with cultural presuppositions in a language so distant from our own that they raise more questions than they answer. So this section analyzes the structure beneath the many images of salvation found in the New Testament and on this basis proposes guidelines for formulating ideas of salvation for our time. All of this relates back to Jesus' active ministry and his suffering and death.

We return to the story of how the various metaphors of salvation that appear in the New Testament were generated. The followers of Jesus encountered God's salvation in him: in the history of his life and ministry, through suffering and death, into resurrection. According to what has been said, this was an extended experience that developed over time. Whatever the disciples might have felt and thought about Jesus during his ministry was tested by his arrest and execution. Only in the light of an Easter experience and the new revealed conviction that Jesus was raised was the Jesus movement able to say that they were saved in and through Jesus Christ. The experience of salvation, then, was itself a product of a narrative, the ongoing experience of Jesus across the time of his ministry, his passion and death, and the new recognition of Jesus present to the community in the Spirit.

Different communities within the Jesus movement expressed their experience of God's salvation in Jesus in a variety of ways. The New Testament contains a pluralism of views of salvation that are irreducible to a single conception or theory. Some idea of the range of these

---

19. This is asserted affirmatively from within Christian faith itself and neither exclusively nor competitively in relation to other religions. That topic will be addressed in its proper place.

conceptions impresses the point. Edward Schillebeeckx carefully analyzed the books of the New Testament and reported on the various
conceptions of salvation that Jesus effected for humankind. Through
Jesus, God adopts human beings as sons and daughters, makes
humans children of God, gives them new birth, makes them into a
new creation. God gives the gift of God's Spirit. Human beings who
encounter Jesus receive new spiritual insight through the Spirit. By
following Jesus they are formed in his image. People gain access to
God in the kingdom of God. How did Jesus accomplish this? He saves
or renders people whole; he redeems people. Humans are freed from
slavery to sin. They are bought back, purchased and paid for by a ran-
som. From a state of alienation from God and other persons, people
are reconciled. Redemption is described as an act of making satisfac-
tion and establishing peace in relation to God. Sins are expiated by a
sin-offering, so that redemption is the forgiveness of sin. It renders
persons just or righteous before God and opens up the possibility of
sanctification. Jesus thus appears as a mediator before God, offering
humans a form of legal aid. Human freedom is bought and paid for so
that people can live in community, love their brothers and sisters, enjoy
a freedom liberated from self-indulgence, and be renewed so that they
in turn can renew the world. Salvation is life in all its fullness, a form
of victory over sinful, dehumanizing, and demonic powers.[20]

The structure of this pluralism, however, bears significance. Pluralism here does not refer to sheer plurality and difference but to a
real unity across a real diversity. Where does the unity lie? The sameness of these salvation theories does not reside in any single one but
in a common Christian experience that can only be described in formal terms: all Christians encounter God's salvation in the person and
teaching of Jesus of Nazareth. And behind that lies the Easter confidence that Jesus is alive with God. This focus of attention on Jesus as
the medium of God's salvation, even when it is construed differently,
constitutes the unity of the Christian experience of salvation across
its differences. Jesus mediates a response to the elementary spiritual
question of meaning. All Christian salvation theories relate back to
this existential being in relation to God through Jesus. Salvation theories in effect "explain" or describe or extrapolate from this experience.

This pluralism, the structure of unity within real diversity, provides a key for developing salvation theories for our time. The pluralism across the writings of the New Testament, the major normative
document for Christian faith, authorizes a pluralism of salvation the-

---

20. Edward Schillebeeckx, *Christ: The Experience of Jesus as Lord* (New York: Seabury
Press, 1980), 468-511.

ories in our time and for the same reasons as they appeared in the New Testament. Each community has to find a language and a set of symbols and concepts that will make salvation meaningful for itself and its historical situation. One can recognize, on a formal level, a certain correspondence between Christians finding God's salvation in their own lives by their encounter with Jesus as he is mediated to them by scripture and the community of faith and the same dynamic movement among the early disciples of Jesus during the course of the first century. This calls for the Christian communities of today to develop salvation theories that fit their cultures the way New Testament theories fit the various communities implicitly represented there. This is to be done by a dialogue with the variety of New Testament soteriologies.

A view of salvation for our time. It seems a bit ambitious to claim to set up a view of salvation for our time when the communities of Christians across the world today display such a profound and unwieldy pluralism. These deep differences among peoples can never be taken lightly; they are considered by many to be unbridgeable. To discuss unity or sameness across cultures, languages, and experiences, then, can be accomplished only in formal and somewhat abstract and analogous terms. Pluralism is never overcome by a single language; but commonalities can be appreciated existentially across differences with the help of language.

Description of a formal structure for understanding salvation today might readily begin with a principle from Irenaeus. The center of gravity of Irenaeus's views on salvation was located within a bigger idea of the incarnation of the Word of God. It included a reflection that has bearing on Jesus' suffering and death. Irenaeus's view combined themes from John's incarnational thinking and Paul's Second Adam: Jesus summed up in himself an integral human life and lived it faithfully to the full, thus restoring it from its fallen condition.[21] A major

---

21. Irenaeus displays his Second Adam thinking this way: "the Word of the Father and the Spirit of God, having become united with the ancient substance of Adam's formation, rendered man living and perfect, receptive of the perfect Father, in order that as in the natural [Adam] we all were dead, so in the spiritual [Adam] we may all be made alive" (Irenaeus, *Against Heresies* 5.1.3, in *The Ante-Nicene Fathers*, vol. 1, *The Apostolic Fathers, Justin Martyr, Irenaeus*, ed. Alexander Roberts and James Donaldson [Grand Rapids: Eerdmans, 1953], 527). The idea of recapitulation, flowing from incarnation, is that the Word of God sanctifies all the stages of life by assuming them all has his own. The creative Word "put Himself in our position and sanctified birth and death and showed forth resurrection" (Irenaeus, *Proof of the Apostolic Preaching*, trans. and annotated by Joseph P. Smith, Ancient Christian Writers 16 [Westminster, MD: Newman Press, 1952], § 38, pp. 70-71).

principle entailed in this incarnational scheme states that the "saved" is that which was assumed by the incarnate Word and lived out.[22] The consistency of this theory led Irenaeus to believe that Jesus was relatively old when he went to his death. If he did not live through old age, old age would not have been sanctified or redeemed. Irenaeus's overall conception need not be accepted on his terms, but it can be used as a suggestive framework for helping to understand how Jesus, even in his suffering and death, but surely not exclusively there, can be appropriated today as salvific.

Human beings experience suffering and death today as a given. The evolutionary story of the rise of life and then the human species shows the interconnectedness of all nature and all life. Violence and suffering are written into the being and maintenance of whole species. On the grand scale, nature itself seems to be a coordinated system of competition and mutual destruction in a process that offers survival by replacement. It may be that the larger design of the whole, which cannot be discerned by science, appeals to the human species to overcome this inbuilt tendency and establish more peaceful relationships within itself and among the species. But the idea of Genesis that this condition of the human is due to a fall from a perfect peaceful condition can only refer to a utopian ideal because it does not correspond to our history. Suffering and death are written into life as we know it and as it has always been.

To recognize suffering and death as an intrinsic part of life does not render life intelligible. Only the narrowest view could overlook the natural resistance to suffering and death. The whole dynamism of organic life strives for existence and more and more freedom from that which would bind it, control and suffocate its expansiveness, injure it, and ultimately kill it. In the dynamics between action and passion, what is done and what is suffered, the two components do not have equal status. The forces that augment and help life to flourish and those that diminish and finally extinguish it do not share the same ontological value. Each individual unit of life recognizes the difference in his or her own case. One form of energy is positive and the other negative. Against the background of the impetus of life itself, the forces of diminishment and death are at best mysterious if not unintelligible.

The negativity that threatens existence itself raises the question of the meaningfulness of existence. There is a form of negativity that

---

22. The principle was usually employed negatively as a criterion for salvation and thus stated negatively: what was not assumed was not redeemed. This principle was entailed in Irenaeus's incarnational paradigm, which was inspired by Colossians and Ephesians.

dialectically spurs development and growth; it does not diminish life or existence in its being but provides a catalyst for larger and fuller forms of being. But that which kills in a consistent and pervasive way undermines the possibility that being holds any ultimate worth and hence ultimate meaning. That which is intrinsically ordered for death and nonexistence can have only immediate, superficial, and transitory meaning. The phenomenon of extinction leads to the conclusion that *ultimately* being is not worthwhile. Moreover, specifically for our modern period, that which is most directly attacked by suffering and death is the creativity of human freedom. The power of freedom to imagine and then create new things of value defines human distinctiveness. By contrast, death flatly undermines the value of being in any ultimate sense, for the person creating and for what they create.

Jesus suffered torture and a violent death inflicted upon him in his innocence. His death was a direct threat to the meaningfulness of his ministry, his life, and his existence. In his passion and death Jesus also most fully recapitulates the negativities that infect the common life of the greatest number of human beings. This is not a slur on the huge amounts of time in which human beings enjoy life and should be grateful for it. It is simply to recall that the inevitability and finality of physical death, not to mention the forms of protracted suffering and living death endured by so many, do call even that joy into question. By Irenaeus's reasoning, Jesus lived his actual human life to the fullest because his own life included innocent suffering and the kind of death that is endured by so many and that, upon reflection, can dramatically call the meaningfulness of being itself into question.

Where in this scenario can one find a redemptive value in the innocent suffering and death of Jesus? Much of the traditional concepts and language that define the redemptive meaning of Jesus' death employ mythological language. That is, they leave history behind with a narrative that unfolds in a world other than our own. In several instances they fail because they predicate value to murderous human acts, suffering, and death itself. Any salvation theory that makes involuntary innocent suffering a good distorts reality and contradicts the message of Jesus about the character of God. There is no salvific negativity: Jesus' suffering and death in themselves are negative passivities, and as such they contain no redemptive value. They represent temptation to despair and need salvation.

We have seen, in our rapid glance at the New Testament and its various soteriologies, that they are all applied to Jesus in the light of the resurrection. The final meaning of Jesus' death is not and cannot be generated by his torture and execution. In these events Jesus is precisely a victim; he has been rendered physically passive; suffering and death are inflicted on him. The only saving act that he can perform in this situation is to trust in God and be faithful to his original vision of the rule of God. Salvation in the end must come from an outside power: he must be raised by God from death; God saves. Within the process of crucifixion, the saving action of Jesus lies in his trust in God. It exists as hope. There can be no theory of salvation based solely on the passion and death of Jesus because these are not good but evil.

It should be clear that this way of dealing with the salvation from God mediated by Jesus by focusing first on the suffering and death of Jesus and then on his resurrection is intrinsically unsatisfying. It separates two dimensions that must be held together. Nevertheless, this way of dealing with salvation has been forced upon us by the tradition. It has the merit of following the story of Jesus as it unfolded and the story of the disciples who lived through this major crisis in their commitment to following him. But the soteriologies of the New Testament show that there can be no ultimate salvation apart from resurrection. The consideration of the passion and death of Jesus in isolation, so to speak, underlines the conviction that his innocent suffering can never be recognized as a good. It cannot be held up as something to be emulated but only as something to be passionately resisted.

In the end, the story of Jesus reveals that salvation consists in the one activity of God, a power that manifests itself in three "times": in the beginning, as the grounding creative power of being itself; in the present, as the power of Spirit that embraces the human person and enables freedom to transcend the self and attend to values outside the self and for the community; and in the absolute future, as the omega point in whom all things will be made whole.

CHAPTER EIGHT

Mission, Spirit, and the Church

With the death and resurrection of Jesus, the historical drama of communicating the rule of God shifted from Jesus to his disciples. These disciples gradually formed a movement that evolved through stages into an embryonic, a fledgling, an early primitive, and gradually a more or less organized church.[1] This was a historical and not a programmed organic development. We have very little exact knowledge about what the Jesus movement looked like during the first two decades after Jesus' death and resurrection. Luke's account in the Acts of the Apostles views things from his later perspective. He writes within a theological framework, and he interpolates stories and speeches into his narrative. For example, in Luke's narrative the church began in Jerusalem. Although there certainly were followers of Jesus in Jerusalem, it is difficult to imagine that other groups of followers of Jesus did not arise in Galilee where his ministry flourished from the start. But little direct evidence confirms this. As a result, much of the reconstruction of the earliest Jesus movement is inferential and hypothetical.

The church in the sense of an autonomous religious organization independent of Judaism did not appear at the same time in all the places to which the Jesus movement had spread.[2] The gradual growth, however, shows that the institutional structure may not be regarded as an addendum to Christianity and Christian self-understanding.

---

1. Some scholars distinguish an earliest movement of the rule of God that evolved into a Jesus movement.

2. Daniel Boyarin insists that the idea of Christianity as an autonomous religion distinct from Judaism did not really materialize until the fourth century. During the Constantinian and post-Constantinian periods, religious boundaries became more important. Before that time the interrelationships between being Christian and being Jewish were much more fluid. While the internal process of institutionalization began with the formation of the Jesus movement itself, the process of erecting external boundaries took centuries. See Daniel Boyarin, *Border Lines: The Partition of Judaeo-Christianity*, Divinations (Philadelphia: University of Pennsylvania Press, 2004). This chapter focuses less on external relationships and more on the way institutional structures grew out of the nascent community's corporate spiritual life.

Offices of ministry cannot be reduced to an expendable or negligible exterior form that is separable from an essential inner faith animating the movement. The slow development of an institutional identity grew from inside the movement of faith. Institution provides the historical mechanism of the communication of Jesus and his mediation of God to the world through successive generations. Understanding Jesus Christ and his message as universally relevant for humankind requires a church that makes this possible. The same divine intentionality that is communicated with faith in Jesus Christ logically includes extension to the church as its vehicle for ongoing dialogue with history. When Alfred Loisy wrote that "Jesus foretold the kingdom, and it was the Church that came," he was not writing ironically.[3] He had a strong sense of development and social formation; he recognized that to survive in history the message of the rule of God needed a historical organ. In short, the development of the church represents an essential element of Christian faith, and the spirituality of following Jesus develops spontaneously into an ecclesial spirituality.

Developments in the world over the past two centuries have created a situation in which long-accepted conceptions about the church are severely tested. At the risk of oversimplifying an obviously complex and regionally differentiated situation, two problems have to be underlined because of their far-reaching implications: the voluntary character of church membership and the fragmented nature of church organization.

For most of the church's existence, its self-understanding included the idea that membership in the church was in one way or another necessary for final salvation. This idea created a number of accompanying problems, such as how to understand the destinies of so many that have never belonged to the church, and these found various theological responses. But through the sixteenth century and deep into the modern period, it was generally believed by Christians that all human beings should belong to the church. During the great missionary expansion in the course of the nineteenth and twentieth centuries, the implicit presuppositions for understanding the church that lay behind the missionary movement were gradually being abandoned by many educated Christians. Several factors were at work here: a recognition of religion's close association with culture, the social-ethical requirement of the freedom of religion from all coercion, a positive appreciation of other religions and dialogue with them, and a conviction that the Christian church is essentially a voluntary organization to which

---

3. Alfred Loisy, *The Gospel and the Church* (1903; Philadelphia: Fortress Press, 1976), 66.

some but not all will belong, even in predominately Christian societies. Given this culture, the very idea of the mission of the church as it was previously understood is now called into question, and the approach to understanding the church becomes apologetic rather than simply didactic. The church now needs to explain itself; ecclesial spirituality cannot presuppose membership in the church but must make the case for it. This in turn calls for a reorientation of the method of the discipline of ecclesiology and the larger imaginative framework within which Christians locate the church.

The second issue, the historical fragmentation of the Christian churches, also sends deep shock waves through ecclesial spirituality. Western Christians and the churches around the world that have been evangelized by the mainline Christian churches of Europe and North America have grown accustomed to the divisions of the church into denominations. In western Europe, which was more or less under the umbrella of one medieval church, the sixteenth century seemed to divide the church into many churches. But those divisions seem slight compared with the fragmentation of the whole church into particular churches that began with the missionary movements of the nineteenth century and have been continued by Evangelical, Pentecostal, and independent churches through the twentieth. This has occurred under the positive imperative for inculturation. But it threatens a loss of Christian identity within the church itself, because the idea of "church" is becoming a generic term for mutually unrecognizable churches more or less loosely related to Jesus of Nazareth. The opposite trend of an unmovable Eurocentric church provides no viable alternative in a pluralistic world culture. This situation demands an approach to ecclesial spirituality that will describe an essential core of a common, unifying ecclesial existence that simultaneously allows cultural differentiation in church self-understanding and organization. Ecclesiology must reflect the spirituality that holds all Christians together and at the same time must celebrate cultural differences.

Such an ecclesiology cannot be developed in a few pages. But this chapter does propose some fundamental elements of an ecclesial spirituality that addresses those issues from a historical developmental perspective. It will not deal with church organization, even though this is crucial for interchurch ecclesiological conversation. Rather, the discussion turns to four essential elements of the spirituality that sustains the church and that can elicit a common commitment from Christians. The first has to do with the relation of the church to Jesus of Nazareth and how the idea of "mission" binds the two together as one. The second turns to the idea of "the Spirit of God," which has always been closely associated with the church. This rudimentary outline of pneumatology, aligned as it is with the church, reflects the trinitarian character of Christian language about God's relationship with human beings. The third idea draws out the relation between a sense of mission and the nature of the church. Although this will not be sufficiently expanded, this relationship contains premises for a more adequate understanding of church organization. Finally, the chapter explicitly takes up the topic of ecclesial spirituality, something that could help bind the churches together in a way that preserves particular traditions.

Before entering into the discussion of the sense of mission contained in the disciples' Easter experience, it is important that one appreciate the logic driving this consideration of church. This chapter does not aim at resolving current problems in ecclesiology. But the way one understands the historical origins of the church, at least in principle, will shape the suppositions of the way they are addressed. This analysis could be called pre-ecclesiological. The idea is to examine the historical development that led from Jesus' ministry to the formation of a church. The carrier of that development was the people who had an experience that Jesus was alive and shared it with others. The engine of tradition is always human action, the lived life of individuals who form groups that support their members and communicate with others and to later generations. But this idea correlates very closely with the notion of spirituality that is operative in this book: the way persons and groups live their lives before transcendence. The church grew within the historical development of the spirituality renewed or generated by the Easter experience. The story of the emergent church is the story of how a Jesus spirituality gradually developed into an ecclesial spirituality, that is, a Jesus spirituality in community with an institutional structure. At this stage in the discussion, a spirituality of following Jesus is in search of an ecclesial spirituality.

Resurrection and Mission

The last chapter outlined the idea of Jesus' resurrection and its central place in Christian religious experience. The discussion that follows integrates the theme of "mission" into the primal Christian experience that Jesus is risen in order to show how it governs the formation and rationale of the church. This effort includes an analysis that explains how Jesus' resurrection includes the idea of a mission of God. This can be shown by reflection on the appearance stories and, guided by them, an imaginative reconstruction of the Easter experience of the original disciples. Even though Jesus may have sent his disciples out to do what he did prior to his death, so that mission can be traced back to the ministry of Jesus, it became a dynamic idea uniting a group of disciples after the resurrection of Jesus was internalized. It might be better to say that a sense of mission was part of the Easter experience itself.

The meaning of mission revolves around the ideas of sending and being sent. One way of determining the meaning of mission in the New Testament is to study the words and the various nuances of the meaning in each context. This is especially relevant to the "apostles" who were more or less official representatives of the group of original witnesses to the events of the whole Jesus affair.[4] The New Testament and other writings provide witness to such roles and to the fact that they were more or less defined, but these roles may have been more loosely circumscribed than has been imagined. For example, the New Testament refers to twelve apostles. But there were more than twelve apostles, and all of the twelve were not apostles in the sense of giving witness beyond Jerusalem or Israel. Examination of the office of apostle falls far short of explaining the sense of mission so essential to the formation of the church.

Another more promising approach to mission lies in a phenomenological effort to project what the disciples of Jesus might have experienced relative to Jesus' public ministry and their participation in it. The "rule of God" formed the centerpiece of Jesus' teaching and action. Although it is hard to be precise and adequately represent the content of "the rule of God" as Jesus mediated it, one can formally circumscribe this symbol as containing God's values and general intention for human existence in the world. Jesus assumed the roles of prophet, teacher, and exorcist, and he communicated God's rule to the lives of those with whom he came in contact. The Gospel stories of Jesus bear ample witness to the idea that Jesus imagined himself being sent by God to be an agent of God's rule becoming effective in the world. The rule of God has a dynamic, eventful character that is felt in history, so that "the kingdom of God is primarily and above all on earth."[5]

Because Jesus operated out of a sense of calling and being sent by God, it was natural for the disciples of Jesus during his public ministry to experience a sense of sharing in this mission. This idea gets formalized in the Synoptic Gospels when Jesus is portrayed as sending the twelve on a mission essentially modeled on his own. "And he called to him the twelve, and began to send them out two by two, and gave them authority over the unclean spirits" (Mark 6:7; also Mark 3:14-15).[6]

---

4. This approach sometimes slides into a juridical mentality that stresses institutional roles in what is presented as a bureaucratic arrangement.

5. Gerhard Lohfink, *Jesus of Nazareth: Who Was He? What Did He Do?* (Collegeville, MN: Liturgical Press, 2012), 25.

6. Virtually the same story has Jesus sending seventy or seventy-two disciples

Jon Sobrino makes a strong historical case that these sendings of the disciples on mission provide the deepest foundations for an emergent church.[7] But even apart from such actual sendings, whether they were historical or not, one has to imagine that the disciples of Jesus shared a sense of his "mission," his urgent sense of calling to follow the imperative of witnessing to the values of God's rule to Israel. In other words, a sense of mission lies at the essential core of the appearance of Jesus, his ministry, and the religious appreciation of him, so that from the beginning "mission" represents an essential element of what will become church.

This elemental insight bears revolutionary potential for some standard self-conceptions of established churches. In theological terms, this insight may be called the priority of the mission to the identity of the church. Mission is the reason for the being of the church. Sobrino writes that "the church's reality lies not in itself but in a mission it is to accomplish."[8] Jürgen Moltmann states that it "is not that the church 'has' a mission, but the very reverse: that the mission of Christ creates its own church. Mission does not come from the church; it is from mission and in the light of mission that the church has to be understood."[9] Theologians aware of the sociological payoff of this theological conception point out how all organizations preserve a healthy tension between the logic of mission and the logic of maintenance. Maintenance attends to the organization's well-being; mission is the goal of maintenance.[10] But the priorities have to be kept straight and the balance retained. Missionary activity of inserting the gospel into the world defines the very purpose of the church. When a church gets settled into culture, it tends to invest more energy in maintenance than mission. This may explain why today, for example, in some places mainline churches are losing their members and Evangelical and Pentecostal churches are surging.

---

out on the same kind of mission. This should be noticed to prevent any hierarchical cooption of responsibility for the mission. See Luke 10:1-16.

7. Jon Sobrino, "Evangelization as Mission of the Church," in his *The True Church and the Poor* (Maryknoll, NY: Orbis Books, 1984), 253-301, esp. 257-65.

8. Sobrino, "Evangelization as Mission," 264. He states further that "the church does not keep itself in existence through history by maintaining its structures but by constantly carrying out its mission" (p. 265).

9. Jürgen Moltmann, *The Church in the Power of the Spirit: A Contribution to Messianic Ecclesiology* (New York: Harper & Row, 1977), 10.

10. "The logic of mission deals with the aim and function of an organization, the purpose for the sake of which it has been established; the logic of maintenance deals with the well-being of the organization itself, its upkeep, security, and perpetuation in the years to come. Both of these logics are essential." Gregory Baum, "Contradictions in the Catholic Church," in his *Theology and Society* (New York and Mahwah, NJ: Paulist Press, 1987), 234.

The driving force on the level of history behind the formation and deep structure of the church lies in Jesus' ministry. Essentially, Jesus' ministry elicited a call to discipleship, so that the response of becoming a follower consists in assuming partnership in his mission. Recall the story of the young man with some wealth who was asked to follow Jesus, but he could not because he was weighed down by possessions and could not quite break free (Matt 19:16-22). The logic is firm: becoming a disciple of Jesus means entering into Jesus' mission and assuming it as one's own. This role has to be played out according to the capacity of each individual, but the fundamental form and dynamics of being a follower entails an embrace of the mission that Jesus represented in his life and ministry. The idea of a mission is no corollary of following Jesus, and mission spirituality does not appear as the conclusion of an inference from Christian belief. Mission spirituality describes the fundamental logic of being followers of Jesus in the first place. "And Jesus said to them, 'follow me'" (Mark 1:17).

The last chapter described how hopes in Jesus' mission were crushed by his criminal execution, but that sometime afterwards in the light of an Easter experience Jesus' disciples were announcing that God had raised him. This new faith-hope was part of the formation of the Jesus movement. It is not surprising that the theme of mission reasserts itself as an essential dimension of this new experience. The theme of mission surrounds the appearance stories. The appearances of Jesus do not merely show that he is alive; they are calling and mission narratives, sometimes implicitly, at other times in direct terms: "Peace be with you. As the Father has sent me, even so I send you" (John 20:21). The climax comes in Matthew's account of Jesus' final appearance and his delivery of the mission mandate: "Go therefore and make disciples of all nations . . ." (Matt 28:18-20).

The symbol "mission" represents a deep structure of what is going on in these narratives and in the history that they characterize. At the epistemological level, the symbol of mission represents the idea that what the disciples experienced as resurrection was also a call of God to something of divine import: the mission of the rule of God in history as revealed by Jesus. It would not be wrong to describe the Easter experience itself as including a recognition that Jesus' mission goes on and a call to join it. Although this is not to be understood in narrow and exclusive terms, it describes what is going on. It also correlates with an objective meta-conception of God's being a dynamic creative presence to human history. God as Spirit permeates history, and this has come to the surface in Jesus of Nazareth and the rule of God he represented. The mission of God in history incarnated by Jesus will go forward, and the stable actualization of that mission provides the reason for the becoming and thus the being of the church.

This dynamism finds its best expression in the two-volume work of Luke, his Gospel and the Acts of the Apostles. In Luke, the theology of the Spirit, God as the dynamic principle of the mission, links the two-volume work about Jesus and the emergent church. Luke's Jesus promises the Spirit; the disciples become the Jesus movement; the Spirit animates the movement. Even though the narrative details provided by Acts of how that post-resurrection mission got under way may be called into question, these details do not impugn the deeper construct: God as Spirit and Jesus now risen are the divine impulse of an expanding force of witness that we describe as mission. The symbol of mission represents a spirituality that envelops the whole Jesus movement, and that spirituality was the power that moved it toward becoming a church.

The Spirit of God

Before turning to the way the experience of being "missioned" by God to carry forward Jesus' ministry of the rule of God developed, we need briefly to explore the symbol of the "Spirit of God." Christians use trinitarian language about God because God has been encountered as creator, savior in Jesus, and sanctifier of life within the church. Although references to the Spirit of God fill the pages of the whole Bible, the Spirit has a special reference for Christians to the generation and continuing life of the church. It is essential, therefore, that some reflection be devoted to the Holy Spirit of God.

The "Spirit of God" refers to God and not to anything other than God. But it points especially to God's presence and power manifested in the world. One way to close in on the meaning of the symbol the "Spirit of God" considers the various usages of the term and then isolates its distinctive meanings and their connotations. Another way, closely aligned with the first, attends to the kinds of experience that elicit an appeal or reference to the Spirit of God. These two approaches complement each other. For example, the Spirit of God refers to God's presence, power, energy, and actualizing stimulus of events. Thus, a narrative account of God creating the world at the beginning of Genesis says that the Spirit of God, symbolizing God's creative power and action, hovered over the abyss and gave it shape or form (Gen 1:1-2). The Spirit of God bestowed order upon what was previously void and without form. From the side of experience, a contemplation of nature such as one finds in Psalm 104 testifies to someone dazzled by the harmonious interconnectedness of natural phenomena and the recurrent patterns of nature and society. The Spirit of God is a response to the question of the source or principle that accounts for the dynamism and integrity of nature. The Spirit of God signifies the power within things that has God as its source. The Spirit of God is the very ground of existence and the source of flourishing life.

The Spirit of God also accounts for events in persons that exceed the normal course of things. The judges, that is, the charismatic leaders of Israel before King David, were inspired and empowered by the Spirit of God. For example, "the spirit of God came mightily upon Saul" (1 Sam 11:26). God's power or Spirit works within the world through agents. Prophets who speak the Word of God act as people empowered to be God's surrogates on particular occasions. When the prophet addressed those in captivity, he said, "The Spirit of the Lord God is upon me, because the Lord has appointed me to bring good tidings to the afflicted" (Isa 61:1). The idea that God acts in history does not mean that God assumes the role of a finite being. The Spirit of God acts in and through the vehicles of nature and especially human beings.

Christians who relate to God through the mediator Jesus Christ see a special relationship between the Spirit of God and Jesus of Nazareth. Jürgen Moltmann states it dramatically when he writes that the story of Jesus Christ begins with the Holy Spirit.[11] The Spirit of God was prior to and involved in the very conception of Jesus of Nazareth. This idea should not give rise to attempts to explain this over against naturalist principles: that would completely miss the point, because God is not a finite entity or cause. God is God, and in a transcendent way, beneath, behind, or within the historical events. The sustaining and enabling power of the Spirit of the creating God operates in a way that cannot be imagined in itself; it appears only in its effects. The Gospel stories of Jesus' ministry consistently bear witness to the power of God as Spirit authorizing his ministry or empowering his exorcisms. Jesus' ministry went forward sustained by the energy of God as Spirit. When Christians affirm the divinity of Jesus of Nazareth, the most exhaustive and comprehensible way of understanding this in the language of the Gospels appears as a "Spirit christology." In Luke's two-volume work on Jesus and the Jesus movement after his death and resurrection, the Spirit of God plays a central role. After Jesus is gone, he "sends" the Spirit of God as the empowering force that enables the movement to go on. If the Spirit of God sometimes appears as the Spirit of Jesus, it is because Jesus' ministry became the criterion for the Jesus movement to dis-

---

11. "Jesus' history as the Christ does not begin with Jesus himself. It begins with the *ruach*/the Holy Spirit." Jürgen Moltmann, *The Way of Jesus Christ: Christology in Messianic Dimensions* (Minneapolis: Fortress Press, 1993), 73.

cern and judge the authentic Spirit of God from its counterfeits. In short, in the community of the followers of Jesus, the Spirit of God surrounds Jesus: before him, in him, driving his ministry, and after him, in the life of the groups of followers he left behind. Jesus cannot be separated from the Spirit of God.

Christians have always linked the Spirit of God with the church. This is due partly to the Lucan narrative of how Jesus promised the Spirit to his disciples, and the story of Pentecost where the grouped disciples were illumined by the Spirit, the church was born, and it began its journey through history. Within the framework of this story, the church becomes the place where the Spirit of God is poured out in a new way. Compared with a Johannine christology, as the "Word of God" became incarnate in Jesus, so too, analogously, the "Spirit of God" became the internal animating principle of the church. As the Jesus movement gradually grew distinct from Judaism in the early centuries, and as the church gained an autonomous institutional status, it became a community in which people could find the saving power of God's Spirit. In Cyprian's view, speaking intra-ecclesially around the year 250, it was not possible for baptism to confer salvation outside of the community that was held together by one authentic Spirit of God. This corresponded to the spirituality of those peacefully within the church. The church was the place where one could encounter God and God's salvation because it was animated, empowered, and held together by the Spirit of God.

Not infrequently theologians complain that the doctrine of God as Spirit is underdeveloped. The reason for this lies partly in the inclusion of the Spirit of God into a doctrine of trinity in the fourth century. Before that the Spirit of God was a topic of several debates: Who did and did not possess the Spirit? Who was able to confer or mediate the Spirit? Was the Spirit of God any less than true God? After the recognition that the Holy Spirit is truly divine, conversation focused on the relationship between the Father, the Son, and the Holy Spirit.

Going back to the primitive meanings of "the Spirit of God" and the experience of the Spirit as God's dynamic immanence and presence to the world, it appears that consideration of the Spirit as one "person" among the three "persons" of the trinity runs counter to the fundamental biblical character of God as Spirit. The symbol of "Spirit" communicates God acting, "outside" of God's self, always effecting something in the world. This traditional meaning of God as Spirit has been preserved in other theological topics, especially those revolving around the Christian life. Augustine presented and highlighted the dynamics of grace, the gift of God's interior help, which is needed for all true self-transcendence because of the curvature of the free human spirit back into itself in an internal bondage of sin. That *auxilium Dei*, that grace, is the Holy Spirit of God at work within a person. Luther too preserved the dynamic power of the Spirit of God that alone can explain a person's turning to accept by faith God's justification. Calvin had a lively doctrine of the Spirit as the illuminator of the mind that allows spiritual understanding and an internal agent that gradually sanctified people through their steadfast lives of faith. No one can live an authentic Christian life leading toward sanctification without the inner support of God as Spirit. Karl Rahner offered an inestimable gift to the Catholic Church when he relocated the emphasis of the term "grace" from its created effect in the human person to the active presence of God who causes that effect. Grace is not primarily a created habit in the spiritual core of a person; grace is primarily God's immediate presence to a person, that is, the Spirit of God.[12] Finally, in Pentecostal Christianity the doctrine of the Spirit retains its fully dynamic role in persons and communities. The doctrine of the Spirit, then, has not been lost to trinitarian speculation, but it needs an expansive recapitulation.

Potentialities for a new Christian self-understanding accompanied by an expanded theology of the Spirit of God are being opened up on two vital fronts at this time: interreligious dialogue and dialogue with science. As to religious pluralism, as a result of developments over the past few centuries, Western culture now allows and encourages Christians to view other religions not as competitors but as valid and viable options for relating to God. But because Jesus Christ still enjoys primacy of place in the Christian imagination as a revealer of God, the autonomous truth of other religions tends to be accounted for by the broad range of the working of the Spirit of God. The details of this conception are many, far from being worked out, and still farther from being universally accepted. But even this minimal statement of initial soundings shows a new viability and importance to the working of God as Spirit, one that will rearrange the furniture in the Christian household.

As to the impact of science on theology, a good way to situate what is going on would be to recall that as Christianity is accepted into new cultures, through a process of historical and cultural symbiosis, it gradually takes on many of the suppositions of the new host, even as it exercises a reciprocal influence on the culture. If the intellectual world of science be considered a culture, it would follow that the church must adjust to the language of science it if wishes to communicate to

12. John Randall Sachs, "'Do Not Stifle the Spirit': Karl Rahner, the Legacy of Vatican II, and Its Urgency for Theology Today," *Proceedings of the Catholic Theological Society of America* 51 (1996): 15-38.

the world that is shaped by it. One of the places where this adjustment is felt most deeply is the story of the evolutionary creation of the universe and of life on our planet. In the scientific story, creation is unfinished business, an open-ended process that has generated human beings and ever more complex interrelationships between peoples and the ecosystem. Where does God fit into this new story and picture of reality? Many theologians spontaneously turn to a theology of God as Spirit immanent within the world as its sustaining ground of being and the dynamism of its becoming. This yields a picture not of God up there watching the world evolve from a distance, but an immanent presence of a personal creative power that accompanies social and historical development. This picture too needs more refinement, but it promises a new importance to a recognition of God as Spirit.

To sum up this overly compact excursus on the Spirit of God, the story of the church is the ongoing narrative of the experience of the Spirit of God as Jesus manifested that Spirit in his ministry. The Spirit of God is that creative power of God that holds finite existence in being, the immanent power of a personal and loving God. On the one hand, the Spirit of God touches the consciousness of Christians as the attraction toward God in personal life and the sustaining power of corporate ecclesial spirituality. On the other hand, in a larger framework, God as Spirit opens up the imagination to God's immanent presence to all humans within their religions. On a grand scale, the Spirit is God's creating power that works in and sustains the finite causality that carries the universe forward in time. Where does the church fit into this big picture?

The Mission Generates a Church

The church is a product of historical development, and we need a narrative to explain it. This narrative will not be the short story of Jesus setting up a church all at once during his lifetime that seems to be implied by Matthew's Gospel (16:13-20). It is a long story that begins with Jesus and stretches well into the fourth century before ecumenical councils begin to consolidate things. One can say that development continues to the present day. A problem of perception on this point revolves around the tendency imaginatively to project back into Jesus' lifetime conclusions about historical events that are derived from later theological interpretations of Jesus as the Christ. The text of Matthew that has Jesus saying "you are Peter, and on this rock I will build my church" (Matt 16:18) offers a good example of this. Scripture scholars generally agree that Jesus did not think of beginning a church and that this text expresses a later theological view representing things that emerged much later. All of this invites a coherent account of the relation between history and an understanding of the church, as well as a reconstruction of how the church developed. The two issues go together, and the latter can illustrate the former.

A historically conscious way of understanding how the church emerged will notice a single defining element of a common faith that united the disciples and spawned their group identity. The spiritual aspect of this group identity is the experience of God's salvation in Jesus. It was shown earlier that God's salvation in Jesus was experienced in many different ways. In all of them Jesus had an impact on how people related to God. The historical aspect of where this would lead the group was subject to normal historical development. The movement or movements gradually grew into an autonomous institution distinct from Judaism. Its nature, as distinct from a more precise description of its identity, can be construed simultaneously from two perspectives. The church understands itself as existing in a double relationship: to history and to God. The relationship to history requires historical and sociological language. The relationship to God requires spiritual and ultimately theological language. Neither analysis alone satisfies; only the two together can give an adequate account.[13] A moment's reflection on Christian experience itself will confirm the two dimensions.

Reflection reveals how the two perspectives and corresponding methods of understanding interact with each other. The sense of mission that lay embedded in the Easter experience gave rise to the preaching and public witness of the disciples that Jesus is risen: it inspired an expansive preaching of Jesus and of the rule of God that drove his ministry. On the one hand, ministry could not continue forward without a group to sustain the effort, and it could not effect its passing to successive generations of disciples without some form of institution. In order to retain existence and identity across time, groups require institutionalization. On the other hand, this movement testified to the divine presence at work within itself as a movement mediated by Jesus of Nazareth, who gradually came to be recognized as the Messiah or Christ, and the Spirit of God as an internal empowering source of energy. The theological foundations of the church are Jesus Christ and the Spirit of God, and their recognition grew out of the mission spirituality spawned by the Easter experience. In this way the two modes of understanding the church mutually influence and complement each other; they are inseparable. But they are also distinct: one

---

13. Edward Schillebeeckx, *Church: The Human Story of God* (New York: Crossroad, 1990), 211-12.

cannot predicate a theological conclusion on the basis of empirical evidence alone; and theological conceptions cannot generate knowledge of empirical facts. Spirituality, the corporate lives of Christians, is the place where these two dimensions interact.

When we pass from questions of how to approach an understanding of the development of the church to its actual historical genesis, it becomes almost as difficult to give specific historical details of how the church actually developed as it is to reconstruct the actual ministry of Jesus. Luke's Acts gives the most detailed account of the earliest history of the Jesus movement developing toward church. But the narrative is heavily influenced by a theological message; Acts does not offer a modern historical account. And no single New Testament source describes the whole Christian movement. For these reasons the historical narrative of the early development of the church still remains murky in its detail.[14] But one can make several broad statements about this development that are enough to make sense of it in a way that has more spiritual power than the naïve picture of Jesus setting up a divinely sanctioned institution.

One way to offer an abbreviated statement of the complex picture of an emerging church would balance the standard picture with details that complexify it. Luke tells of a Pentecost experience that launched the movement in a supernatural way from Jerusalem. Yet that picture can be modified at two points. The scene can be read as a symbolic account of a common extended experience of the power of God as Spirit that accompanied the Easter experience. In other words, the "event" of the Spirit's initiating intervention was a protracted affair over a more or less extended period of time. And one might suppose that the Jesus movement also took off in Galilee where Jesus performed his ministry. When such a premise is factored in, the idea of a single grand narrative for the developing church originating in Jerusalem is replaced by a broader movement of many developing communities.

The first stages of the Jesus movement, from Jesus' death to the crisis in Antioch in 48-49 that had to be adjudicated by Jerusalem, resist reconstruction in any detail. The heavily theological character of Luke's witness does not substitute for firsthand sources. This leaves basic questions unanswered. Did the Jesus movement actually begin in Jerusalem or in Galilee or both places simultaneously? Did it understand itself as one movement in different places, or was it made up of distinct groups loosely related to one another? Was it completely embraced by temple

---

14. Hal Taussig provides an overview of the scholarship on the origins of Christianity over the past few decades ("The End of Christian Origins? Where to Turn at the Intersection of Subjectivity and Historical Craft," *Review of Biblical Literature* 11 [2011]: 1-45).

and synagogue, or did it also have independent cells? All will agree that there were itinerant missionaries, apostles, prophets, and teachers who circulated and spread the message of Jesus. And these were balanced by stable groups of householders who in some way maintained a common identity as followers of Jesus.[15] But how did they relate to their fellow Jews, and what exactly set them apart?

A common thread through these two decades is the common meal. It is present in the meals of disciples with Jesus during his ministry and their meal together before his death recounted in all four Gospels. It is present and highly developed theologically in Paul's First Letter to the Corinthians (1 Cor 10-11). Luke has a short description of the church in Jerusalem during this period: "And day by day, attending the temple together and breaking bread in their homes, they partook of food with glad and generous hearts" (Acts 2:46). Even if this picture represents a later period of the developing movement, it is difficult not to imagine that the common meal, and all that went on during it, was a major institutional factor in a developing identity.[16] But in this case and more generally, one cannot presume that the answer to these questions in one community applies to others. Communities had their own characteristics, and the responses to these questions would vary according to circumstances.

From the beginning, therefore, pluralism has to be factored into this process of development. This in turn implies unevenness in the timeline of the developmental process itself. It was not the same in every

---

15. Elisabeth Schüssler Fiorenza, *In Memory of Her: A Feminist Theological Reconstruction of Christian Origins* (New York: Crossroad, 1983), 160-204. John Dominic Crossan calls the two groups "itinerants" and "householders." The former represents a more radical commitment to the Jesus movement and the other a more sedate routinized internalization of this spirituality. See John Dominic Crossan, "Itinerants and Householders in the Earliest Kingdom Movement," in *Reimagining Christian Origins: A Colloquium Honoring Burton L. Mack*, ed. Elizabeth A. Castelli and Hal Taussig (Valley Forge, PA: Trinity Press International, 1996), 113-29. Schüssler Fiorenza shows that women were counted as leaders in both forms of spirituality or ways of being a follower of Jesus.

16. As Schüssler Fiorenza puts it, "the Christian house churches had the same unifying center: the communal banquet or meal which regularly gathered together all members of the group for table companionship. Eating and drinking together was the major integrative moment in the socially diversified Christian house community" (*In Memory of Her*, 198). One can imagine that the practice had its origins in earlier forms that recalled meals with Jesus and/or the Last Supper. Hal Taussig summarizes the research done on the Greco-Roman banquet over the past few decades and the relevance the meal had in the assemblies of associations within the empire at this time (*In the Beginning Was the Meal: Social Experimentation and Early Christian Identity* [Minneapolis: Fortress Press, 2009]). It provides a much more concrete way of historically imagining how groups of Jesus-followers organized themselves and developed socially in ways that preserved communion and still allowed participation in temple and synagogue.

case; it did not follow a common timetable. Thus, the significant event at Antioch, usually dated around 48 to 50 (Acts 15), in which the Jesus movement more or less "officially" opened up Christian membership to Gentiles while bypassing circumcision, had significant import for future development. But that influence was felt differently in different churches. For example, some new communities in the eastern Mediterranean may have been more Jewish in character, while others may have been more Greco-Roman, and still others mixed.[17] The effects of the policy would differ according to circumstances. We are also becoming more aware of how deeply Hellenistic influences were already at work in Palestine in Jesus' own time. Thus, while we can more or less distinguish strata of a developing church through dating and "placing" the writings of the New Testament, it is difficult to make generalizations about any single portrait of "the whole church" in the earliest years of its development. Perhaps the most important generalization of all that can be made is that the church was a product of history: the church was not born with a single stable organizational structure but developed several structures, which relied on the resources of each community and borrowed from contemporary models. In other words, the most important lesson about the church that can be learned from its development from Jesus' time to the early centuries of life in Greco-Roman culture is the fact of development itself.

Without pretending to define what these common features were in detail, one can get a sense of embryonic elements that will constitute all the churches by noticing five structural elements found in all organizations. First, the nature and purpose of the church revolved around Jesus as the Christ, the new sense of the Spirit of God that he released into history, and the salvation people experienced in their faith commitment to him. Second, the organizational plan of the churches drew from other associations or organizations of identity groups common in the empire. It would be strange if associations of the Jews in the Diaspora did not strongly affect emergent Christian groups. Third, the initial members of the Jesus movement were Jews, and across the early centuries Jews were the most prominent members of the church, even though the ratio between Jews and Gentiles in different regions and communities would vary considerably and evolve.[18] Fourth, the

---

17. Raymond E. Brown, "New Testament Background for the Concept of Local Church," *Proceedings of the Catholic Theological Society of America* 36 (1981): 1-14. Typologies of different churches can be constructed according to several different themes: cultural membership, representation by New Testament book, christology, organizational structure, and so on.

18. See Rodney Stark, *The Rise of Christianity: A Sociologist Reconsiders History* (Princeton, NJ: Princeton University Press, 1996).

principal activities of the communities were religious: gathering for common meals, to listen to the reading of scriptures, hear commentary on them, have common prayer, read letters from other communities, hear and recite stories about Jesus, and sing psalms or newly composed hymns. We are learning more about how the common meal and various adaptations of the Greco-Roman banquet may have been a principal vehicle for these activities to happen. Fifth, the emergent churches, on the one hand, related to the empire like other religious associations; on the other hand, they were related to Judaism, which enjoyed official tolerance. This too entailed variations in different cities and provinces across the decades of the genesis of the church.

One of the main obstacles for today's members of the church to accepting the seemingly chaotic, uneven, and pluralistic character of its development lies in an apparent lack of criteria for distinguishing the value of various features. This problem arose in the New Testament itself in the so-called pastoral epistles, which promoted leadership and order. The principle of functionality provides a way of understanding how and why certain elements of the church were originally set in place. This principle means that the developing Christian movement appropriated or created those institutions that would serve the nature and purpose of the church. This is a dynamic principle that implicitly recognizes some essential nature or purpose of the church in its faith commitment to Jesus Christ and faith's experience of empowerment in the Spirit identified by him. This principle also provides a norm and criterion for the church's "self-construction." Organizational elements were appropriated or created as needed to preserve identity and promote the mission. Today this principle allows one both to appreciate the pragmatic and changeable character of the historical dimensions that the church assumed and to recognize that they are expressions of a centering and defining norm.

To conclude this discussion of the historical genesis of the church, the following three propositions characterize that development and are relevant to a diagnosis of its increasingly fragmented existence today. First, it has to be insisted that the church does not relate extrinsically to faith in Jesus Christ and the salvation he mediates. Jesus did not set up a church, but church has an intrinsic, necessary relationship to the movement begun with his ministry. Jesus addresses human beings by revealing God and a way of life that actively relates a person to God. This corporate spirituality gradually constructs a church, for without a church the existential message would cease to exist in history. Second, such a church, then, is essentially missionary: mission represents an element defining its nature as reaching out to communicate with the world. Wherever the church is, it is mission. This has particular relevance for established churches that seem to lack vitality or concern for the world around them. Third, the church from its beginning has always and essentially been pluralistic. Pluralism means unity amid difference or differences within a core of sameness. Authentic churches can never be so separated from other churches that they fail to recognize what they have in common with them. This pluralism is best exemplified in the very constitution of the church provided by the New Testament. There the individual writings of the New Testament, which represent widely different churches across cities, cultures, and exact time periods, are held together between two covers in the book that unifies them all.[19]

Ecclesial Spirituality

Spirituality encompasses the way people live their lives with respect to the transcendent ground of their being.[20] The phrase "ecclesial spirituality" refers to the way Christians live their lives as a group or a community. Ordinarily Christians belong to churches, and churches at root are nothing else than the corporate spirituality of their members bonded together in a community organized by institutional structures. Although in our postmodern culture many people with self-conscious religious spiritualities are estranged from religious institutions, more from the institutions than from the religious component, without structures spiritual traditions would die. When spirituality remains religious in character but leaves a community, it gives up the depth of a community's support, the coherence of corporate reflection, and the richness and solidity of a tradition. One can conclude that "the quest for God is too complex and too important to be reduced to a private enterprise."[21]

The purpose of the church as an institutional community could be well defined as housing and nurturing ecclesial spirituality.[22] Such

---

19. Gerd Theissen, *The Religion of the Earliest Churches: Creating a Symbolic World* (Minneapolis: Fortress Press, 1999), 249-85.

20. Spirituality may or may not be religious. Sandra Schneiders is not optimistic about nonreligious spirituality: "it is usually a privatized, idiosyncratic, personally satisfying stance and practice which makes no doctrinal claims, imposes no moral authority outside one's own conscience, creates no necessary personal relationships or social responsibilities, and can be changed or abandoned whenever it seems not to work for the practitioner. Commitment . . . is easily circumvented by a spirituality which has no institutional or community affiliation." Sandra M. Schneiders, "Religion vs. Spirituality: A Contemporary Conundrum," *Spiritus* 3 (2003): 173.

21. Schneiders, "Religion vs. Spirituality," 177.

22. The apologist for the church has to admit that, as self-evident as it may seem, this is not the usual way in which the church is described. Too often the churches as institutions behave as if the preservation of the institution is an end in itself.

a spirituality should be deeply personal: each person is an individual, and the church is meant to empower the faith-life of each of its
members. This is accomplished precisely in community. The shared
or corporate spirituality of the community differentiates an ecclesial
spirituality from that of the private fellow traveler. This corporate
spirituality should be a mission spirituality for the reasons outlined
earlier: the essential characteristic of Christian life comes from Jesus'
life and ministry. Jesus reveals God and opens up a way of human
life that unites a person with God and leads to human fulfillment.
Some form of following Jesus lies at the bottom of every Christian
spirituality. Since the mission of the rule of God defined Jesus' own
life and ministry, it also shapes the nature and purpose of the church.
Ordinarily, when one joins and assumes membership in an organization, a person internalizes and participates in the nature and goal of
that organization. So too here: to be a Christian implies participation
in the mission of the church. In one way or another Christians identify themselves with a mission spirituality, and this usually includes
a public responsibility, sometimes manifested simply in the form of
showing up and bearing witness.

However, this does not address the serious problems that affect
religious institutions. One way to approach those issues runs through
the tension between structure and *communitas*.[23] Structures refer
to "the patterned arrangements of role sets, status sets, and status
sequences consciously recognized and regularly operative in a given
society and closely bound up with legal and practical norms and
sanctions."[24] *Communitas* by contrast refers to the spontaneous character of the full life of the group that overflows structures and more
freely responds to stimuli within the community and to the world
outside it. *Communitas* in this sense transcends the structured life of
the group and at certain points may threaten the ordered life; it has
a primal energy of its own. Structure orders the energetic life of the
community; *communitas* is the source and origin of all structures and
precisely that which is structured. This tension is an intrinsic dimension of the church; it is something good, a dynamic, tensive, and cata-
lytic source of the church's life.

Healthy ecclesial spirituality exists in a balance between the energy
of the community and the controlling function of structure. The bal-

---

23. This distinction was developed by Victor Turner and Edith Turner, *Image
and Pilgrimage in Christian Culture: Anthropological Perspectives* (New York: Columbia
University Press, 1978). Carl Starkloff applies these categories to the study of the church
("Church as Structure and Communitas: Victor Turner and Ecclesiology," *Theological
Studies* 58 [1997]: 643-68).

24. Starkloff, "Church as Structure and Communitas," 649.

ance between these two dimensions is variable; it will be different in different societies and always shifting as a church moves through time and culture. In the West at the present time, the community has assumed a much more active voice than in the past, partly due to the increased education of church members. This is readily seen in the relationship between clergy and faithful. For example, in matters of authority, earlier clear distinctions of competence seem less apparent today: between those who teach and those who learn, those who lead and those who follow, those who have authority and those who are obedient.[25] Authority has become thoroughly ambiguous and troublesome in the modern world generally. Religious authority has become even more complex in a globalized, postmodern context. These issues affect the spiritual life in the ecclesial community. Spirituality in Western culture transcends clericalism and authoritarianism, and yet it seems to be open to genuine religious leadership. To bear authority, such leadership has to appeal to freedom. Any person with a mature religious sensibility will consider a demand for blind obedience as spiritually inauthentic. Genuine religious authority can only represent transcendent authority by holding up opportunities for a commitment of Christian freedom to high ideals and to service inside and outside the community.

Baptism, which initiates people into the church community, commissions them in a community of shared responsibility for ministry. This idea is called the priesthood of the faithful, a phrase that goes back to the earliest church.[26] In brief, the baptism that introduces one into the church as the community that extends Jesus Christ's presence in history makes them responsible members of the community. This responsibility is not homogeneous but differentiated: all do not do the same thing. But all are called to participate in helping to build up the community. The relationship between the nature of the church and its mission gets translated into practical tasks of maintenance and mission within every church community. An ecclesial spirituality of ser-

---

25. Sociologist José Casanova, addressing principally the Catholic Church, argues that since the eighteenth century the "secular societal morality as been the one challenging, informing, and influencing church morality" instead of the other way around. This appears in the spheres of gender and sexual morality most clearly, but also in other spheres of interchange between the church and secular aspects of life. See his "Societal and Church Morality," in Charles Taylor et al., *Church and People: Disjunctions in a Secular Age,* Cultural Heritage and Contemporary Change, Series 8, Christian Philosophical Studies 1 (Washington, DC: Council for Research in Values and Philosophy, 2012), 127.

26. "But you are a chosen race, a royal priesthood, a holy nation, God's own people" (1 Pet 2:9).

vice in and on behalf of the community will be measured by practical effectiveness.

Ecclesial spirituality can be closely associated with the full life of the community just described under the sociological distinction of *communitas*. This association opens up some of the distinctive qualities and functions of ecclesial spirituality. More than any other definable factor, ecclesial spirituality accounts for the unity of the church across denominational and other boundaries. Paul formulates a premise of ecclesial existence that is clear, pointed, and filled with promise: "There is one body and one Spirit, just as you were called to the one hope that belongs to your call, one Lord, one faith, one baptism, one God and Father of us all, who is above all and through all and in all" (Eph 4:4-6). This describes a unity that, practically speaking, transcends all divisions within the church. It names that which all Christians share. When the enumerated elements are taken together, they define the dynamic essence of Christian faith in relation to which everything else seems secondary. With the exception of baptism, all these qualities reside within Christian spirituality or *communitas*. The essence of the church thus lies in organized ecclesial spirituality.

The tradition of the church is carried in Christian spirituality. Behind the landmarks of creeds, doctrinal definitions that resolved crises, and the confessions of faith that identify specific churches, lies the continuity of Christian life and practice. The carrier of the tradition of the whole church and the particular churches is ecclesial spirituality.[27] The socially and historically expansive and yet concrete and existential character of ecclesial spirituality enables it to provide the meaning and import of objective doctrines and practices. At the same time, tradition embodies them in the life of the community.

Ecclesial spirituality also provides the clearinghouse for the unity of the church in a way that preserves distinct traditions and differences in structure. When Paul's description of the definition of the unity of the church is translated from objective terms to the lived spirituality of Christians, it becomes immediately apparent that this unity can obtain within differences. All it needs is recognition, because it is already present in virtually all Christian life or spirituality. In other words, Christian unity actually exists across the differences between the churches. It needs only a corporate will to act upon it.

Finally, ecclesial spirituality helps to clarify a way of conceiving the practice of the mission of the church in a time of religious pluralism.

---

27. This social, historical, and existential notion of tradition is developed by Maurice Blondel in the essay "History and Dogma," in his *The Letter on Apologetics and History and Dogma*, ed. and trans. Alexander Dru and Illtyd Trethowan (New York: Holt, Rinehart & Winston, 1964), 219-87.

Because of an acceptance of pluralism among cultures, the strong ties between religion and culture, the inherent freedom of religion, and a certain embarrassment over past religious imperialism, the appetite for Christian missionary communication with other religions has waned. But is not a desire to communicate the Christian message an intrinsic dimension of Christian faith itself?

Here again Christian spirituality can provide a model for a policy regarding Christian missionary activity. Such activity has to be dialogical and be free of every hint of coercion. Free spiritual dialogue among people of different faiths provides a natural and spontaneous model for such interfaith dialogue. Take, for example, the stories of the ordinary faithful encountering other religious people as a paradigm for how the mission of Jesus Christ might be formally set to practice by the churches. Mrs. X of one faith meets Mrs. Y of another faith in the workplace or the neighborhood. They may become close friends, and in the course of their relationship they share their religious convictions. In so doing they communicate with and in some measure influence one another quite profoundly without ever feeling or suggesting a desire that the other convert. Such an event is interreligious dialogue at the grassroots level, and it provides a picture for church policy to emulate. Today the mission has to enter into dialogue with the religions and with the world of secular life. Mission spirituality carries this forward according to the historical situation and the abilities and place of all the members.

CHAPTER NINE

Trinity and the End of History

Christian self-understanding is constructed of two stories, the small story of Jesus of Nazareth and the large, sacred narrative of the origins of reality through to its end. The story of Jesus is told in the Gospels. The second metanarrative is told in doctrines that grew over centuries by simultaneously borrowing from the whole of scripture and submitting it to reflection and debate. In this way the large sacred story of salvation history grew out of reflection upon lived Christian spirituality of following Jesus. In this searching narrative approach to Christian spirituality, the doctrines of the trinity and eschatology "round off," sum up, and conclude the large Christian story of God and God's dealings with the world and humankind. This chapter will show how they relate back to their common source in spirituality.

This searching narrative framework does not represent the standard way of appreciating doctrines. The doctrine of the trinity usually refers to the analytical understanding of God as the one integral God whose inner being is made up of three distinct "persons." The term "person" here has a special meaning generated historically from biblical sources but in Greek philosophical language to indicate a real distinct element of the Godhead without being a discrete conscious being in the sense that "person" carries today. Eschatology is the branch of theology that speculates about the end of time and the destiny of humankind at the end of its worldly existence. What happens to these doctrines when one looks at them as the conclusion of the Christian story from the perspective of Christian spirituality?

Trinity, as a doctrine, concludes the Christian story in two quite different senses. First of all, the formula is the product of the community's debate that continued over the course of the first centuries. From the beginning, the Christian movement used language that expressed in terms of Father, Son, and Spirit how the community encountered God. This gave rise to questions and extended discussion about the nature of "the Son" and "the Spirit" that played so intimate a role in the experience of God. In 381 at the Council of Constantinople, the Christian church concluded its discussion with the formula of three persons within the one single divine nature or being of God. That gives the function of summing up a logical sense: the formula concluded the debate by providing common language for belief in the character of God who created, saved through the person of Jesus, and was present within the community as Spirit.

But the doctrine also has another symbolic character of summing up of the story of the Christian encounter with God. This book has considered God as creator, as present and at work in Jesus for human salvation, and as a presence and dynamic force within the Christian community. The doctrine of trinity recapitulates that story of an expanding community's experience of God into a short formula. It holds together all the resonances of the drama by which a tradition was constituted. It recalls the long story of Christian tradition that began some time back in the Middle East with the events that would constitute Israel. Even at the time when the Old Testament began to take shape, the metaphysical story told of God as creator, savior, and immanent companion on the journey of life.

Eschatology also has a narrative base because it attempts to speak about the end of the story. We will have to attend carefully to the epistemology underlying this kind of language: What do we know about the end-time and how do we know it?

These doctrines should reflect the narrative shape of Christian spirituality. But this has not always been the case. Over the centuries their influence has been both negative and positive. Regarding the doctrine of the trinity, the overt statement of the doctrine that there are three persons in one God communicates something akin to tri-theism when each of the persons is considered so distinct as to be a separate "person." This in turn sets up a conundrum of how three can be one, or one three, which occupies so much of trinitarian theology, and thus leads the imagination away from the story of God's engagement with human lives. Much more positively, the doctrine of the trinity can be read as the concentrated story of God's presence to and interaction with humankind in a way that has relevance for all.

Regarding the doctrines of eschatology, one can chart analogous negative and positive possibilities in the way people conceive of the end of all things. On a negative side, Christians frequently have anthropomorphic conceptions of what lies beyond history, and these generate fantastic scenarios about the end of history. Understanding doctrines always entails the imagination, but in this case the tendency is particularly dangerous. But, more positively, Christians can understand the end-time in utopian terms of God's aims, as they are revealed in Jesus, coming to fulfillment. And the plenitude of fulfillment can then bend back to relativize the present and provide vision for new and better human conditions even in the proximate future. In both cases these doctrines should draw out positive dimensions of Christian spirituality and thus contribute to Christian self-understanding. The goal of this discussion is to show how these doctrines grew out of Christian spirituality, so that, when we reflect on them, they draw out the import of Christian behavior.

The discussion has four parts. It is important to begin with an overview of how the doctrine of the trinity developed, even though this has to be brief and schematic in character. That will be followed, in a second section, by the way in which this doctrine can be understood to recapitulate Christians' story of their encounter with God. The third sections turns to eschatology. And, finally, the fourth section briefly indicates how these doctrines draw out the implications of Christian spirituality.

The Story of the Development of the Doctrine of the Trinity

Beginning with the death and resurrection of Jesus and the disciples' Easter experience, the development of the doctrine of the trinity took roughly 350 years. This was a long and complex discussion; it was not unified and controlled but spread out over diverse times, places, authors, vocabularies, and community sentiments. It was filled with misunderstandings on a formal level due to the same words or transliterations of words bearing different meanings within different communities. Yet one can clearly discern over the centuries some stark alternatives that are appreciated in various degrees by different authors in their contexts. One can also draw this debate into our own context and appreciate it anew; indeed, we have to do this for the doctrine to be meaningful and responsibly appropriated. It is true that the story of the development of the doctrine of the trinity requires extensive analysis. But the goal here is not adequately to represent that development but only to communicate the fact of development itself and its unfolding through a series of logical stages that appealed to Christian spirituality. The doctrine did not fall down from heaven.

The point of departure for this development consists in the store of various metaphors and images that the Hebrew Bible contains for indicating the presence of God in the world and the modes of God's appearance to human beings. For example, in chapter 3 of the Book of Exodus, God appears to Moses in the form of nonconsuming fire localized in a burning bush. Fire functions as a literary symbol for the presence of God (Gen 15:17). Other symbols and metaphors communicate different modes of God's activity or power. The last chapter discussed how "Spirit" represents God's creative and life-giving energy; like the wind it is invisible and yet effective. God speaks and it is accomplished, so that God's "Word" too indicates a power that accomplishes what God wills and says (Gen 1:3). God's "Wisdom" regulates the world: Wisdom personified, like a consulting agent, orders things sweetly according to God's will. She was with God at the foundations of the universe (Proverbs 8). God rules Israel, and the only way to conceive of and speak about how that works is with the language at hand drawn from experience. One has to recall the humble beginnings of the most powerful religious symbols. Their power comes from their authenticity in communicating profound experiences that are truly analogous and common.

When the disciples began interpreting who Jesus was after his death and resurrection, they used the language at hand. The presence of God to him and the power by which he acted were described with familiar symbolic language: the Spirit of God was upon him; he represented and embodied God's Wisdom; he was God's Word of revelation to us; in him was found God's glory. When we read in Proverbs the words of Wisdom speaking: "The Lord created me at the beginning of his work, the first of his acts of old" (Prov 8:22), we recognize the figurative language of personification. When we read in John's Gospel, "In the beginning was the Word, and the Word was with God, and the Word was God" (John 1:1), it is hard to tell whether this is metaphor or indicative speech, because metaphor uses literal predication. Is it perhaps metonymy, where "Word" is used for the speaker, God? Or is it, again, personification? Hypostatization consists in making a personification into a real, distinct, or individual being. The first stage of the development of the doctrine of the trinity consisted of christological interpretation that passed from figurative language about God at work in Jesus to nonfigurative or nonsymbolic or directly referential language. The reasoning was straightforward: if John said "the Word was with God" (John 1:1), obviously the Word must be distinct from God. It is hard to tell when or in what authors or communities the shift occurred. But in the second century the Word of God, that which was incarnate in Jesus, became a form of being distinct from Yahweh, yet so closely associated with God that "the Word was God" (John 1:1).

Many things followed the hypostatization of the Word of God. Three were of major importance. First, the Prologue of John's Gospel provided the predominant language in which christology developed. The proposition that "the Word became flesh and dwelt among us" (John 1:14) as Jesus of Nazareth crowded out other christologies, especially the Spirit christologies of the Synoptic Gospels, and monopolized the terrain of the debate. Second, hypostatization of the Word raised the question of a second God for Judaism, which clung to its monotheism as to a raft on the sea of polytheism in the Roman Empire. A frequent description of the cultural context in which christology developed cites the tension between Greco-Roman polytheism and Jewish monotheism. In the West today it his hard to imagine how the Mediterranean religious world was filled with gods and lesser divine beings of every sort. The incarnation of gods was not difficult to imagine. Jews had a right to be nervous. Third, however, in contrast to polytheism, the Jewish Christian imagination held firmly to a single and all-embracing, transcendent God. But it was difficult to imagine how this God of heaven and earth could be incarnate in Jesus and, in effect, localized in a creature, not to mention suffer. Almost spontaneously, then, the divine Word that was incarnate in Jesus was thought of as less than Yahweh, less than the Father. So-called modalists strongly defended the divinity of Jesus by implying that truly God was incarnate in Jesus.[1] But this way of speaking was rejected because God as Father could not possibly endure suffering. This strong antipathy to the idea that the creator and ruler of the universe could be incarnate in Jesus and even suffer as Jesus did implicitly confirmed a subordinationist christology. The Word of God was such that it could be incarnate in Jesus and suffer accordingly; he was in that respect less than the Father. One could say that subordinationism was the condition for the possibility of asserting Jesus' divinity; it had to be divinity in a lower case relative to Yahweh or the Father.[2]

The Council of Nicaea represents the next logical stage of this debate. When at the beginning of the fourth century Arius made explicit the subordinationism that lay under the surface of christological construction, he did so in a way that elicited a strong reaction. For example, in Arius's imagination "Word" was another term for "Wisdom," and Wisdom was hypostatized. Thus, the text of Proverbs, "The Lord created me at the beginning of his work, the first of his acts of old" (Prov 8:22), meant that the Word was a created "divine" being and thus less than God. But this offended a fundamental aspect of Christian spirituality. One encountered salvation in Jesus, but salvation can come only from God; therefore, if Jesus is not the incarnation of true

---

1. Modalists defended the divinity of Jesus. The Word of God incarnate in Jesus, therefore, was not "other" than the Father, but rather a manifestation or distinctive mode of God's presence to Jesus. In short, this view could not imagine differentiation within the one God.

2. It is crucial to recall that although this development is being represented as a logical debate, the whole of it rested on the foundation of religious—read spiritual—sensibility. The final appeal of arguments was always something like: "But if that were or were not the case, what would that mean for our basic faith and spirituality, our salvation?"

God, then neither is experienced salvation really salvation. This fundamental conviction can be parsed in many ways, resulting in seemingly different arguments. But this logic of salvation underlies them all. On its basis Nicaea declared that not less than true God was operative in Jesus. But this could not be the Father: that was still unthinkable. Logos, or the Son, then, was truly divine and of the same nature or character of being as the Father. This assured the reality of salvation and secured the solution to subordinationism. And, on the basis of the hypostatization of Logos and its distinction from the Father, it ratifies the basic principle upon which trinitarian theology rests: distinction within the Godhead.

The final stage of the developing doctrine regarded the Spirit of God. The story of how the Spirit of God was also conceived and affirmed as not less than God and thus truly divine draws on a logic analogous to the thinking relative to the Word. If the Spirit experienced within the community was not also truly God, it could not be God's saving presence and power. The affirmation of the real divinity of the Spirit, together with the divinity of the Word of God incarnate in Jesus, provides the basis of the doctrine of the trinity. Three aspects and functions of God acting—God creating, self-revealing in Jesus, and sanctifying in the community—became associated with principles really distinct from each other. The threefold operation of God is projected as coming through distinct persons from the one source who is God. How this "threeness" within the life of God operates is more difficult to explain than to assert, and this accounts for the intricacies of trinitarian theology. The topic is quite subtle and usually requires a mastery of each theologian's conceptual apparatus. But it is not difficult to understand the spirituality of salvation that supports the process of the development of the conceptions.

As a conclusion to this analytical story of the development of the idea of the trinity, the following four sharply stated propositions show the significance of the development itself. First, the doctrine is a product of development and is entirely dependent upon christology.[3] Logically, one gets to trinity through christology, and not christology through the trinity. This is a significant detail because it forbids an ahistorical way of thinking that is quite common, namely, understanding Jesus of Nazareth as a "divine figure" *because* he is the incarnation of the second person of the trinity. Second, the doctrine is a doctrine about God and not a proper name for God. This too contra-

---

3. In fact, it was the product of a particular christology, the Logos christology that was most forcefully stated in the Prologue of John's Gospel. Other christologies in the New Testament writings do not so readily sustain trinitarian thinking in the form in which the doctrine developed.

dicts a common usage among Christians. Third, no trinitarian theology can be allowed to compromise monotheism: as Gregory of Nyssa insisted, there are not three Gods.[4] Fourth, the point of the doctrine from the beginning to the end of its development is soteriological—that is, it concerns salvation. Salvation names the inner experiential core of Christian spirituality: being in relation with God. The point of the doctrine of trinity is to support with coherent grounds the reality of God's action for salvation in creation, in Jesus, in the church, and beyond it in the world at large.[5]

The Story of the Christian Community in the Doctrine of the Trinity

How important can a doctrine be if no one understands it? Much of the difficulty with the doctrine of trinity applied to God has its roots in a mathematical imagination that conceives of it in terms of the conundrum of three equals one. "A triune God" refers to God's inner life that is made up of three distinct persons. Conceiving of this doctrine about God in this way, as a puzzle, is fundamentally wrong in almost every respect. But considering how the doctrine developed and attending to the logic of each decision in the story of its development give rise to another way of interpreting this doctrine. The key is to notice how the development of the doctrine really responded to crucial issues of Christian spirituality. Because of this, the doctrine lies at the center of Christian faith, and people can understand the coherence of the doctrine, if not the internal life of God to which it refers.

The point of a doctrine appears in the reason why it was developed in the first place, in the problem to which it responds, and in the answer it announces. The point of the doctrine of the divinity of the Word of God defined at Nicaea was to preserve the reality of Christian salvation mediated by Jesus as coming from God. To the Alexandrian party that negotiated the Nicene view, this is what Arius had endangered with his view of an incarnation of a demigod. What is said of the Word in this respect can be extended to the Spirit. Either the Spirit is truly the Spirit of God, or that which we experience at work in the community is less than God and less than salvific. By affirming that true God is at work in Jesus and within the Christian community the doctrine preserves the integrity of Christian faith and the realism of

---

4. Gregory of Nyssa, "On 'Not Three Gods,'" in *Nicene and Post-Nicene Fathers,* vol. 5, *Select Writings and Letters of Gregory, Bishop of Nyssa* (Grand Rapids: Eerdmans, 1892).

5. I draw this question of "the point" of an assertion from Schubert M. Ogden, *The Point of Christology* (Dallas: Southern Methodist University Press, 1992). The question forces attention to the existential (salvific) relevance of a given theological construction.

its saving character. In both cases this is what was at stake; in both cases this is what the church intended to preserve.

Trinity also functions relative to the Christian community. All communities and organizations, because they exist in time, have a narrative of their coming to be and continued existence. Everything that exists in time has its identifying story. This story of Father, Son, and Holy Spirit represents the identity of the Christian community simply because it recalls the narrative of the community's genesis and development. The formula of the trinity is the shorthand symbol that encodes the story of the Christian community. The Creed synopsizes this story in an extended short formula; the doctrine of the trinity compresses it into the central symbol of faith. For the community, Father, Jesus the Son, and Spirit recount the historical encounters with God that gave rise to the Jesus movement and the Christian church in history. The symbol recapitulates the fundamental ideas that emerged out of a spirituality of following Jesus over time. Each of the three forms of encounter with God adds a constitutive element in the story of the genesis of Christian faith.

God is encountered first of all as sovereign ruler of the universe. Historically, this refers first of all to Yahweh: savior, creator, sovereign, and Israel's God. This faith in God can be pushed further back or deeper down by the archeology of creation faith to a conception that God is creator of all that is, of finitude itself, so that all that is has its ground in God by creation. This is not an exclusively Christian experience, and not even a specific religious experience itself, but more like a dynamic of human consciousness that accounts for all religious experience. This is the human source for mysticism, the openness of the human spirit that knows no boundaries in its transcendent questions, its sense of utter contingency and dependence, and the awesome experience of the gratuity of being itself. The creator God, who implicitly subsists within the question of ultimate meaning, becomes its answer: the whence of our being, the ground of our existence, the whither of our destiny.

God was and still is encountered in Jesus of Nazareth. Insofar as Jesus is recognized within the framework of the religious question, the question of human being and meaning, he appears as a religious figure. His identity revolves around the way he offers a response to the religious question. That answer is salvation, that is, meaningful fulfillment of existence. It is crucial to notice that the term salvation, which has been drenched in our society by unthinking emotional religious behavior, really responds to a radically secular question: the meaning of being itself. That meaning was portrayed in Jesus' ministry; confirmation of it was effected by Jesus' resurrection and the disciples' appropriation of it in an Easter experience. Like creation, resurrection occurs by the power of God. Thus, God was at work in Jesus' life and destiny, and Jesus is savior because what he reveals of God is universally relevant: it concerns everyone. In short, Jesus is one in whom God's revelation of ultimate meaning is encountered: Jesus is divine because he mediates God's salvation; and he mediates God's salvation because of the presence and power of God at work in him. The two entail each other.

God is also encountered as Spirit within the Christian community. The Spirit of God was not encountered for the first time in Jesus or in the Jesus movement. God has always been active in creation and thus history because the Spirit of God continues to move over the face of reality (Gen 1:2). But God as Spirit was experienced with new intensity in the wake of the Jesus affair, and the New Testament is filled with Spirit language attesting to the community's resonance with the Spirit of God in a new, vital, and saving way. As was drawn out in the last chapter, the Spirit extends God's work in Jesus out into history through the mediation of the community of followers. The internal presence of God as Spirit to all reality gives Christians confidence that God can be truly encountered in other religions, and the many different guises of God "appearing" can be instructive for Christians.

This is the Christian story. In its reference to God it elicits what is called in technical theological language the economic trinity, that is, the actual dialogue of God over time with people who ended up becoming a Christian church. God has engaged this particular community in a way that cumulatively was experienced as God creating, God reaching into history through the agency of Jesus of Nazareth, and God's accompanying the community of his disciples from within.

The doctrine of the trinity, in sum, recalls the inner structure of Christian spirituality and the story of its coming to be in history. In both cases, personal and ecclesial, it also preserves the realism of the faith within the spirituality. At all three junctures the doctrine of the trinity says that God really is as God appears in Christian faith experience. God is really present to creation, really operative in Jesus' person and ministry, and really present accompanying the Christian community as church. Frequently enough the doctrine of the trinity is referred to as an impenetrable mystery. Actually, the development of the doctrine is quite readily comprehensible if one takes the time to notice the spirituality from which it arises. The doctrine is no mystery; God is mystery.

Eschatology

For many centuries, theology covered the topic of eschatology by commentary on a series of Christian beliefs about death, judgment, and the final destinations of human life represented by the symbols heaven and hell. Under the pressure of developments in the study of scripture and theology, the area of eschatology has assumed new dimensions. The turn to the human subject and spiritual experience as a clearing house for the meaning of doctrines has reoriented consideration of the end-time. Thinking has moved from a consideration of beliefs about what will happen objectively after death to a discussion of human existence in time, moving toward an absolute future, and the way Christian faith illumines where we can place our hopes relative to the whither of our lives and of reality itself. A few paragraphs do not provide enough space to survey all the ramifications of this shift, but it is possible to indicate the direction and importance that this development has had for spiritual self-understanding. Eschatology provides a distinct standpoint on reality that adds depth to spiritual meaning by steadfastly locating human existence in time, in a history that is moving forward and generating new forms of being.

Interpreting eschatological beliefs. This discussion has to begin with some considerations of what eschatology deals with. The traditional doctrines and commentary on them frequently left believers with the impression that we know something about reality on the other side of our deaths and more generally at the end of history. In direct contrast to that impression, it needs to be stated firmly that we have no knowledge whatsoever about what transpires in the realm of God's transcendence. The term "knowledge" in its ordinary sense refers to concrete sense data and extrapolation from it. The discussion here is analogous to that of Jesus' resurrection: our imaginations, by being tied to the sensible reality of this world, tend to misrepresent the transcendent sphere by conceiving of it in terms of the knowledge of the things of this world. We can talk about the other side of death, of judgment before God, of salvation and loss, of reward and punishment, of ultimate truth about ourselves and reality itself before God. But this language is almost purely formal and abstract because of its lack of concrete data. Quite literally, we do not know what we are talking about, because these matters share in the absolute and incomprehensible mystery of God. Honesty and realism require these straightforward confessions of ignorance. Without them, what we do and can say about the end-time from the perspective of religious faith will lack all credibility.

Turning to a more positive account, as in all matters of transcendence the turn to the subject and religious experience of revelation opens up new meaningful dimensions of eschatological doctrines. What Christians believe about the end-time is rooted in faith and mediated to faith by the revelation of God made real and present to us in Jesus of Nazareth. An earlier chapter discussed the cognitive value of spirituality and faith. Faith, as a human disposition that includes our intellect and reason, is illumined by various forms of encounter with God's gracious presence. Faith penetrates into reality because, as a form of reflective human consciousness, faith consists of reality or being that is conscious of itself. Faith participates in being itself because it *is* reality consciously present to itself. Faith that is deliberate is not pure unknowing projection. It includes a heightened awareness of the self spiritually, that is, in the face of transcendence.

When Christian faith is directed into the future to shed some light on its mystery, especially in the light of Jesus' resurrection, it generates hope. Hope looks like faith turning forward and reaching into the future. While hope does not know the future, it shares the light of faith's assurance and commitment in the presence of the unknown: the existence of God, God's benevolence, God's faithfulness to the end, and in particular the conviction that Jesus' resurrection is a revelation of the true character of God. Eschatology, then, is a product of faith and hope together, and both of them are fueled by the revelation to faith of God's encompassing the future of human existence. Like creation-faith, hope in the future spills over to include the whole of reality. Based on hope, eschatology seeks to draw all finite created reality up into itself.

This short epistemology provides a framework for considering the implications for spirituality of what Christians say about the end-time. How are we to approach and interpret the statements of Christians about the future condition of humanity after death? What method makes these statements possible? What do they mean?[6] These questions draw out in direct explicit terms the logic of eschatology. The language of the end-time expresses Christian faith and hope. It expresses the human subject's projection into the future of that which Christians already experience now in their faith and spirituality. But unlike the projection of Freud, this projection is not gratuitous and self-serving but rests on the self-authenticating faith generated by Christian experience and confirmed in an active spirituality. The analyses of theologians like Rahner show how the openness of the human spirit, which

---

6. Karl Rahner addresses the logic of these eschatological statements ("The Hermeneutics of Eschatological Assertions," in his *Theological Investigations*, vol. 4 [Baltimore: Helicon Press, 1966], 323-46).

is itself a form of being, participates consciously but in a nonconceptual way in the infinite range of being itself. This makes the projection of faith more than launching empty ideas into the void. Put in logical terms, hope experiences transcendence now, as constitutive of the self. It then spontaneously reasons in this way: if reality and God are as my faith affirms and my spirituality confirms them to be, then the absolute future must be continuous with what surrounds me now.

Thus, hope draws the content of eschatological statements from faith's conviction and spirituality's acting it out. Faith's conviction reaching into the future runs along a path that resembles the disciples' experience of Jesus' resurrection. This results in a conviction about an objective state of affairs that cannot be imagined, but that completely engages the existential self. This in turn reflects back on the community of faith and the whole of humanity and fills reality with meaning.

Giving an account of our hope. The First Letter of Peter offers the frequently quoted maxim that we should be able to give an account of the hope that is within us (1 Pet 3:15). Essentially, Christian hope is drawn from the narrative of Jesus: his ministry, his death, and his resurrection. But this has been elaborated over the centuries by continual reflection. Reflection on what Christians hope for has in turn generated various doctrines about the end-time. Rather than commenting on those doctrines, what follows provides an outline of how hope illumines and energizes Christian spirituality.

We can begin by returning yet again to a description of hope drawn from Karl Rahner that establishes this human disposition as constitutive of what it means to be human.[7] Hope, as he describes it, refers to the fundamental openness of the human spirit. When compared with the other two virtues that frequently define Christian life, faith and love, hope is prior to both. By this Rahner means that hope designates a region of human existence from which both faith and love are elicited. Hope reaches back into the human spirit as inner freedom that characterizes reflective consciousness. The infinitely capacious seeking of intellect and faith, and of desire and love, is generated by a searching openness that defines the human spirit as such. The word "hope" draws to the surface of consciousness the inner resources of the human spirit that flows forth in the acts of freedom recognized as feeling, knowing, desiring, willing, and doing. Hope on this structural level describes a characteristic at the core of being human: spiritual being that is free, open, and reaching out to other forms of being.

---

7. Karl Rahner, "On the Theology of Hope," in his *Theological Investigations*, vol. 10 (New York: Herder & Herder, 1973), 242-59.

Hope exists primarily in individuals, and only derivatively in communities. Time imposes upon it a narrative character. Because this hope exists in time, it operates in the present and the present's inclusiveness of the past, but always in the direction of the future. The foundational character of hope just described alters somewhat the simple formula that hope is faith directed toward the future. Hope more accurately describes the openness of the human spirit in and across time but always oriented to the future. This integration of time into the description of the very nature of the human spirit transposes faith into a new key. Using the analogy of music, the melody remains the same, but the difference of range effects a total or all-embracing shift in the delivery of its sound and its reception. Placing hope in the position suggested by Karl Rahner's anthropology analogously shifts the performance of faith. Faith can no longer be looked upon as a static once-for-all assent, act of trust, or commitment. It becomes a living thing always in time and subject to it, always looking forward to the new, and as it moves forward always receiving new data, facing new challenges, and adjusting itself to being in a new place. For example, the shift from a theology of faith to a theology of hope as represented by Jürgen Moltmann's classic *Theology of Hope* is sharp and distinctive.[8] It is theology in a new key of life in history, of historical consciousness, of a historical evolutionary ontology that constantly must adjust to novelty.[9]

The eschatological dimension of reality cannot be understood solely in terms of the absolute future. On the one hand, hope has a utopian character, because that which is hoped for is ideal fulfillment. This perfection in turn bends back to criticize the present, showing that nothing in place is absolute, that everything in history is subject to critique and reform. On the other hand, the eschatological also has a sense of being present ontologically and providing depth and divine substance to the becoming of each moment. John Zizioulas highlights this dimension in a distinctive way relative to the life of the church. The eschatological dimension is mediated through the iconic character of the church. The Spirit gives life. "The epiclesis [calling upon] and the presence of the Holy Spirit mean that in the Eucharist the being of the

---

8. Jürgen Moltmann, *Theology of Hope* (Minneapolis: Augsburg Fortress, 1993). See also Edward Schillebeeckx, "Epilogue: The New Image of God, Secularization and Man's Future on Earth," in his *God the Future of Man* (New York: Sheed & Ward, 1968), 167-207.

9. Process theology offers an understanding of Christianity that is analogous. One of the major differences between Moltmann's theology of hope and process thinking lies in the almost exclusively evangelical idiom of much of his writing, whereas process thought has more science and philosophy behind it.

church is not founded simply on its historical and institutional base, but that it dilates history and time to the infinite dimensions of the *eschata* [final and transcendent things], and it is that which forms the specific work of the Holy Spirit."[10] The Spirit renders present a transcendence of the finite, historical, worldly, and natural that releases them from their intrinsic limits. The Spirit introduces finite reality into transcendence, the really real, the infinite life and love of God. The church is constituted in and through eschatology because God as Spirit constitutes the church. Zizioulas writes, "What I mean by 'constitutive' is that these aspects of pneumatology must qualify the very ontology of the church. The Spirit is not something that 'animates' a church which already somehow exists. The Spirit makes the church *be*."[11] The eschatological, therefore, is not just out there in front of the church but sustains it in being. Eschatology has a mystical dimension that requires an iconic imagination, that is, an ability to recognize an appeal of transcendence in a tangible artifact or event.

In the theology of Moltmann, the centering ground of hope lies in the resurrection of Jesus. God's promise to humanity of a freedom that one can hope for finds its exemplar in Jesus' resurrection, and Moltmann's theology of hope emanates from that event. Jesus' resurrection represents God's absolute power of breaking open history into newness: it is God raising real death into new transcendent life. This symbolizes and thus makes real God's absolute promise to history. History can no longer be considered to be completely bound by the laws of nature or history; it cannot be condemned to more of the same; there are grounds of hope for something really new and surprising by the power of God's grace.

But this promised power of resurrection should not be isolated and reserved for a transcendent event of the absolute future. The two insights into the eschatology of Moltmann and Zizioulas unite to shape the ongoing attitude and response of Christians to the character of everyday reality. The eschatological is constituted by the Spirit that embraces all reality at any given time, supplies finitude with a divine source of creativity, and promises a divine reception in the absolute future. The eschatological not only promises a future but also empowers human beings to work for that future in the present. The end-time and eschatology function almost like teleology in holding out an abso-

---

10. John D. Zizioulas, *Being as Communion: Studies in Personhood and the Church* (1985; repr., Crestwood, NY: St. Vladimir's Seminary Press, 1997), 22.

11. Zizioulas, *Being as Communion*, 131-32. What Zizioulas says of the church is not confined to it. Since the Spirit of God suffuses all reality, what Zizioulas describes in terms of liturgical experience within the church also describes the structure of being itself.

lute future, but it is not programmed as in organic development. This future is always receding in concrete history, but drawing human freedom forward in a constructive striving for it. Unlike Aristotelian teleology, the limits of nature do not confine the future: the Spirit of God can transform boundaries of nature as it has done in emergent species. In the framework of eschatology, historical consciousness is something that is not threatening but welcomed. It corresponds to an open history and an open freedom, released by the Spirit of God into creativity of the things of value as measured by the criteria of Jesus' ministry.

Finally, an eschatological perspective always harbors the question of the value of the things of this world relative to an absolute future, and implicitly the value of what freedom creates in history. Does it have substance in the face of the corrosion and the absolute forgetfulness of time? Is the new creation that is promised by God in resurrection one that leaves the old behind, or does it transform this world and all that is finite and temporal? The answer to this question makes all the difference for an estimate of the meaningfulness of human freedom and what it creates. And this in turn reductively leads back to spirituality and the ultimate meaningfulness of human existence in this world. Are human lives as they are in history ratified? Or should we think of existence in time as merely penultimate and provisional relative to an utterly new being?

The very question phrased in this way answers itself. If there is no continuity between the constructive works in this world and the absolute eschatological realm, then what we do has no ultimate value. One can, of course, retrieve immediate value relative to immediate satisfactions. But an ultimate transcendent meaning of the exercise of human freedom now requires some causal connection with the end-time. This should not be construed in a Pelagian mode of self-salvation. Reflection in the context of present-day reality renders that idea ridiculous. Rather, one has to think in terms of the Spirit of God releasing and empowering eschatological freedom in the construction of values that will make up a dimension of the final rule of God. This gives freedom an ultimate and absolute value.

Significance for Spirituality

Do the contours of trinity and eschatology as they are interpreted here throw any light on spirituality, the way people live their lives? These ideas originally developed out of Christian spirituality. How do they reflect back on Christian life?

This introduction to Christian spirituality and faith began with a call for narrative and searching reflection. These chapters have been written to accommodate that imperative. The quality of a searching and seeking narrative is reflected in these outlines for trinitarian and eschatological synthesis. The idea of trinity bears a narrative structure: it follows the Creed in telling the Christian story of the encounter with God in history that led to the church. The approach through narrative spirituality shifts attention from attempting to analyze the inner nature of God to recounting the history of the community's encounter with God, and this strengthens its realism. It is truly God who is encountered in creation, in the person and ministry of Jesus, and in the vibrant life of a Christian community. This encounter with God constitutes a person's salvation, which is as real as the encounter itself.

Trinity thus understood does not add to the spirituality underlying the ideas of God as creator, God as revealing word and savior in Jesus Christ, and God as sanctifying Spirit in the community of faith. It rather presents these encounters as dimensions of the Christian story that gives Christianity its historical identity. One cannot stress too much the way a community's story provides its existential identity. Trinity is the central doctrine it is because it holds the experiences of God as creator, in Jesus, and as companion in history together in the larger sacred narrative that a person identifies as his or her own.

Eschatology provides the other bookend of Christianity matching the doctrine of creation. We have more to go on with the doctrine of creation than with that of the end-time. But like creation, eschatology too has to be understood within a dynamic framework of process in which faith projects the end of the story of humanity as we know it. Eschatology reorients the perspective from which one approaches reality, from a static framework of space and an analytical understanding of recurring patterns to a dynamic framework of time, movement, and becoming. We live in time, and history continually moves and develops. As in process thought, reality appears first as being that is always becoming, so that one has to look carefully across distances and lengths of time to find constants within the fluidity of change. They only appear by analogy. Here faith's understanding operates within the framework of linear time. It embraces an ontology of change, evolution, and constant movement into the new. Anthropology becomes historical reflection. This does not break the human umbilical cord to physical nature and the other species. These constitute our world, our habitat, our environment, and ultimately our history and ourselves; nature is God's vehicle for our creation. Nature and history are symbiotically related, so that spirituality includes responsibility for and stewardship of nature. This framework respects present-day experience and ratifies the searching character that marks faith itself.

Eschatology as it is understood here will begin to have an impact on spirituality when the ideas of movement, change, and development toward a future replace a static framework of self-understanding. We are always moving toward a future. This movement unfolds as human action: aims, decisions, and performance. One's spirituality is itself a process of moving forward in time that involves goals and the means to attain them: immediate goals, larger goals, the direction of one's whole life. In this framework each one is a responsible actor, more or less but always in some degree in charge of one's life. People define themselves through the process of receiving the world into themselves, conceiving values, and committing themselves to them.

One particular aspect of eschatology has particular relevance for spirituality, and Juan Luis Segundo has emphasized this point more strongly than most commentators. His contribution revolves around his continuous eschatology and the impact it has on the conception and orientation of human freedom and spirituality itself.

Segundo insists on the continuity between what we do with our freedom in history and what will be preserved, what will last, in the end-time. In his view, "eternal life can only be fashioned with the materials, that is, the values of this one."[12] Grace and resurrection mean the transformation of material fashioned by or through human freedom into something permanent and everlasting.[13] Human freedom cooperates with the Spirit of God in fashioning the eschatological rule of God. If this were not the case, the creative aspect of human freedom would be a deception and an illusion. God raises up human freedom through evolution and bestows upon what it creates out of love eternal permanence and solidity. Segundo quite explicitly uses the language of cooperation and synergism, not as two equal partners but in terms of grace liberating and sustaining freedom. "In the building up of God's kingdom, not even God will supply the results that were not procured in a creative, realistic way by God's co-workers seeking to be *as effective as they could be.*"[14]

---

12. Juan Luis Segundo, *Grace and the Human Condition* (Maryknoll, NY: Orbis Books, 1973), 71. He states further, "To put it in other words, we must reunite eternal life and the construction of history. Eternal life is *the new earth*" (p. 72).

13. Segundo, *Grace*, 73: "Hence it is the *earth* that we are looking forward to and that is identical with eternal life. It is our earth and our history and our effort transformed by the gift of God's grace. Through this gift our transient and mortal earth acquires perduring incorruptibility and immortality, the qualities that come from on high. Grace elevates the human earth and human history." Segundo was indebted to Pierre Teilhard de Chardin in his formulation of these perspectives, not exclusively but substantially.

14. Juan Luis Segundo, *The Humanist Christology of Paul* (Maryknoll, NY: Orbis Books, 1986), 124; see also 157.

These fundamental ideas about anthropology, grace, and the human condition neatly correlate with Segundo's conception of spirituality. He distinguishes between a "trial" spirituality and a "project" spirituality. A trial spirituality conceives of human freedom minimally as choice, and of human life as a trial consisting of a field of opportunities to choose the ways of God versus the ways of perdition. The finite world has no value in itself apart from being the staging area for the trial whose outcome leads to real life or real death. A project spirituality, by contrast, conceives of freedom as commitment and creativity, and the world as the raw material for evolutionary construction. Human freedom is meant to contribute to the reign of love in the world.[15] The constructive conception of freedom and spirituality underlying a project spirituality fits perfectly with the language of a mission spirituality used earlier. The two reinforce each other and represent a distinctive spirituality adapted to a postmodern situation and audience. In this way eschatology provides the ontology for a narrative theology and reinserts spirituality squarely into time and history. This is a spirituality of finding God in history: first, in one's personal history and then, as a spirituality of service, in taking responsibility for history. In the end, this becomes a spirituality of participation in the eschatological rule of God.

In sum, these reflections reinforce an activist spirituality. The historical framework and the narrative interpretation provide a natural context for a spirituality of following Jesus of Nazareth in service of the rule of God. Spirituality consists of shaping one's behavior so that it is aligned with God's will as this is revealed in the pattern of Jesus' ministry. And, in the power of God's Spirit, it participates in the movement of evolutionary creation toward an end-time.

---

15. Juan Luis Segundo, "Ignatius Loyola: Trial or Project?" in his *Signs of the Times: Theological Reflections*, ed. Alfred T. Hennelly (Maryknoll, NY: Orbis Books, 1993), 149-75. Also Juan Luis Segundo, *The Christ of the Ignatian Exercises,* Jesus of Nazareth Yesterday and Today 4 (Maryknoll, NY: Orbis Books, 1987).

Index